# A.D. LIVINGSTON'S

# MASTERING THE CAST-IRON SKILLET

## From Charred Chicken to the Perfect Pan-Seared Steak

### A.D. Livingston

LYONS PRESS

Guilford, Connecticut

An imprint of The Rowman & Littlefield Publishing Group, Inc.
4501 Forbes Blvd., Ste. 200
Lanham, MD 20706
www.rowman.com

Distributed by NATIONAL BOOK NETWORK

Content from *Cast-Iron Cooking* copyright © 1991, 2011 by A. D. Livingston
Content from *The Curmudgeon's Book of Skillet Cooking* copyright © 2006, 2011 by A. D. Livingston

A few of the recipes used in this book were adapted from the author's cooking column in *Gray's Sporting Journal*. Acknowledgements to other authors and books are made in the text as appropriate.

British Library Cataloguing in Publication Information available

**Library of Congress Cataloging-in-Publication Data available**

ISBN 978-1-4930-4526-6 (paperback)
ISBN 978-1-4930-4527-3 (e-book)

∞™ The paper used in this publication meets the minimum requirements of American National Standard for Information Sciences—Permanence of Paper for Printed Library Materials, ANSI/NISO Z39.48-1992.

# CONTENTS

## A Manly Tradition

## Cast-Iron Skillet Specialties

## 1. Hearty Breakfast   11

## 2. Beef and Pork   21

## 3. Burger   34

## 4. Birds   43

## 5. Venison and Other Game   54

## 6. Fish and Shellfish   70

## 7. Exotic Meats   93

# 8. Vegetables and Fruits    104

# 9. Bread, Corn Bread, and Biscuits    120

# 10. Gravy    136

# 11. Blackened Fish, Fowl, and Red Meat    145

# Dutch Oven and Other Cast-Iron Specialties

## 12. Dutch Oven    155

## 13. Stovetop Dutch Ovens    164

## 14. Cooking Cajun    171

## 15. Mexican Cooking, Cast-Iron Style    179

## 16. '49er and Sourdough Cooking    184

## 17. Yankee Cooking, Cast-Iron Style    190

## 18. Large-Batch Cooking    194

# Other Cast-Iron Pieces

# Appendix

# Metric Conversion Tables   216

# Index   217

# About the Author   226

# A Manly Tradition

**I** hide my favorite frying pan whenever my mother-in-law comes for a visit. This good arm-and-hammer woman doesn't merely wash the dishes, singing and humming and enjoying the soap suds as she goes. She grits her teeth shut as she scrubs and scours, and within thirty minutes she can make even a well-blackened pot or pan look downright spick-and-span. The woman means well, but, of course, scrubbing a cast-iron skillet is well-nigh (but not quite) the worst thing that you can do to it.

I have the opposite problem with my good wife. A modern woman, she doesn't scrub anything. Instead, she merely stuffs pots and pans into the dishwasher along with the dishes and silverware—which is, to be sure, even worse than scrubbing cast-iron ware. Even well-seasoned skillets and Dutch ovens go into the machine, sometimes piled on top of everything else. Or under everything else. Whatever

The skillet or frying pan is the most popular piece of modern cast-iron cookware.

doesn't come out clean simply gets another cycle or two. Of course, everything stays in the steamy machine until the next washing. Although I allow that dishwashers with convenient pull-out racks are quite handy for storing glassware, be warned that cast iron ought to be stored bone-dry, as will be discussed a little later.

One of my sons doesn't wash anything, with or without mechanical aid, and he can somehow mess up the nonstick surface of a cast-iron skillet while merely scrambling half a dozen chicken eggs for a light breakfast. Then he leaves the mess on a hot stove to harden. The boy shows a talent for cooking, and, for that reason, I try not to fuss at him. But maybe the time has come for him to get his own skillet. He will, I'm sure, start off with Teflon. After wearing out several dozen of these, at considerable expense, he will come to his senses, and, remembering his father's smother-fried round steak, he will discover the wisdom of the old ways. Cast-iron cooking is an American tradition, started no doubt at hearthside by the colonial goodwives and spread across the country by the brave, hardy women who followed the pioneers westward. But, alas, it's a tradition that must be carried on by us menfolks. Recall the mountain man, the '49er, the cowboy, and, perhaps, the firemen of Nantucket.

## Understanding Cast Iron

After iron ore has been smelted in a blast furnace, the immediate product is called pig iron. It can be refined further into wrought iron or steel, or it can be cast into pots, vats, Dutch ovens, and so on, in which case it is called cast iron.

Unlike steel, cast iron has no great tensile strength, and it tends to be somewhat brittle. Nor can it be easily forged. But it is easy to sand cast, and it happens to withstand high temperatures. Thus, it is ideal for use in cookware that is used on red-hot coals in a fireplace or at a campsite.

Further, cast iron is a rather porous material, and it will take what is called a seasoning or "sweetening." In short, it more or less absorbs oil, which, in cooking, forms a protective coating on the surface, so that a drop of water will dance on it. Cast iron is the original no-stick material, and it lasts until the sweetening is lost by mistreatment. Sweetening and caring for cast-iron cookware are discussed a few paragraphs below.

Moreover, cast-iron cookware heats evenly and holds heat for a long time, as compared with aluminum. Partly because of its thickness, cast-iron cookware isn't as likely to have hot spots, and it isn't as likely to burn food on the bottom.

One disadvantage is that cast-iron cookware is quite heavy, partly because thin pieces would be more difficult to sand cast. A 12-inch skillet, for example, weighs 7 pounds, and an 8-quart Dutch oven with lid weighs 16 pounds. Clearly, this stuff isn't for the backpacker, although it might be a purely excellent choice for a remote camp, simply because it is very versatile, quite durable, and will cook everything from sourdough bread to beaver stew.

Another disadvantage is that a cast-iron piece will sometimes crack if it is heated fast and unevenly. For this reason, large cast-iron vats and wash pots are usually partly filled with water or lard before they are heated. Cracking usually isn't a problem, however, with the smaller pieces. Most cast-iron cookware can be put directly onto a hot bed of campfire coals without a problem. It won't warp like lighter cookware. Further, cast iron is the only cookware that withstands, time after time, the heat required for cooking "blackened redfish" and similar dishes.

# Tender Loving Care

Because I stood my ground as a bachelor for a good many years—thirty-nine to be exact—some people believe that I am stubborn and somewhat set in my ways. This is not the case. It's simply that, in some matters, there is a right way and a wrong. As for cast iron, there are no ifs, ands, or buts about it: Either a skillet sticks or it doesn't.

Of course, my mother did some cooking on a cast-iron skillet even after we got an electric stove. Moreover, my father had seven sisters who all cooked great food. Strangely, however, I didn't learn how to take proper care of a frying pan from my kinfolks. To be sure, I had observed my mother and my aunts wiping out a frying pan without putting it into the harsh, brown-soap dishwater. But the reasoning didn't sink in until I went to Auburn University.

During my college days, I quickly learned something of the art of cooking in a skillet on a one-eyed hot plate. But I had trouble with food sticking, and none of the engineering students were of much help. I took a job as a co-op engineering student at the nuclear bomb plant at Oak Ridge, Tennessee. While there, I shared a room with a fellow named Windell Nix, from the foothills of the Smokies in East Tennessee. A student of nuclear physics, Nix told me that I was washing the frying pan too much.

"My grandmother," he said, adding proof to the theory, "has got a 13-inch cast-iron skillet that hasn't been washed for over a hundred years."

I laughed.

"I'm serious," he said, puffing up a little. "All she does is wipe it out with a cloth or paper toweling. You see—" He paused to light his pipe.

"I suppose she's married to the guy who hasn't cleaned the cake out of his pipe for twenty years?" I said.

But I smoked a pipe myself, and I knew all about what a good cake could do to make the smoke cool and mellow. So, I took Nix's word for the molecular theory of pipe cake and cast-iron seasoning, and quickly became a believer in keeping washing powders and scrub pads out of my frying pan.

Immediately, the results became self-evident, and I've been eating good ever since.

In any case, once your cast-iron cookware takes a good seasoning, you simply must care for it. Scrubbing it with detergents and scouring pads will surely take out the seasoning. It can be rinsed in hot running water and wiped out immediately in case your dog has licked it or you have some other reason to suspect that it has germs in it. If, heaven forbid, it has chicken eggs or other food caked in it, try putting hot water in it and simmering it on a stove eye for a while. Then wipe it with a paper towel and rinse

it in hot water. Dry it out thoroughly and coat it very lightly with bacon drippings. If you are lucky, it will be fine. If not, you'll have to start all over, as directed a little later.

As already indicated, putting a cast-iron piece in a dishwasher is very bad, partly because of the harsh detergent, the water jet, and the drying process. The worst thing you can do, however, is to leave it inside the machine (after the washing and rinsing cycles) in a very humid, hot environment.

After frying with cast iron, I merely pour off the grease and wipe the pan clean with a rag or paper towel. Then I store it in a dry place. Some kinds of cooking, as when baking cornbread, require that the surface of the cast iron be well greased. These pans are treated just like pans used for frying. Some other methods of cooking, as when making a stew in a Dutch oven, will not leave a well-defined coat of oil on the surface. Lightly, I scrape the food out of these with a wooden spoon or rubber scraper; then I may rinse it under hot running water while wiping it clean with a sponge. Immediately, I dry the pot and sit it on the stove eye, or in the oven, at very low heat for a few minutes. This warm environment will help dry the surface. Next, I put a very light coat of bacon drippings or cooking oil on the piece, inside and out, before putting it away.

In storage, by the way, it's best to give each piece its place and not stack it under or over something else. Never store a piece with a lid on it.

## How to Sweeten the Pot

If foodstuff sticks to a cast-iron piece, be assured that it has been mistreated in one way or another, or else it was not properly seasoned to begin with. Fortunately, such a piece can be scoured out and re-seasoned. First, the pan is washed out thoroughly with (in this single instance) soap and water, then coated with grease and heated for a long period of time in the oven. All the manufacturers' information that I have seen, as well as suggestions in almost all cookbooks, say to coat the iron all over with a light coat of vegetable oil. I tried this several times—and ended up with a sticky surface that covered only part of the bottom of the pan. In one book, I noted that a specific brand of oil was specified. I bought some. But it didn't work either, not for me. I finally quit trying to follow the experts' directions and switched to ordinary bacon drippings. After all, I reasoned, our forefathers didn't normally have vegetable oil at hand. They had suet, lard, goose grease, or bear fat.

While writing this short work, by the way, I discovered that Lillian Bertram Marshall, in her *Southern Living Illustrated Cookbook*, had reached the same conclusion regarding vegetable oil. She pointed out that a bacon rind or hog skin was a good way to grease a cast-iron piece—a practice that was also used in the *Foxfire* books. But, alas, these days not many of us have a piece of hog skin handy when we need it. So, if you have neither skin nor bacon drippings, try wiping the pan inside and out with a piece (or half a strip) of bacon. Smoked bacon is great, but I would not recommend using salt pork or salt pork rind on cast iron.

In any case, after cleaning the piece and coating it with animal fat, put it into an oven at about 300 degrees for several hours. Cool the piece, wipe it out with a paper towel or rag, coat it again with animal fat, and bake it again at 300 degrees for several hours. After the first seasoning or two, the pan can be used for frying fish or chicken, provided that ¾ inch of oil is used in the pan. Cooking in rather deep oil several times will in fact further the sweetening. It's best not to use the piece to fry eggs, to make country steak, or to simmer a thick stew until the cast iron has been seasoned *several* times.

There is no hard-and-fast rule to follow about the baking times and temperatures required to achieve a proper seasoning, and in fact baking isn't always necessary. A pan can also be seasoned on top of the stove, or in a campfire. Usually, however, the oven is the best way to go and the easiest.

Remember that new cast-iron pieces are coated with a thin film of wax before they are shipped from the factory. The wax helps prevent rust and keeps the piece looking new. For cooking purposes, however, the wax must be removed and the piece must be seasoned, as directed above. Once a piece takes a seasoning, it will cook good indefinitely, and in fact it will get better with age, provided that it is properly used. In time, cake may appear on the sides of the pan, but this doesn't hurt a thing, in my opinion. In the book mentioned above, Lillian Marshall says that if a heavily caked piece of cast iron is run through a regular cycle in a self-cleaning oven, it will come out looking like new. Damned if it doesn't!

Getting a piece of cast iron very hot either by accident or for blackening a steak or a fish fillet may take out the seasoning. Usually, these pieces will take a new seasoning readily, but, of course, the best practice is to keep your blackening griddle separate from the other pieces. Use it only for blackening, and, after it has cooled, coat it *very* lightly with oil.

I must add that sticking isn't the only problem with cast-iron cookware that isn't seasoned properly. An ill-seasoned piece can impart a metallic taste to food. Of course, this usually occurs when meat is stewed for a long time in tightly covered pieces, such as a Dutch oven with a good lid. And, more often than not, the trouble will be in the cast-iron lid. In any case, be sure to season the lid and the sides of a cast-iron piece.

One major manufacturer of cast-iron cookware says that iron getting into the food can be good for your health. Maybe. But I for one don't want enough of it to alter the taste of my food. How much iron will leave a properly seasoned cast-iron piece is questionable, at least to me. Frankly, I never see pits in my skillet or Dutch oven—a claim that I can't make for aluminum cookware.

Acidic foods tend to remove the seasoning from cast iron, resulting in a bad taste and discolored food. Never marinate meat in cast iron, especially if the marinade contains vinegar, buttermilk, or lots of salt.

Rust can be a problem with cast iron, but it usually results from improper storage together with inadequate seasoning. And from dishwashers.

# Cast-Iron Skillet Specialties

Black iron is one of the oldest types of cookware in existence today. Columbus brought some with him to the New World in 1492. . . . Before that, during the reign of Edward III, from 1327 to 1377, iron pots and skillets were considered part of the "Crown Jewels."

—*Diane Becker Finlay*

**A** skillet is merely a cast-iron frying pan. Usually, but not always, a skillet has pouring spouts, or indented lips, set 90 degrees on either side of the handle. It was designed to hold enough oil or fat for frying, and of course frying is its main function. But remember, a cast-iron skillet, with a built-in handle, can also be used in the oven without danger of burning a plastic or wooden handle.

Skillets come in various sizes, from 5 inches in diameter up to 15 inches. A 15-inch skillet weighs over 9 pounds, and anything much larger would be too heavy for easy handling. A 20-inch skillet-like piece has recently been put on the market, but it doesn't have a regular handle; instead it has lifting nubs on either side. I don't think this is a true skillet, and it is discussed later. At the other extreme, a 5-inch skillet comes in handy for frying a chicken egg for breakfast, but it isn't much good for cooking bacon. There are some other tiny skillets on the market, but these were intended to be used as ashtrays or spoon holders. If I had to choose one size skillet, it would surely be 10¼ inches wide. This is an ideal size for cooking on most stove eyes. But larger skillets will be needed for cooking some specialties, such as jambalaya.

Normally, skillets are round. But a square model is available. I like the square shape for cooking on coals or on a campfire, and I sometimes balance a square skillet on two bricks in my kitchen fireplace. A square skillet, however, on a round stove eye doesn't set too well with me aesthetically, although it is surely the best design for cooking bacon.

In any case, if you've got a well-sweetened cast-iron skillet of reasonable size, you can cook up some purely excellent victuals on the stovetop, by a campfire, or at the hearth. In short, a well-sweetened cast-iron skillet will cook anything that can be cooked in

A rectangular skillet comes in handy for cooking bacon.

aluminum, stainless steel, or various Teflon-coated wares. Usually cast iron will cook better, too.

## What's What

A recently published book on cast-iron skillet cookery had lots of recipes for stovetop Dutch ovens—enough for me to question the honesty of using the word "skillet" in the title. The confusion doesn't stop at the title, either. As I browsed about in the text, a recipe called Skillet-Roasted Clams with Garlic and Parsley caught my eye. Turns out that the clams weren't really roasted in a skillet. The term "roasting" implies cooking with dry heat, usually uncovered in an oven or over an open fire or bed of coals. Instead, the clams in this recipe were actually steamed—and in a Dutch oven, not in a skillet as promised in the name of the recipe. A skillet was not involved in the cooking in any way whatsoever. Moreover, this clam recipe was published in a chapter on outdoor cooking, in which four of the five recipes called for a Dutch oven, not a skillet.

Another book on cast-iron cooking set forth a recipe called Pan-Fried Catfish. In the preamble to the recipe, the author says, "In the Southern food lexicon, catfish is nearly always fried, and you certainly need a trusty, seasoned good ol' cast-iron skillet to fry it." Yet, the list of ingredients for the recipe calls for 7 to 9 cups of oil for deep-frying—and the directions clearly say to add the oil to a 4- to 6-quart cast-iron Dutch oven (presumably a stove-top model). No skillet is used in the recipe in any way whatsoever. What the hell is going on?

Here are a few related terms that should perhaps be put into focus before we start cooking.

**Skillets and Frying Pans**. These interchangeable names apply to shallow metal pans used to fry or sauté meats and other foods. They range in size from 4 inches to about 15 inches across the top of the pan. Since the sides slope down, the bottom will have a smaller diameter. A few models, however, do not slope, being perfectly cylindrical. Although some skillets come with a lid, the cooking is usually done uncovered—or should be. A good deal depends on the size of the skillet and the material from which it was made. These features are discussed under other headings later in this chapter.

**Sauté Pans**. Similar to skillets, these pans are often made of aluminum, stainless steel, or copper, and a few are made of enameled cast iron. Some have straight sides, but most curve up from the bottom and are a little deeper than a skillet. This curve, together with a long handle, makes the sauté pan much better for fancy skilletmanship such as tossing the food into the air to turn or cool it. Very large sauté pans have a long handle on one side and a D-ring handle on the other. Sauté pans can, of course, be used for panfrying. I might add that some of the illustrations in cookware catalogs show the sauté pan with straight sides and the skillet with curved sides. It's the curve that matters, not the name. Thus, my skillet might well be another cook's sauté pan.

**Chicken Fryers**. These great pans are deeper than skillets but not as deep as a stove-top Dutch oven. Thus, in function they sort of split the difference between deep-frying and panfrying. They can also be used as a regular skillet, but the high sides sometimes get in the way and make the pan heavier. Most chicken fryers come with a matching lid, which I really can't recommend when using the pan for frying. I like these, used without the lid, for frying enough fish fillets to feed eight to ten people.

**Spiders**. Although old cast-iron skillets are sometimes called spiders, the real ones have three legs and long handles. These were designed to sit in a bed of coals without mashing them down. Frankly, however, they don't work too well in a campfire, where the ground under the coals is likely to be soft and uneven, in which case a flat skillet balanced on rocks or other support works better (more on campfire cooking at the end of chapter 12). Spiders are really at their best for use at a fireplace designed for home or cabin cooking, where they can easily be shuffled in and out of a shallow bed of coals spread out on the hearth.

**Electric Skillets**. These skillets, usually square in shape, plug into standard 120-volt electrical outlets. They usually have a dial temperature control and, in general, work great for frying at medium-high heat. They come with a fitted lid, making them suitable for cooking most one-skillet dishes and for cooking and warming buffet-style foods. Most of these skillets are quite attractive and can be used for serving. I like to have one of these in the kitchen, even if I seldom reach for it.

**Griddles**. These are flat pans with a shallow lip around the circumference. They work great for some of the skillet recipes in this book, such as blackened fish, but won't work for frying simply because they won't hold enough oil. Round and oval griddles usually have a handle like skillets, but the larger rectangular ones have D-handles on either end. Some of the modern griddles, some pleasingly oval in shape, have a rough, unmachined cooking surface and were intended, I gather, to be used for keeping such foods as fajitas warm while serving. I've never actually seen one of these used for serving, except in an eatery that specialized in fajitas. Fajita pans are nonetheless great for reducing weight and space in camp cookery, and those with a smooth cooking surface do a good job of breakfast bacon and eggs for one or two people.

# Skillet Cooking Techniques

While the self-made, well-seasoned skillet cook may not need much of the information in this section, I feel that discussion will be helpful just to make sure we are on the same page, if for no other reason. If the novice picks up an idea or two, or if the expert is forced to clarify his thinking a little here and there, so much the better.

**Skillet-Fry, Panfry.** These synonymous terms refer to frying meats and other foods in a skillet with a little oil. How deep? Personally, I like for the oil to be deep enough to cover about half the thickness of the food. For thin fish fillets, half an inch will do. For chicken breast, a little more will be required. (For safety, however, do not fill the skillet more than half full of oil.) Many of the recipes in this book are cooked by the skillet-fry method. Others are sautéed in a lesser amount of oil, as discussed next.

**Sautéing.** Steaks and chops cooked in a small amount of oil without any sort of dredging or batter are really sautéed instead of fried. Generally, the sauté works better with very tender cuts of meat that require no beating to tenderize them, or with fish fillets. Sautéing can be accomplished on medium heat (often with butter) or on high heat with oils that have a high smoke point, such as peanut oil. There are no hard-and-fast rules, however, and one man's sauté might well be another's fry. The key is in cooking with only a small amount of oil, and without a batter or dusting. The sauté, I might add, leads to superior gravy, as in such dishes as steak au poivre.

Remember also that the sautéing works best with an open skillet. Yes, covering the skillet will help reduce grease spatter going onto the stove, but it will also partly steam the food, tending to produce a soggy surface instead of a crispy one. (But also see the comments under "Braising.")

**Deep-Frying.** In this popular method of frying, the food is cooked in enough oil to completely cover the food. Usually, this will be 3 or 4 inches, but the proper depth is relative. Two inches of oil will deep-fry tiny bay scallop eyes, but not a large chicken breast. More oil is better, within reason, because it helps maintain a hot temperature (about 375°F) when the food is added to the fryer. Also, deep-frying is best done without a lid to cover the foods. If covered, the food will be partly steamed, yielding a soft crust instead of the crunch usually associated with fried foods. In any case, this method of cooking is not recommended for skillet cookery. If filled more than half full with oil, a skillet can easily boil over and cause a grease fire. (Tips on fire prevention are found in "Skillet Safety" at the end of this chapter.) The rather deep, skillet-shaped utensils called chicken fryers can sometimes be used for deep-frying, but a deeper pot is better.

**Chicken-Fry, Country-Fry**. These terms are usually used with beefsteak but can also be applied to venison and other good eats. Essentially, a chicken-fried steak is cut thin, pounded to tenderize it, dusted with flour (or sometimes dipped in egg and rolled in flour), and fried until nicely browned and crisp. It is then topped with a white country gravy, made by pouring most of the cooking oil out of the skillet and then making a gravy with a little flour and some milk. The steaks are plated and the white gravy is poured over them at the table—but only at the last minute. This method combines the flavor of the gravy with the crunch of the steak's crust.

**Smother-Fry**. This term applies to meats—usually tough cuts—that have been breaded and fried in a skillet. Most of the pan grease is poured off and a thin gravy is made. The meat is then put back into the skillet, covered tightly, and simmered until tender. Sometimes sliced mushrooms and such are also added. The technique is similar to braising, except that the meat is breaded before frying. Smother-frying does not yield a steak or chop with a crunchy crust (as can chicken-frying), but the gravy is usually more flavorful, and more plentiful, and goes nicely with mashed potatoes or rice.

**Braising**. This excellent cooking technique is similar to smother-frying except that the food is not dusted with breading or dipped in a batter before being fried. Instead, it is sautéed until browned on all sides, then cooked on low heat in a small amount of liquid, usually water or stock, until it is tender. Braising works best in a skillet with a tight-fitting lid. The food should be stirred and turned from time to time, adding more liquid as needed.

**Parboil**. Some tough meats are boiled (or, better, simmered) until tender. Then the pieces are breaded and skillet-fried until nicely browned. The technique is often used for cooking tough old squirrels. I seldom apply the technique myself, but my father's parboiled squirrel was memorable. The technique is also used to partly cook some of the tougher foods for a stir-fry or a kabob broil, so that the cooking time in the skillet or wok is equalized for all the ingredients.

**Sweating**. This term is being used these days to indicate a form of cooking vegetables in a little oil or cooking fat until they are done but not at all browned—the opposite of caramelization. The cooking should be done over rather low heat, and the food is well covered, first with foil and then with a lid to the skillet. I seldom have a need to use this term—or apply the technique without having a name for it. Any time you "sauté" onions until they are translucent but not browned, you are getting pretty close to "sweating," whether you know it or not.

**Trying Out**. This term refers to a method of melting chunks of animal fat on low heat to render or separate the oil from the tissue. Trying out pork fat, for example, yields lard for cooking purposes and delicious cracklings for noshing, as described in more detail under "How to Make Cracklings" in chapter 9. Fat from bear, duck, and some other animals can also be used.

**Broiling**. This term should refer to meats or other foods cooked under a broiler, with the heat coming from the top. The term "pan-broiling" can reasonably be used in skillet cookery, however, especially when one of the raised-rib pans is used.

**Grilling**. This method of cooking is accomplished on a rack or grid over a fire, hot coals, or other heat source. Some meats cooked in a dry skillet or a skillet with a raised-rib bottom are said to be grilled, but not in this book. Many food writers also confuse grilling, which is a quick method of cooking, with barbecuing, which is a long, slow method. The term grill is also applied to a large, flat cooking surface used in short-order restaurants, and, hence, foods cooked on such a heat source are said to be grilled. Because of the confusion, I try to avoid the term (along with the term "griddle") in this book.

**Roasting**. This term means cooking a rather large piece of meat, uncovered, in an oven or over an open fire or coals. It's a dry method of cooking, suitable mostly for tender meats. Tougher cuts are better when cooked by a wet method such as braising. The term has limited use in skillet cookery, but it is used from time to time, as in "roasting chestnuts."

**Simmering**. In this method of slowly cooking foods, a liquid is often used to tenderize tough meats. Note that simmering does not mean boiling, although small bubbles may break the surface here and there. At sea level, water boils at 212°F; it simmers at about 185°F. In some cases, the lowest heat on the kitchen range will be too hot to simmer properly. A flame tamer—usually a flat piece of metal placed between the pan or skillet and the burner—will solve the problem. A skillet can be tightly covered while simmering. If it is left open, more water may have to be added from time to time.

**Browning**. To cook meat in a skillet on high heat until it is browned all around, usually with the aid of a little cooking oil, is called browning. The cuts of meat can include roasts, steaks, cubes, or burger. With burger, however, the purpose is often to separate the grinds so that the meat doesn't cook in chunks. In this case, the meat is usually cooked to a gray, not to a brown. (See chapter 3 for more on cooking burger.) So, don't always take the cooking instructions literally.

**Searing**. Searing means to cook meats briefly on high heat to help seal in the juices. The term is close to browning, but a higher heat is implied. Searing is usually used before longer cooking by some other method and is especially useful when cooking roasts and thick steaks. The term does not often apply to cubed or ground meats.

**Caramelize**. This culinary term originally applied to sugar that has been heated until it melts and turns lightly brown. These days it is widely used in cookbooks, in magazine articles, and, especially, on television shows to refer to everything from burnt onions to seared steaks. I suppose the term is useful, but I hold suspect any word that ends in -ize. The old term "brown" used as a verb as in the directive "brown the onions" is a shorter word and a better one.

**Skillet in the Oven**. Although used primarily on top of the heat, a skillet also makes a good pan for cooking in an oven. A cast-iron skillet is especially useful for this since it has an ovenproof handle. Many people consider a cast-iron pan the very best for baking corn bread, and even biscuits. When cooking thin fish fillets, I sometimes sauté them on top of the stove and then put them under a preheated broiler to brown the top, all without turning the tender fillet even once. I do, however, want to point out that "oven-frying" is one of the more absurd terms in culinary lingo. You have to use oil to fry anything.

# Skillet Safety

Hot skillet handles, popping grease, and accidental contact with the rim of the skillet cause many minor burns—but grease fires are the biggest hazard. The following are some talking points to help minimize the danger. Ignore them at your peril.

**Oil Level**. Never fill a skillet more than half full of cooking oil, and never overcrowd a skillet with fish, chicken, or other foods to be fried. Pictures in magazines and on television shows often err in this direction. A full skillet not only contains more oil to burn, but is also more likely to boil over and catch fire from the stove burner, especially when using gas heat.

**Temperature and Smoke**. Always stay alert for smoke and adjust the temperature of your skillet accordingly. You can see the smoke and you can smell it, and usually you can sense when a skillet is too hot simply by the sizzle it makes. If you are smart, you'll have a modern smoke detector in working order in the kitchen. Yeah, yeah. I know. Smoke detectors can be a pain in the neck, as they often sound off long before you think there is danger of an outright fire, but, even so, they are a good reminder that you need to watch your skillet closely.

**Extinguishing a Grease Fire**. Once the oil in a skillet catches on fire, smoke will quickly ruin the paint job in a kitchen and possibly in the rest of the house. The impulse of most cooks will be to grab the skillet handle and rush for the back door to get the fire out of the house. Sometimes the handle is too hot to hold onto, or the fire licks back onto the hands, causing the skillet and burning oil to be dropped on the floor, causing a larger fire or burning the cook, or both. Sometimes opening the back door with one hand while trying to hold the burning skillet with the other will cause an incoming draft of air, causing the fire to sweep back onto the cook's hand and face.

Some people keep a small fire extinguisher in the kitchen, which of course is a very good idea. Just be sure that it will handle a grease or oil fire. My personal choice—which I have exercised more than once—is to keep a box of baking soda handy. When sprinkled into the hot skillet, the soda will cause a gas that quickly extinguishes the fire. I always keep a box of soda within easy reach of the kitchen stove, and it's hell to pay for anyone who hides it in a cabinet.

Some other people say to cover a burning skillet with a lid, which is, I suppose, better than making a run for the door, but I have never had to do this. Most cast-iron skillets are hard to cover tightly because of the pouring spout on either side.

One of the worst things you can do to a skillet fire is to pour water into it. Oil and water don't mix and will cause an even more dangerous fire. Since skillet fires are so common, I would suggest holding a family fire drill on this matter, emphasizing the use of the fire extinguisher or the box of soda, or both.

Camp cooks don't have to worry about the kitchen paint when the skillet catches on fire. The best bet is to let it burn. That way, all you'll lose is a little oil and a few fish or whatever you were frying.

**Pot Holders, Mittens, and Cooking Gloves**. Every Christmas, I get two or three sets of pot holders, some lovingly hand-sewn and some made in the shape of a mitten. Yet, I can seldom find one when I need it quickly! Often, I'll make do with a dry—never wet—dishcloth or towel. (Wet cloth will quickly cause hot steam, which will burn you or cause you to drop the skillet, or both.) What I really want for cast iron, however, is a pair of cooking gloves. These give a sure grip and are designed to withstand some heat—and the handle of a cast-iron skillet gets very, very hot. There are several of these on the market, and I like to think of them as being made of "asbestos," but most of them are probably some sort of leather and cloth combination. I also have a set of rubberized cooking gloves that came with my old Showtime Rotisserie, but I usually save these for use when shucking oysters, where the waterproof feature is needed. Bottom line: Get yourself a good set of cooking gloves and have them at hand before you start cooking with cast-iron skillets. Many of the other skillets have a longer and cooler handle.

**Trivet**. A short-legged or otherwise raised stand is handy for holding hot skillets and pots, thereby keeping them off the surface of the table or countertop. Having a trivet at the ready will not only protect the table or countertop but will also permit the cook to get rid of a hot pan in a hurry, making it a safety device.

**Frying Explosive Foods**. Some foods can pop violently when cooking in hot oil, sometimes resulting in painful burns on the cook's hands and arms, and even the face of one who likes to hunker down over the skillet. Chicken livers and fish roe are especially prone to pop. A lady friend of mine advised me to wrap mullet roe in aluminum foil before frying it. Well, it stopped the spattering all right, but the roe was more steamed than fried. Some people will want to cover the skillet to contain the spatter, but that too alters the frying process. My best advice is to fry as usual—but be careful, stand back, and use long tongs to turn the chicken livers.

**Treating Grease Burns**. I hesitate to give medical advice on this matter, partly because the popular remedies for grease burns, like those for snakebite, seem to change every time I read up on the subject. My best advice is to run clean cold water over the burn as soon as possible to cool it down. Ice helps, but a steady stream of cold water is better. If the burn is at all serious, see a doctor as soon as you can. Secondary infection is a big problem with burns, and these can set in days after the accident.

Years ago, when I lived out in the country, I caught myself on fire at two o'clock in the morning, while cooking a very late supper. While holding a book open in my right hand, I put a skillet on the rear eye of the stove—but I turned on the front burner by mistake. Then I leaned against the stove to continue reading, and, before I knew it, my shirt was on fire. I ran up through the house, tearing off the shirt (a synthetic thing) and a cotton T-shirt, planning to roll myself in a quilt on the foot of the bed to smother the flame. Fortunately, I got the shirt off without having to use the quilt, but in the process I burned my right hand in addition to my back. I washed down with cold water and immediately drove my car—an old Volkswagen with a stick shift—to the emergency room of a small hospital about 20 miles away, sitting up straight to keep my back off the seat and working the gear with my burned right hand while steering with my left. The burns hurt pretty bad before I got treatment, but I think I did the right thing. These days I would probably call 911 instead of trying to drive myself.

Clearly, a skillet can be a dangerous utensil—and cooking with one on high heat is a full-time job. Never leave the skillet handle sticking over the edge of the stove, especially if you have small children on the floor or good ol' boys wrestling in the kitchen.

# CHAPTER

## 1

# Hearty Breakfast

**T**hese days too many people eat cold cereal, Pop-Tarts, or store-bought doughnuts for breakfast, none of which require cooking. Even so, chicken eggs are still the mainstay of the American breakfast. Several egg grades and sizes are widely available in our supermarkets, but I really prefer eggs from yard chickens that are free to scratch in the dirt and chase insects in the grass. To me, these eggs have a brighter yolk and a better taste.

Most of the eggs eaten in this country are from chickens, but other kinds are popular in some other parts of the world. In China, duck eggs are highly regarded. I like them—especially those from a mallard. Other bird eggs include the whoppers from the ostrich and emu on down to the small ones from quail. In times past, wild bird eggs have been eaten on islands and along seacoasts, and, not too many years ago, some city bakeries purchased them from hunters in very large numbers.

I like to cook chicken eggs in a well-seasoned cast-iron skillet or griddle, but I would quickly recommend a nonstick Teflon skillet for tenderfoots. Since most egg dishes are best cooked on low heat, a Teflon or other nonstick skillet will do a good job and isn't as likely to stick.

In any case, here are a few recipes to try, along with some talking points for basic scrambled and fried breakfast eggs. A few breakfast recipes not requiring eggs are also included. Some breakfast staples, such as biscuits and redeye gravy, are covered in other chapters.

# SCRAMBLED CHICKEN EGGS

I don't offer a firm recipe for scrambled eggs, partly because the technique is far more important than nonessential ingredients like milk or cream. All you need is good fresh chicken eggs, fresh butter, and a little salt and freshly ground black pepper.

Lightly whisk the eggs in a bowl to break down and blend the whites and yolks. (Some people use a little water, milk, or cream to help break down the eggs, but these are not necessary if you have a good arm.)

Melt the butter in a skillet on low heat. Add the eggs and cook slowly, stirring slowly with a wooden spoon. As small curds begin to form, increase the stirring and decrease the heat to very low. Cook and stir until the eggs are creamy and set to your liking. (Note that high heat will produce harder scrambled eggs.) Serve hot with sea salt and freshly ground black pepper.

Most people like scrambled eggs for breakfast, along with toast and a little bacon, ham, or sausage. I confess to eating them for lunch or even dinner—and as a sandwich filling between soft white bread halves spread with mayonnaise.

# FRIED CHICKEN EGGS

The best fried eggs are cooked on low heat, preferably in a nonstick skillet. I use salted butter for frying eggs because it tastes good and works just fine on low heat. If I have cooked bacon to go with the eggs, however, I am likely to pour off the excess drippings and fry the eggs in what's left.

For sunny-side up, break the eggs directly into the skillet. Cover with a lid and cook for about 5 minutes, more or less, depending on the size of the eggs and the heat, until the whites of the eggs have set and the yolks look cooked around the edge. If you have used a nonstick skillet, tilt it carefully over the serving plate and slide the eggs out with the yolk up and intact. A good spatula will also work, being sure to slide the egg off instead of flopping it over.

For over-easy eggs, do not cover the skillet with a lid. When the whites are set, carefully slide a spatula under the egg and turn it over in the skillet. Cook for about 30 seconds. Slide it out onto the serving plate or platter with the aid of a spatula.

For hard-fried eggs, proceed as above for over-easy, but cook for 60 seconds after the turn.

# EASY WILD MUSHROOM OMELET

Here's an omelet that doesn't require fancy skilletmanship. Note that beating the eggs a little before cooking makes a light omelet—but beating too much will make the eggs spongy and airy. (But see the note below.)

6 large chicken eggs
1 pound fresh chanterelle mushrooms, sliced
2 tablespoons butter

2 tablespoons olive oil
1 tablespoon chopped fresh herbs, to taste (optional)
salt and black pepper to taste

Beat the eggs lightly with a whisk, mixing in the salt, pepper, and chopped herbs. Melt the butter in a 12-inch nonstick skillet, add the olive oil, and heat to medium-high. Sauté the mushrooms for about 5 minutes. Add the eggs and cook, without stirring or scrambling, until almost set. Fold over with the aid of a spatula and serve with bacon, toast, and other breakfast fare. Feeds from 2 to 4, depending on appetite and go-withs.

*Note: There are several kinds of omelets. A classic French folded omelet, for example, is folded with two sides over the middle, usually covering a filling of some sort. Souffléed omelets are made by beating the egg whites until they are airy, then folding in the yolks before cooking. Flat omelets are usually served like pancakes, being a little too thick to be folded. A Western omelet is usually a flat one containing ham, onions, and bell peppers, all finely chopped. Most good family cookbooks will have recipes and cooking directions for several kinds of omelets. There are also many similar dishes, such as the one below.*

# HANGTOWN FRY

I've cooked several recipes for an old California Gold Rush recipe called hangtown fry. All of them were very good, if properly made, but my last version was my favorite (as is often the case). The dish should be cooked in a rather large skillet, about 11 inches. Ideally, the fried oysters should fit loosely into the skillet in one layer. Of course, much depends on the size of the oysters, with the best ones being just right to sit on a saltine. If you prepare too many for the recipe, fry them separately and serve them on the side. Although I consider this to be a hearty breakfast dish, it can also be served for lunch or dinner.

**2 dozen medium oysters, freshly shucked**

**6 large chicken eggs**

**2 more large chicken eggs for the batter**

**6 ounces cured ham, sliced and diced (⅜-inch squares)**

**2 ounces salt pork, diced (⅜-inch squares)**

**¼ cup clarified butter (maybe more)**

**¼ cup milk**

**1 medium to large onion, grated**

**2 cloves garlic, mashed and minced**

**flour**

**cracker crumbs (crushed saltines)**

**Tabasco sauce**

**salt and freshly ground black pepper**

**parsley for garnish (optional)**

Bring all the eggs to room temperature. Try out the salt pork in the skillet. When the cracklings are crisp, drain them on a brown bag and set aside. Whisk two eggs in a bowl. Shuck the oysters and shake them in a bag with a little flour. Dunk them into the beaten egg and shake in fine cracker crumbs.

Heat the butter in the skillet along with the leftover salt pork drippings. Sauté the ham for a few minutes, drain, and set aside. Fry the oysters a few at a time and drain on a brown bag, using more butter as you go if needed. When all the oysters have been fried, fit them back into the skillet without overlapping. (If you have too many, set some aside to be served separately.) Add the ham.

Lightly beat 6 chicken eggs in a bowl, adding in the milk, grated onion, and garlic. Pour the eggs into the skillet on medium heat. Cook until the eggs are set, lifting here and there to let the eggs run to the bottom. Put a drop of Tabasco sauce on each oyster, and sprinkle in a little salt and freshly ground black pepper. Then carefully fold the mixture, as when making an omelet, and transfer to a heated serving platter. Sprinkle on the cracklings and garnish with parsley sprigs.

Enjoy with hot coffee, hash browns, and sourdough biscuits. This fry will feed 2 gold miners or 6 modern San Franciscans. Anyone asking for catsup to pour onto the fry will be shot.

# EGGS YBOR CITY

This dish calls for chorizo, a spicy pork sausage brought to the Americas from Spain. Today there are many variations in Mexico, South America, Florida, California, and other areas influenced by the early Spanish settlers. For this recipe, similar sausages can be used. I like one made from a mixture of venison and fatty shoulder of wild pigs, along with some red pepper flakes, sage, salt, and black pepper. Chorizo is often used in soups and stews, or in various other recipes.

This particular dish is from the old Spanish section of Tampa, called Ybor City, where it is still cooked and sometimes used as a fast supper dish. I like it for breakfast. If you can't get authentic Cuban bread, try either a French or Italian loaf. Note that the dish will need no salt or pepper if your sausage is spicy enough.

**6 large chicken eggs**      **¼ cup cream**
**4 ounces bulk chorizo or country sausage**      **Cuban bread, toasted**

Sauté the bulk chorizo in a medium-hot skillet for 5 or 6 minutes, until it is crumbly. (If you are using link chorizo instead of bulk, peel off the casing and chop it finely before the sauté.) Pour off most of the grease that cooks out of the sausage.

Lightly whisk the cream into the chicken eggs. Pour the mix into the skillet with the sausage. Scramble lightly, stirring for 5 or 6 minutes on medium-low heat until the eggs are set but still fluffy. Do not overcook.

Serve with toasted Cuban bread, buttered. This recipe makes a hearty breakfast for 2 good men. For lunch or supper, serve with some tomato-based salsa of your choice.

# VENISON CHOPS AND CHICKEN EGGS

Here's a breakfast that can be made with slices of venison loin or tenderloin, or with small chops cut from the hind leg. The meat should be cut ½ inch thick. Allow 3 chops and 3 chicken eggs per person, if you are feeding hunters or other hearty eaters.

venison chops

large chicken eggs

all-purpose flour

salt and pepper to taste

cooking oil or bacon drippings

Sprinkle each chop on both sides with salt, black pepper, and flour. Beat both sides with a meat mallet or the edge of a heavy plate. Let sit for a few minutes. Then repeat the sprinkling and beating.

Heat a cast-iron skillet and wet the bottom thoroughly with cooking oil or bacon drippings. Cook the chops for 3 or 4 minutes on each side. Remove the chops to drain and add more oil or bacon drippings as needed, along with a little water. Add the chicken eggs, cover the skillet, and cool for 3 or 4 minutes. Do not turn.

Plate the eggs sunny-side up and top with the chops. Deglaze the skillet with a little more water and scrape up the grimilles with a spatula or wooden spoon. Reduce the liquid to a gravy and pour it over the eggs and venison chops. Eat with Texas-size biscuit halves. A little butter and wild grape jelly or honey will help finish off any remaining biscuits.

# FISH ROE BREAKFAST

Any good fish roe with small berries can be used for this recipe. My favorite is from bluegill, shellcracker (redear sunfish), or similar panfish. Exact measures aren't required, but equal parts of roe to chicken egg by volume will be about right.

roe

chicken eggs

scallions

bacon

salt and pepper

Break the roe sacs and put the fish eggs into a bowl, discarding the membrane. Whisk the chicken eggs in a separate bowl. Chop the scallions, including about half of the green tops.

Fry a couple of strips of bacon in a skillet. Remove the bacon and pour off most of the grease. Sauté the onion until it is clear. Add the roe, stirring with a wooden spoon, and cook for a minute or two. Pour in the whisked chicken eggs and cook on low heat, stirring constantly, until set and nicely scrambled. Salt and pepper to taste. Serve along with camp biscuits and bacon.

**Note:** *If you don't have fresh roe, steam or simmer a fish fillet for a few minutes, flake up the meat with a fork, and whisk into the eggs. Leftover fish can also be used.*

# SOPCHOPPY PANCAKES

If you want to feed pancakes to a crowd, it's best to cook on a large rectangular griddle or at least on a flat circular griddle. A regular skillet won't hold many pancakes, and the deep sides make them difficult to turn with a spatula. Still, pancakes cook quickly and a skillet will make a stack in short order. I prefer to cook one pancake at a time in an 8-inch cast-iron skillet, but larger pans can be used.

I don't really have a recipe that I use religiously, and, I'll have to admit, I usually use a pancake mix from the supermarket. If you have a trusty recipe for pancake batter, perhaps from sourdough, use it instead of the mix. (I set forth some off-the-beaten-path recipes in my work *The Whole Grain Cookbook*, including those made with teff, buckwheat, rice flour, and so on.)

Apart from the batter, a few rather small wild blueberries or huckleberries are nice in breakfast pancakes, but the larger cultivated berries are acceptable. Several kinds of wild blueberries and huckleberries grow in several sizes in the scrub lands around Sopchoppy, Florida. My title for this recipe, however, comes from the wonderful sugarcane syrup that is made in the area. I buy a gallon whenever I visit thereabouts. Some parts of the country will cry foul here and champion the use of some sort of local sorghum, or even maple syrup. Most of the latter (or at least what is sold to tourists) is far too thin for pancakes, at least to my thinking. I want a thick syrup or honey that isn't quickly sogged up. But suit yourself. It's also hard to beat the tupelo honey harvested from the river swamps of northwest Florida.

**pancake batter (from a mix
or your favorite recipe)**
**fresh blueberries or huckleberries**

**fresh butter**
**pure cane syrup or tupelo honey**

Mix the batter according to the directions on the package. It helps to mix the batter in a bowl with a handle and a pouring spout. Heat the skillet medium hot and coat the bottom with butter. Slowly pour a little of the batter into the skillet, or use a ladle or large spoon if you must. (Start with about ⅓ cup of batter for each pancake.) Pour steadily so that the stream is into the middle of the pancake. Cook for a minute and sprinkle on a few blueberries. When the bottom starts to set (peek by lifting up the edge with your spatula), carefully turn the pancake and cook the other side.

Put the pancakes on a serving plate or platter. When you get 3 or 4 (or whatever you deem a serving to be), put a pat of butter between each pancake and on top. Serve hot with the thick syrup or honey of your choice. Bacon or sausage and hot coffee complete the breakfast.

# HASH BROWN POTATOES

Frozen supermarket hash brown potatoes are partly cooked and cut into short strings so that they mat together when cooked. I like fresh hash browns much better, made with diced raw spuds. The measures below will feed 2 people, perhaps with a little left over for the dog. Both the onion and the diced red bell pepper can be omitted. Any kind of cooking oil can be used, but I prefer bacon drippings, especially from the bacon to be served with the hash browns.

**1 pound finely diced potato**

**2 tablespoons minced scallions with part of green tops**

**1 tablespoon minced red bell pepper**

**salt and freshly ground black pepper**

**2 tablespoons bacon drippings or vegetable oil**

Heat the bacon drippings in a cast-iron skillet. Add the potatoes, scallions, and red bell pepper, and cook, stirring and shaking the skillet as you go, for a few minutes. Sprinkle with salt and pepper. Spread the mix evenly and press down lightly with a spatula. Reduce the heat to low and cook for about 10 minutes, shaking the pan with one hand, and then press a time or two with the spatula in the other hand.

When the bottom is nicely browned, turn the potatoes with the aid of two spatulas—or by flipping if you feel frisky and don't have too much oil left in the skillet. Add a little more bacon drippings if needed and brown the other side. If the resulting pattie has held together, cut it into pie-shaped pieces for serving. If the pattie has torn apart, serve it as hash.

# SKILLET BACON

Of the several ways to cook bacon, the jackleg will usually prefer to sauté it in a skillet simply because it's more of a hands-on approach and lets one appreciate the sizzle and the aroma. (Never mind who has to clean the stove.) A square skillet works a little better if it's large enough to hold the bacon slices without curving them, but any large skillet will do.

Heat the skillet on medium-high heat, then lay in a few slices of the bacon—but do not overcrowd, cooking in several batches if necessary. Cook for a few minutes, then turn one strip at a time with tongs. (It isn't necessary to try to flip the whole works with a spatula.) Cook for a few more minutes and turn again, considering each piece for doneness and perhaps adjusting the heat a little. Cook and turn until the bacon is as crisp as you like it. Note that some of your guests will want it crispy, others want it limp and chewy. The compleat cook will take pleasure in cooking both kinds to perfection. In either case, drain the bacon on brown bags before serving.

A good deal depends on the quality of the bacon, and on the cut. I prefer mine to be on the thick side. In fact, the best is sold in slab form so that the cook can slice it to order.

Old-time cooks used to strain their bacon drippings into a small grease pot to be used in cooking corn bread, camp potatoes, and so on. I still do this on a limited basis, but, unfortunately, many people consider any animal fat to be pure poison these days.

# COWBOY CAMP COFFEE

Excellent coffee can be made without machines that spit and sputter and steam and drip. All you need is a pot or even a bucket (I have even used a salamander bait bucket). A large skillet is not ideal, but will do. Be warned, however, that the water should not be boiled or left on the fire for a long period of time, which turns the coffee into strong mud.

Any good brand of coffee will do. I like a New Orleans mix of half coffee beans and half chicory root, but suit yourself. Most of the cowboys of old used Arbuckle's coffee beans, which came with a stick of peppermint candy in the bag. This is not a bad idea for camp or on the road.

**½ cup freshly ground coffee**          **½ cup cold water**
**1 quart water**

Bring the water to a boil in a pot, bucket, or large skillet. Add the coffee grounds, remove the pot from the heat, and steep for a few minutes. (Do not bring to a boil after the coffee grounds have been added.) Gently pour in ½ cup of cold water and let stand perfectly still for a minute or two. This will cause the grounds to settle to the bottom. Pour the coffee carefully into cups, trying not to disturb the grounds. If all of the coffee will not be consumed right away, it's best to pour it off the grounds and keep it in a separate container. It can be reheated as needed.

*Note: If you have eggshells, crumble one and add it to the pot or skillet during the boil. It will help settle the ground. Other recipes include a little salt, and one practitioner recommends tapping the side of the pot or pan with a spoon or some such metallic object, apparently to help settle the grounds.*

# CHAPTER

2

## Beef and Pork

For the most part, really good steaks and chops are ideal for cooking in the skillet. Tougher cuts can also be used, sometimes following a Plan B approach in case Plan A doesn't pan out just right, and these less-expensive meats can be even more rewarding to the jackleg cook. This chapter deals mostly with thin cuts of beef and pork. Ground meats are covered separately (in another chapter). Also, some of the recipes in the game chapter (chapter 5) can easily be used to cook beef and pork. Best of all, I hope the recipes and methods set forth in the chapter on gravy (chapter 10) will inspire more people to try the old ways, with a skillet in one hand and a wooden spoon in the other.

Some of the recipes below illustrate the terms "chicken-fried," "smother-fried," and so on in more detail than we set forth (previously), and the techniques can be used with other recipes. Learn the best way to cook a chicken-fried steak, for example, and the lesson can easily be adapted for venison chops in camp cookery. That's the great attraction to skillet cookery, so that every jackleg can easily add a pinch or two of his own secret ingredient without changing the results too drastically. In short, properly prepared chicken-fried steak is good with or without a little chopped parsley in the gravy.

# STEAKS COGNAC
# À LA JOE DOGS IANNUZZI

Here's a recipe cooked by Joseph "Joe Dogs" Iannuzzi at a safe house in Florida, where he was awaiting important news concerning his fate. In his *Mafia Cookbook*, Joe Dogs said he wanted to serve something special, just in case it would be his last supper. The recipe calls for four filets mignons of about 8 ounces each. Since I have trouble finding these in my neck of the woods, and don't have Mafia money to order them via airmail delivery, I usually cook the dish with four regular rib eyes cut 1½ inches thick.

| | |
|---|---|
| 4 tender steaks of about 8 ounces each | ½ cup very good cognac |
| 8 rather large mushrooms, sliced | 3 tablespoons extra-virgin olive oil |
| 2 medium to large onions, chopped | salt and freshly ground black pepper to taste |
| ½ cup beef stock | |

Heat the olive oil in a 12-inch skillet and cook the steaks, turning once, until they are done to your liking. (Medium rare for me.) Stack the steaks on a heated platter and set aside.

Add a little more olive oil to the skillet if needed. Quickly sauté the onions and mushrooms for about 8 minutes, stirring several times. Add the beef stock, cognac, salt, and black pepper. Flame the skillet to burn off the alcohol. Then simmer until the liquid is reduced by half. Put the steaks back into the sauce and reheat, turning once.

Serve with a baked potato and vegetables of your choice. Joe Dogs recommends his Asparagus Hollandaise, but I'll settle for simply steamed asparagus, cooked only a short time to retain a slight crunch. Of course, a good red wine and a chewy Italian bread go nicely with the dish.

*Note: A number of other recipes for skillet steaks are also good, such as steak au poivre and steak Diane. I can't cover all these here, but I would like to call attention to an old recipe for cooking in a dry skillet and to a recipe I like to use for cooking for myself in a 6-inch cast-iron skillet, both covered below.*

# A. D.'S UN-LUCULLAN RIB EYE

Not having as many servants as Lucullus, the Roman epicure who insisted on a full table even when dining alone, I confess to cutting back a little when cooking a steak for myself only. I think it's best to drink the brandy after dinner instead of burning it in some showy recipe like steak Diane, which I would be more likely to cook for a lady love.

| | |
|---|---|
| **1 rib eye steak about 1½ inches thick** | **black pepper and salt as needed** |
| **soy sauce** | **olive oil** |

Grind some black pepper onto each side of the steak, pressing it into the meat with your fingertips. Put the steak into a small container and pour a little soy sauce over it. Let it sit at room temperature for an hour or so while you get the potatoes, salad, bread, and so on ready. (If longer, put the container into the refrigerator.)

Drain the soy sauce off the steak and discard (unless you opt for gravy). Heat the skillet on high until it spits back at you. Add a little olive oil to the skillet. When the oil starts to smoke, put the steak in with your tongs, centering it nicely. Set your timer for 3 minutes. Do not turn the steak. When the timer buzzes, turn the steak with tongs and cook for another 3 minutes. Sprinkle the top with a little salt.

Put the steak onto the plate with the go-withs and cut it in half to bleed out some juice to sauce the bottom of the plate. Pour yourself another glass of good red wine. Cut yourself a bit off the end of the rib eye and enjoy.

*Note: If you want to be more Lucullan with this simple dish, drizzle the steak with a little very good olive oil and a squeeze of fresh lemon a moment before serving. Call it Tuscan Steak and open another bottle of Chianti.*

# COUNTRY STEAK

I allow that broiled T-bone steaks or grilled New York strips are hard to beat for dinner or supper, along with baked potatoes and salad. For breakfast, however, I'll take country steak and gravy every time. I normally use round steak for this dish, but about fifteen minutes before this writing, my wife cooked up a batch of top sirloin to feed our strapling sons and a spend-the-night hulk or two. The flavor and texture were just right. For cooking this kind of steak for four people, I recommend a 12-inch cast-iron skillet. A griddle can be used for the steak itself, but doesn't work if you want lots of gravy, which ought to be a requirement for anything called country steak. Here's a recipe that has been used in my family for generations, and it is almost exactly like one used by my good wife's people.

| | |
|---|---|
| beefsteak, ¾ inch thick | salt |
| cooking oil | pepper |
| flour | water |

Trim the steak and pound it with a meat mallet, the edge of a heavy plate, or the mouth of a heavy glass bottle. (I use the edge of a plate, pounding in a crisscross pattern; my wife uses an old, heavy 2-quart bottle, which she holds with both hands.) After you've worked over the meat, pour some flour in a plate and flip-flop the steak in it. Then pound the steak again and flour it again. (Keep the flour plate handy.) Cut the steak into 3-inch pieces. Heat a little oil in a heavy skillet and cook the steak pieces on both sides until well browned. Remove the steak pieces to a heated serving platter. Pour off most of the grease. Draw a cup of water and have it ready. Using a tablespoon, put some flour into the skillet and stir it into the remaining grease and pan dredgings. Stir continuously on medium-high heat until the mixture is browned, as when making a roux. Add water and stir until you have gravy of a consistency that suits your fancy. Salt and pepper to taste. The gravy can be served over the meat, or it can be served over rice or biscuit halves. For breakfast, I prefer biscuit halves. I don't require biscuits made from scratch if I've got a really good mix at hand. But I don't much care for the refrigerated canned biscuits.

*Variation:* The above recipe is what we usually make for breakfast. If we cook country steak for another meal, I usually add some onions to the gravy. Peel and dice a medium onion. Brown the onion for a couple of minutes in the skillet before adding the flour. Then proceed as usual. I am especially fond of this onion gravy, made quite thick and a little heavy on black pepper, served over fluffy white rice.

# DRY SALT STEAK

This unusual method of cooking steak seems to seal in the juices better than other methods, and the results are not as salty as one might think. A popular family cookbook directs the reader to wash the cooked steak before serving. Don't do it! I normally use rib eyes or chuck eyes about 1½ inches thick for this technique. Any good steak will do, but those with lots of marbling work best.

*Note: This method does make some smoke. If you don't have a good vent over your kitchen stove, it may be best to save this method of cooking for the patio. It's also a very good camp recipe, thanks partly to the Spartan list of ingredients. I normally use a sea salt for this recipe, but regular table salt works just fine. Avoid very coarse salt, however.*

**good beefsteak**     **sea salt (regular grind)**

Sprinkle a thin coat of salt onto the skillet, almost covering the bottom. Heat the skillet until it is very hot. Dry the steak with a paper towel and lay it onto the salt. Sear without turning for 4 minutes. Turn and cook the other side for 4 minutes. It should be crispy brown on the outside and rosy moist inside. Serve hot, along with potatoes, salad, and whatever you like with your steak.

# STEAK TERRY GUNN

One of my favorite recipes for good steaks (rib eye, T-bone, or porterhouse) appeared in a book called *Angler Profiles* (which also set forth the world's best fried fish recipe—mine). It was submitted by a fly-fishing guide and tackle shop owner in Arizona named Terry Gunn. Terry says to start with a steak thicker than 1 inch and to cook it on a flat iron surface, such as a griddle or skillet bottom. The flat surface, he says, and I agree, seals in the juices better than ribbed surfaces. The ingredients are as simple as can be, with the reader given the option of choosing his own seasoning salt.

**prime-cut thick steak**     **Lawry's (or other) seasoning salt**

Pat the steak with your favorite seasoning salt. Heat the skillet to the hottest possible point, Gunn says. Sear the steak on both sides, then reduce the heat by 20 percent. Turn the steak frequently—at least once every minute. (Frequent turning will help keep the juices in the middle of the steak instead of letting them drip out, Gunn goes on.) Press on the steak with your finger to determine the level of doneness, Gunn says. I say it takes a total of 3 minutes on each side for a steak that is 1½ inches thick. Then let it coast a little before serving. So . . . there you have it: the best steak that you have ever tasted, Gunn insists. I consider this to be a good way to cook a steak in camp, where a little smoke from the sear won't alarm the local fire department.

# HERTER'S MINNESOTA STEAK

In my book *Good Vittles*, I set forth a French skillet specialty called steak au poivre, and I can't repeat it here. Since then, I've experimented with a similar skillet steak as cooked by George Leonard Herter, co-author of *Bull Cook* and *Authentic Historical Recipes and Practices*. Herter was a great champion of beef suet, which he claimed was the only sensible substance to use for frying fish. Beef suet is difficult to find these days, and most grocery store employees don't even know the meaning of the term. It is, for the record, a beef shortening rendered from fat, especially from the good fat around the kidneys and other choice spots. Here's the complete list of ingredients for Herter's version:

| | |
|---|---|
| **steaks** | **salt** |
| **beef suet** | **pepper** |
| **butter, melted** | |

Put ⅛ inch of beef suet into a skillet. Salt and pepper the steaks to taste. Bring the skillet to heat and sear each side of the steak, then fry for 3 minutes or so on each side. Blot each side of the steak with a paper towel, then put the steak on a heated platter. Butter each side of the steak and serve hot.

I usually cook Herter's recipe after finding some T-bone steaks that weren't well trimmed and have lots of fat skirting the meat. I trim the fat closely, cut it into ½-inch cubes, and fry enough of it, on low heat, in my cast-iron skillet until I have ⅛ inch of "suet." (Note that one T-bone steak will not always provide enough suet in which to cook itself, and more beef fat may be needed.) When you are finished rendering the suet, you'll have some small crackling-like balls left in the pan. Drain these on a brown paper bag and set them aside. Sear and fry the steak by the directions above, or, if you prefer, cook the steak on rather high heat and omit the searing step. Crumble the leftover beef cracklings and sprinkle them over a tossed salad, or use them to top the sour cream on your baked potato.

*Note: People with cholesterol problems should beware of this recipe. The beef suet as well as the butter will up the count considerably.*

# CHICKEN-FRIED STEAKS

These are tender steaks, often beaten or cubed, that are dredged and fried with a crispy outside. Then they are topped with a skillet gravy, often a white one. Beef steaks from chuck, cut from ⅜ to ½ inch and duly beaten, are best for this recipe.

<table>
<tr><td>beef chuck steaks (about a pound)</td><td>water</td></tr>
<tr><td>peanut oil</td><td>chicken egg</td></tr>
<tr><td>all-purpose flour</td><td>salt and freshly ground black pepper</td></tr>
<tr><td>milk (at room temperature)</td><td></td></tr>
</table>

Sprinkle the steak on both sides with salt, pepper, and a little flour, then beat it with the edge of a heavy plate or saucer. Turn and repeat several times until the meat is quite tender. Lightly whisk the egg and a little milk. Dust the steaks with flour, dip in the egg mixture, let the excess drip off, and then dredge in flour. Shake off the excess flour and set the steaks aside while you heat about ½ inch of peanut oil in a skillet.

Fry the steaks for 2 or 3 minutes on each side until golden brown and a little crispy, turning once. Remove the steaks to a heated serving platter but do not cover.

Pour off most of the skillet oil, saving about 2 tablespoons. Slowly add 2 tablespoons flour, stirring with a wooden spoon. Stir in about 1 tablespoon of water and reduce the heat. Slowly stir in 1 cup of milk, or a little more depending on how thin you want the gravy. Cook and stir for a few minutes, shaking the skillet as you go, until you have a nice white gravy.

Pour the gravy over the steaks (or into a gravy boat) and serve hot, along with mashed potatoes and vegetables of your choice. It is important to hold the gravy until the last minute. That way, you'll have a rare treat of a crunchy steak in a flavorful gravy.

# SMOTHER-FRIED STEAKS

Here's a method for cooking very tough steaks, perhaps from an animal of maturity and character, as they like to say in Texas. It's a great recipe for camp cooking, if you have the patience and the skill to simmer the steak in the gravy long enough without burning it. In a sense, it is the exact opposite to Chicken-Fried Steaks, which just goes to show you that there's more than one trick in the skillet cook's bag. Note that the previous recipe works best with comparatively tender cuts of meat; this one, with tough cuts. The Chicken-Fried Steaks recipe offers a certain crunch with the gravy; this one, however, makes the best possible gravy. (For more on gravy, see chapter 10.)

| | |
|---|---|
| **tough steaks** | **cooking oil** |
| **chopped onion** | **salt and freshly ground black pepper** |
| **chopped fresh mushrooms** | **water** |
| **flour** | |

Dust the steaks with flour, salt, and pepper. Beat each steak on one side, then turn and beat the other. Sprinkle with flour and beat again. Heat a little oil in a skillet, getting it hot enough to spit back at you. Give the steaks a final dusting with flour and quickly fry for 2 or 3 minutes on each side, turning once, then remove from skillet. Cook in several batches, if necessary.

Pour off most of the cooking oil, keeping about 1 tablespoon. Sauté the onion and mushrooms until the pieces start to brown around the edges. Add a little water to deglaze the skillet, scraping up any grimilles that have stuck to the bottom of the pan. Make a paste with flour and water, then slowly pour it in, stirring, until you have a thin gravy. Bring to a light boil, then put the steaks back into the skillet. Lower the heat, cover tightly, and simmer for 2 hours or longer, until the steaks are fork tender. Stir from time to time and add more water as needed. (If you don't have a tightly fitting lid, use whatever you can rig; then stir and add water more often.)

Serve hot with rice or mashed potatoes, along with green beans and other vegetables or salad, and maybe some chewy French bread to help sop up some of that wonderful skillet gravy.

# TWO-SKILLET STROGANOFF

A number of recipes exist for beef Stroganoff, named after a Russian diplomat, and most of them are suitable for cooking in a skillet. Some experts say that the real stuff does not contain mushrooms or tomatoes in any form. I'll opt for the mushrooms, but the tomatoes are rather late additions to the dish and are therefore questionable on historical grounds. Moreover, Stroganoff is usually served with rice pilaf as well as with noodles and hot boiled new potatoes. (I'll take mine over noodles, thank you.) All of the recipes, however, must contain sour cream, and most are made with very tender beef, usually loin or tenderloin.

| | |
|---|---|
| 1½ pounds beef tenderloin | 1 medium onion, minced |
| 8 ounces sliced mushrooms | 2 tablespoons whole wheat flour |
| 1 cup beef stock or water with bouillon | 1 tablespoon dry bread crumbs |
| ½ cup sour cream | salt and freshly ground black pepper to taste |
| ¼ cup butter or more (divided) | rice, egg noodles, or new potatoes, cooked separately |

Cut the beef into strips about ¼ inch wide. Roll these in flour and set aside. Heat about half the butter in a 10-inch skillet and sauté the mushrooms and onions. Set aside. Heat the rest of the butter in another skillet and quickly brown the beef strips, cooking a few strips at a time.

In the large skillet, combine all the browned beef strips with the mushrooms and onions. Add the beef stock and bread crumbs, along with some salt and pepper to taste. Simmer, covered, until the meat is tender, or about 10 minutes, adding more stock or water if needed.

Add the sour cream and bring to a quick boil. Remove from the heat and serve, quite hot, with rice, boiled new potatoes, or noodles, sprinkled with parsley or chopped fresh dill. Feeds 4 to 6. Forget the vodka, but I'll take a little red wine with my serving.

*Note: Excellent Stroganoff can also be made from tenderloin of bison, deer, or other big game, such as bear.*

# VEAL PARMIGIANA

Here's a dish I like to cook with veal cutlets or venison tenderloin, a strip of meat found on the inside of the backbone. (As described at the end of chapter 5, the twin tenderloins of deer can and should be removed during field dressing, making them a good choice for deer camp cookery. No aging or marinade is required. Like veal, the tenderloin doesn't have much flavor, but—also like veal—it responds well to the coating of Parmesan cheese, which is best when hard, aged, and freshly grated.) It's customary to pound veal cutlets about ¾ inch thick down to about ¼ inch thickness, or less. You can also cook this with pork loin cutlets, or with any tender venison steak.

1 to 2 pounds ¾-inch veal cutlets, pounded
½ cup clarified butter
1 cup fine dry bread crumbs
1 cup freshly grated Parmesan cheese
2 chicken eggs

a little water or milk
½ teaspoon dried basil (optional)
salt and pepper to taste
tomato sauce or salsa (optional)

Mix the bread crumbs, grated Parmesan, salt, pepper, and basil on a sheet of plastic wrap or aluminum foil. Dredge the cutlets in the mixture one at a time and shake off the excess. Lightly whisk the chicken eggs in a bowl with a little water or milk. Dip the cutlets in the beaten egg, letting the excess drip off. Then dredge the cutlets again in the bread crumb mixture. Let sit at room temperature for about 20 minutes, but do not chill.

Heat the clarified butter in a skillet and fry the cutlets, 2 or 3 at a time, for about 2 minutes on each side, or until brown and crisp. Serve hot with a tomato sauce or tomato-based salsa (mild, medium, or hot) of your choice, or try it plain if you relish the pronounced flavor of good Parmesan.

# FINGER-LICKING PORK CHOPS

Prime T-bone pork chops are best for this recipe, but boneless loin chops will also work.

| | |
|---|---|
| fresh pork T-bones | peanut oil |
| flour | salt and black pepper to taste |
| chicken egg | water |

Mix some salt and pepper into a little flour. Whisk the chicken egg in a wide, shallow bowl. Flop the pork chops, one at a time, in the egg and dredge in the seasoned flour.

Heat ½ inch of peanut oil in a skillet on medium high. Fry the chops, 1 or 2 at a time, depending on the size of the skillet, until nicely browned and cooked through. Drain on a brown bag.

Pour off most of the grease and deglaze the skillet with a little water. Add a little flour, stirring constantly with a wooden spoon, and cook until the gravy is the way you want it.

Serve with mashed potatoes, vegetables, and bread. Because pork chops can be on the tough side, a steak knife is recommended for cutting these chops on the plate. Better yet (unless you are feeding snooty guests), simply eat them hand to mouth, a technique that eliminates a lot of work and facilitates the gnawing of the T-bone.

# BORNEAN PIG CHOPS

Here's a culinary treat that I found in (and adapted from) Richard Sterling's book *Dining with Headhunters*. Sterling, in turn, got it from a native of the jungle called Eetwat, who foraged and processed wild pepper. Wild pigs, I understand, abound in the jungles of Borneo, feeding on local fruits. Highly prized as table fare, they are hunted by the rather nomadic Punan peoples with poisoned dart and blowgun. Anyhow, I tried Eetwat's recipe with loin chops from a Florida pineywood rooter; green peppercorns from a local supermarket (bottled in brine); the juice of two large Parson Brown oranges (a variety developed on Timucuan Island in Lake Weir, where I once lived); peanut oil from the Wiregrass area of Alabama, where I was raised on a peanut farm; and wild onions that grow profusely along the roadways of North America. Use chops from a domestic pig if you must, cutting them about 1 inch thick, and try scallions with green tops in lieu of wild onions—or ramps, in season.

2 pounds loin chops

juice of 2 oranges

¼ cup sliced scallions or wild onions with part of tops

¼ cup green peppercorns, crushed

¼ cup peanut oil

2 cups flour

2 tablespoons salt

2 tablespoons black pepper

Mix the flour, salt, and black pepper in a brown bag. Shake the chops to coat all sides. Heat the peanut oil in a large cast-iron skillet. Brown on both sides, cooking in two or more batches if necessary. Remove the chops, putting them on a brown bag to drain.

Sauté the scallions for 5 or 6 minutes. Place the chops back into the skillet, add the orange juice, cover, and simmer until the chops are almost done (still pink inside).

Remove the chops, add the crushed green peppercorns, and reduce the pan liquid until you have a nice sauce. Pour the sauce over the chops, let sit for a minute or two, and serve with rice and steamed vegetables of your choice.

# LEFTOVER ROAST BEEF HASH

Roast beef from the rump end, usually cooked in an oven or large pot, is likely to be rather dry, especially the second time around. It can be sliced thinly and used in sandwiches, preferably with lots of mayonnaise, or it can be reworked in a moist hash. In this recipe, the meat and vegetables are all cut into ½-inch dice. The amounts of each ingredient don't have to be exact. The hash also works with leftover venison, buffalo, and so on.

| | |
|---|---|
| 1½ cups diced leftover roast | ¼ cup minced fresh parsley |
| 1½ cups diced potatoes | ¼ cup butter |
| 1 cup diced onion | salt and freshly ground pepper |
| ¾ cup diced green bell pepper | hot water |
| ¾ cup diced red bell pepper | flour (if wanted) |

Heat the butter in a large skillet and brown the onion. Add the red and green bell peppers, parsley, and potatoes. Cook for a few minutes, stirring a time or two. Add the diced beef, salt, and pepper. Heat through. If you want more gravy, as for serving over rice or pasta, stir in a little flour and water. Serve hot.

*Note: If you have some of this hash left over, reheat it the next day with more water or stock and call it a slumgullion, a stew, instead of a hash.*

# CHAPTER

## 3

# Burger

**G**round meats are frequently cooked in a skillet, either as patties or meatballs, or loose in such recipes as chili and spaghetti sauce. The modern cook now has several ground meat choices from the larger supermarkets, including ground beef chuck, ground beef round, ground turkey, ground pork, ground lamb, and so on.

I normally prefer to purchase market-grind meats—those that are prepared on location in the store—to prepackaged meats ground and packaged at another place, often hundreds of miles away, requiring more handling and time in distribution and more large-batch exposure to contaminants. But with a market grind, much depends on the individual store and the butcher, it seems to me. I'm talking about freshness, fat content, and meat scraps, in addition to contamination. Thus, I prefer to deal with a personal butcher in a shop that specializes in meat.

The best bet, however, is to prepare your own burger meat. That way you'll at least know what you have. Here are some talking points.

**Sausage Mills**. I highly recommend that the cook purchase one of the several electric or hand-cranked sausage mills that are on the market these days. The food processors and other high-speed zappers may work, but I don't want to risk making a mush of good meat. The sausage mills go slower and produce a more uniform grind. It's best to start with large chunks of meat and grind it shortly before it is needed. (This will produce a fresher grind, more likely to be free of harmful contaminants.) Cut the big chunks into 1-inch cubes and grind in a sausage mill fitted with a ³⁄₁₆-inch wheel. Finer or coarser grinds can be obtained with different-size wheels. My book *Sausage* sets forth more advice on this matter, along with some sausage recipes suitable for the skillet.

**Mixing the Burger**. Do not overwork the mixture when adding bread crumbs, chicken egg, spices, or other ingredients. The mix ought not to be smooth or too dense. If adding spices to the mix, let it sit for about 30 minutes to absorb the flavors.

**Shaping the Pattie**. It's best to shape burger patties by hand—but don't press them tightly. Preshaped burgers or those made in a kitchen press are all right, but I really prefer to make my own the way I want them. Each burger should be a little different. Most of the market patties are too thin for my liking. They are also too geometric—either too perfectly round or square.

**Cooking the Burger**. Many jackleg chefs and short-order cooks press on a burger with a spatula as it cooks in a skillet or on a griddle. The idea is to press out the red juices, making the burger seem to cook quicker. Although I am guilty of the practice from time to time, I know better. If you want a juicy burger, do not compress the meat during mixing, while shaping the pattie, or during cooking. Period.

**Browning the Meat**. In preparing such recipes as spaghetti sauce, chili, and so on, many recipe writers instruct the reader to begin by browning the burger meat. While the instruction is clear enough to most of us, the term "brown" is not accurate. Gray would be the better term, but its use as verb would take most readers aback instead of clarifying the matter. In any case, the purpose of "browning" hamburger meat is not, as a rule, to change the color or to partly cook it; instead, the process separates the meat grinds and thereby helps keep it from cooking in chunks.

Some people add a little oil to a skillet before browning the meat, but this is usually not necessary, especially if a rather fat meat is used in the grind, such as beef chuck. Others will take pains to pour out any fat after the meat has been browned. I prefer to use a little water instead of oil to help start the meat without sticking. It works nicely, cooks away, and doesn't increase the fat content.

# HAMBURGER STEAKS FOR TWO

I once knew a cowpoke from Okeechobee City, Florida, who wouldn't eat beef unless it was ground up. He had good teeth, and, so far as I could tell, he was perfectly able to chew. I decided that maybe he had never eaten a really good steak. What his wife cooked, I told myself, was hard and dry. I was wrong, of course, and, after eating her ground steak, I at least understood the man's position. Here's pretty much what the good woman did to make a believer out of me:

| | |
|---|---|
| 1 pound lean beef, ground | coarse black pepper |
| grease | hot black coffee |
| diced onion | whole wheat flour |
| salt | |

Mix salt and pepper into the ground beef. Shape the meat into an oval patty about 7 inches long. Heat a little grease in a cast-iron skillet. Brown the ground beef steak on one side for 5 or 6 minutes. Turn carefully. While the other side is browning, put a little whole wheat flour into the frying pan on one side of the oval steak. (There should be enough fat or pan liquid to moisten the flour; if not, add a tad of butter.) Stir the flour with a spoon and clear a spot for the onions. Stir the onions while they brown. If you've timed it right, the steak should be almost ready about now. Pour a little hot coffee atop the flour, and quickly stir in the onions. Let it bubble a few minutes, then spoon the gravy over the steak. Turn the steak over and halve it with your spatula. Check for doneness. I like mine medium rare, with a touch of pink showing in the center of the meat, provided that I've got freshly ground lean beef instead of old packaged (and repackaged) "hamburger meat." If you want yours well done, turn the heat to high and pour in a little more coffee. Quickly cover the skillet with a lid, thereby holding in the steam, and cook for a few minutes. When steamed this way, the steak can be well done without being too dry. But it's best if you don't overcook the meat. Serve the gravy over the steak. Feeds 2.

# VERSATILE VENISON BURGERS

Burgers made from ground venison without added fat are quite tasty, but they can be on the dry side and tend to come apart during cooking and turning. Here's an easy recipe for keeping them succulent and intact. I don't offer exact measurements, but anybody who has ever made hamburgers won't have much trouble. It's best not to crowd the burgers in the skillet, cooking in more than one batch if need be. For practice, go one burger at a time in a small skillet.

| | |
|---|---|
| freshly ground venison | a little vegetable oil or spray |
| cream of mushroom soup | salt and freshly ground black pepper |
| finely minced onion | hamburger buns |
| dry red wine (optional) | |

Mix the onion, salt, and black pepper into the ground venison, along with a little of the mushroom soup. Shape the mixture into loose patties about ¾ inch thick. Heat a skillet and add a little oil, or spray, to keep the burgers from sticking. Cook the burgers on medium heat for about 5 minutes. Turn carefully with a thin spatula and cook for another 4 minutes. (I often use two spatulas, placing one on top of the burger to help hold it together on the turn.)

Add some of the mushroom soup to the skillet, using a tablespoon to place it around the sides of the burgers and on top. Use a generous amount of the soup—enough to give you ½ inch (or a little better) of liquid in the skillet. Add a little red wine, if you have any left. Cover and simmer on very low heat for 5 minutes. Turn carefully and simmer for another 5 minutes, adding a little more soup or red wine if needed. Carefully remove the burgers and place them on buns, topping with a little of the pan gravy, thinly sliced onion, a sprinkle of grated cheese, thin tomato slices, sautéed mushrooms, or whatever you like on your burgers.

Plan B. If your burgers don't hold together, break up the patties in the skillet, add more mushroom soup, and spread the mix over open-faced hamburger buns. Call the mess Pete's Sloppy Joes if your name is Pete—or Joe's Sloppy Petes if your name is Joe—and serve proudly, without letting on that the dish is a failed burger.

Plan C. If you are feeding sophisticated folks, spoon the venison and soup mix over egg noodles instead of hamburger buns. Add a dollop of sour cream and call it Russian Venison Stroganoff. If you want to eat French instead of Russian and have some more wine, use crème fraîche instead of ordinary sour cream and serve over pasta (al dente, of course) with a chunk of chewy bread on the side. Red wine all around.

# RUSSIAN MEAT PATTIES

Said to split the difference between an American hamburger and a Swedish meatball, a Russian specialty called *kotlety* is served up with a sauce called *podlivka*. There are many versions of both sauce and pattie. This recipe, making use of sour cream, is adapted from Kira Petrovskaya's *Russian Cookbook*. It can be cooked in any good skillet and is ideal for large electric skillets.

| | |
|---|---|
| 1½ pounds lean beef | 2 tablespoons sour cream |
| 1 medium to large onion, grated | 1 chicken egg lightly whisked |
| 2 or 3 slices stale white bread | a little milk |
| dry bread crumbs | salt and pepper to taste |
| butter (used twice) | 2 or 3 tablespoons water |

Trim the crust off the bread. Soak the bread in a little milk for a few minutes, then squeeze it out and set aside. Cut the meat into small chunks and run through a meat grinder with a medium or fine blade (no larger than ³⁄₁₆ inch). Mix in the stale bread, squash the mix all together with your fingers, and run it through the grinder again. Add the grated onion, salt, pepper, and chicken egg, stirring as you go with a wooden spoon.

Heat the skillet to medium hot. Add about ¼ cup of butter. As the butter heats, shape the meat mixture into small balls or ovals, somewhat smaller than the typical hamburger. Roll the balls in dry bread crumbs, then flatten them loosely with a chef's knife, making patties instead of balls. Cut a crisscross on either side. Cook the patties a few at a time in the butter for 4 or 5 minutes, then turn carefully and cook for another 4 minutes or so. (Overcrowding the skillet will make them difficult to turn.) Put the cooked patties on a hot platter or plate. Cook the rest of the batch, adding more butter as needed.

When all the patties have been browned, turn the heat to high and add a little fresh butter to the skillet along with 2 or 3 tablespoons of water, stirring and scraping any tidbits (grimilles) off the bottom of the skillet. Reduce the heat and stir in 2 tablespoons of sour cream. Pour the sauce over the patties and serve hot. Feeds 4 to 6 ordinary people—or 2 Russians.

# BULGARIAN BURGERS

I found this recipe in Atanas Slavov's book *Traditional Bulgarian Cooking*. It is typical of the almost infinite ways that different kinds of ground meats can be mixed. Try ground venison burger instead of lamb.

2 pounds ground lamb

1 pound ground beef

2 medium onions, minced

½ cup chopped fresh parsley

2 chicken eggs

1 slice white bread

4 teaspoons flour

1 tablespoon butter (more as needed)

½ teaspoon cumin

salt and freshly ground black pepper to taste

warm water

Remove the crust from the bread and give it to the dog. Soak the bread in a little water for a few minutes. Squeeze out the bread, shred it, and place it into a large bowl. Mix in the meat, eggs, spices, onions, and parsley, along with ¼ cup of water. Use your hands to squash and knead the mixture, then shape it into 8 burgers about 3 inches wide and 1 inch thick.

Place the flour in a plate and carefully set each burger in it. Turn the burger to coat both sides and shake off any excess flour. (Add more flour to the plate if needed.) Heat the butter on medium-high heat and cook each burger for about 4 minutes on each side. Use more butter if needed.

These burgers can be eaten as a meat pattie, perhaps topped with mushroom sauce or gravy made in the skillet. The patties also work as a bun filler, using as you would a regular burger. The flour will give the burger a little different texture, however, so consider using a little more mayonnaise or other condiment than usual.

# SEMINOLE BURGERS

The Seminole Indians made a bread of pumpkin and flour, as discussed in chapter 9. This dough was rolled out flat and fried, but sometimes they used rounds of dough to encase meat patties. Then the whole thing was fried. Ground beef, venison, or other good red meat can be used.

2 pounds ground red meat
½ cup minced onion
salt and black pepper to taste

1 recipe Seminole Pumpkin Bread dough (chapter 9)
cooking oil

Mix the ground meat, onion, salt, and black pepper. Shape into 6 patties. Roll out 6 rounds of dough about twice as wide as the burgers. Put a burger into each round of dough, fold in the edges, and pinch shut.

Heat an inch or so of oil in a skillet. Fry each burger until golden brown, turning several times. Serve hot. These are easy to hold and eat, making them ideal for feeding children in camp.

# ONE-SKILLET DINNER

Many are the recipes for cooking a whole meal in a single pot or even a skillet, and many people cook up some such dish without following a recipe, depending on what we have at hand that needs using up. A lot of these recipes call for ground meat, partly because it's easy to use, readily available, and liked by almost everyone except vegetarians and vegans. A large skillet with a lid is usually best, and a square electric skillet is ideal. Here's a recipe for openers, but remember that exact measures aren't necessary. In other words, you can dice up a medium onion without measuring to see whether or not it makes exactly 1 cup.

1 pound hamburger meat
2 cups diced celery with part of green tops
2 cups diced potatoes
1 cup diced onion
½ cup diced red bell pepper

½ cup diced green bell pepper (or jalapeño)
½ cup diced mushrooms
salt and freshly ground black pepper
water or beef stock

Add a little water or beef stock to the skillet, then brown the meat and onion, stirring as you go with a wooden spoon. Add the potatoes, celery, bell peppers, and mushrooms, along with salt and pepper and some more water. Reduce the heat to a simmer, cover tightly, and cook for 20 minutes or so. Serve hot. A loaf of bread completes the meal.

# EASY SKILLET CHILI

Here's a recipe that I like to cook in a cast-iron skillet whenever I want only a small batch of chili or do not have a large pot handy.

For the cracklings, cut the salt pork into slices down to the rind. Then cut the slices into ¼-inch dice. Discard the rind, or use it to make your own pork rind for fishing. (Simply place the rind in highly salted water and store in the refrigerator. Cut into strips, or perhaps frog-shaped chunks.)

Regular ground beef can be used, but a coarse grind works better. I like to use chuck ground with a ½-inch wheel. If you can't simmer the chili for at least 2 hours, however, use a regular hamburger grind. The chile powder used in the recipe does not contain spices and should not be confused with chili powder.

2 pounds chili-grind beef
2 ounces salt pork
¼ cup minced onion
2 cloves garlic, minced
4 tablespoons pure chile powder
(ancho or New Mexico)

1 tablespoon freshly ground cumin seeds
¼ teaspoon dried Mexican oregano
salt and freshly ground black pepper to taste
water or beef stock

Cook the salt pork in a large skillet until the pieces give up most of their fat and are crispy. Drain the cracklings and set aside, resisting the temptation to eat one or two.

Brown the ground beef in the skillet. Stir in the onion and garlic. Sprinkle on the chile powder, cumin, oregano, pepper, and salt. Add enough water or beef stock to barely cover and stir well. Heat almost to a boil, then reduce the heat and simmer for 2 hours or longer, uncovered. Stir and taste from time to time with a wooden spoon, adding more liquid as needed.

Toward the end, cook down until the chili is quite thick. Serve in bowls, topping each serving off with a dollop of sour cream and a sprinkling of the cracklings.

# A. D.'S PASTA HELPER MEATBALLS

The best spaghetti sauces are simmered for hours in a cast-iron pot or large skillet, stirred from time to time with a wooden spoon. Recipes abound, and most cooks will have a family favorite or otherwise will brown some burger meat and pour in a can or two of prepared tomato-based sauce. Here's a quick variation, without tomato, that I like to make.

| | |
|---|---|
| 1 pound hamburger meat | bacon drippings or cooking oil (olive oil will do) |
| 1 small can cream of mushroom soup | salt and black pepper to taste |
| fettuccine (or similar pasta or egg noodles) | Chianti |

Cook the fettuccine according to the directions on the package, preferably al dente. Using your hands, squash some salt and pepper into the burger meat. Shape the meat into small balls—no larger than 1 inch across—and set them aside on a flat surface. (The balls should hold their shape nicely but should not be compressed.)

Heat about ¾ inch of oil in a skillet. Put some meatballs into the skillet but do not overcrowd them. Fry for a few minutes, turning a time or two, until nicely browned. Drain the balls on a brown bag. Repeat until all the meatballs have been fried.

Pour the oil out of the skillet and deglaze with a little Chianti. Stir in the can of mushroom soup. Add the meatballs back to the skillet. Cook for a few minutes more, stirring constantly but gently. Fill each plate with hot fettuccine and top generously with meatballs and gravy. Serve hot with some chewy Italian bread, a colorful tossed salad, and some more Chianti.

*Note:* *A topping of freshly grated Parmesan cheese goes nicely with this dish.*

# CHAPTER

# Birds

**I** have included a few hunter's birds here instead of putting them in the chapter on game, partly because many of these, such as quail and pheasant and mallards, are farm- or pen-raised these days, either for home consumption or for marketing in our super- markets, or for sale by mail-order. Other fowl, such as the guinea hen, are available and may even be regional barnyard favorites. Although this approach opens the doors to almost limitless and tempting culinary adventure, there are practical limits to the coverage in a book like this. Reluctantly, I've decided not to include recipes for the very large birds such as ostrich and emu, which are usually compared to beef, not chicken. Nor do I include very many recipes for duck or goose, simply because these are better (as a rule) when roasted in the oven instead of cooked in the skillet on top of the stove.

Fact is, chicken is the main bird for these times, at least in North America. So, let's get on with it.

## SKILLET-FRIED CHICKEN

You don't need a long list of secret spices to fry good chicken. Salt and black pepper will do, preferably fine sea salt and freshly ground black pepper. You don't even need a deep fryer or a "chicken fryer." A 10- or 12-inch cast-iron skillet will do—and may be better if you insist, as I do, on having the bottom of the chicken in contact with the bottom of the pan. You do need good chicken, a whole bird, preferably from the barnyard or at least free-range style. Many modern cooks, accustomed to buying supermarket bird parts and fast-food fare, won't know how to pluck and cut up a bird properly, and probably won't even recognize some of the best parts, such as the pully bone and the back.

Most modern housewives or even jackleg cooks aren't going to catch their own bird, wring its neck, pluck it, and singe it. But it's still easy to purchase a whole fryer, plucked and drawn, in the supermarket. For best results, cut it into the following pieces: two drumsticks, two thighs, one back, one pully bone (cut from the front of the breast), two breast halves, two wings, one rib assembly (we used to call it the crag in my family), one neck, and, sometimes, one head, along with a liver, gizzard, and heart, if these parts are included with the bird, as they damn well ought to be. If you proceed with an unplucked farmyard bird, note that the gizzard, an ovoid-shaped organ, should be split along one side and turned inside out, dumping the contents. I read in a cookbook on British country cooking that the two gizzards should be separated, but unfortunately, most American birds have only one gizzard.

Having such a variety of pieces, all crisply fried and piled on a platter in the center of the table, is part of the whole chicken experience. Each family member will have favorite parts, and sometimes the head of the table must be firm to maintain order and manners. In most families, the breast is usually reserved for any guest at the table. The pully bone goes to one of the kids.

For the best skillet fry, use a cast-iron piece and fill it with about ¾ inch of peanut oil. The oil should almost but not quite cover the chicken pieces. This works much better than a deep-fry method simply because the bottom of the chicken will be in direct contact with the bottom of the skillet. This in turn will produce a well-browned spot, one on either side, a feature that is not obtained when deep-frying.

The recipe for the world's best chicken? Well, it need not have a long list of ingredients. Here's all you need.

| | |
|:---:|:---:|
| 1 fryer, cut up | fine sea salt and freshly ground black pepper |
| all-purpose flour | peanut oil |

Sprinkle the chicken pieces with salt and pepper, then shake a few pieces in a bag with some flour. Using your fingers, shake off the excess flour, and set the pieces aside.

Heat about ¾ inch of peanut oil in a cast-iron skillet until it starts to quiver. Hold a drumstick by the small end and touch the big end into the oil. If it sizzles, it's hot enough (about 350°F or 360°F if you have a thermometer handy). Put several pieces into the skillet, being careful not to overcrowd. Cook for about 8 minutes or so. Using tongs, lift up a piece to see how it looks. If crisply brown, turn to cook the other side. Note that each piece should be considered separately because thicker pieces take longer to cook and don't brown as quickly. Be careful when frying the liver; it may pop and splatter hot grease on you.

As soon as a piece is ready, lift it from the skillet and put it on a brown bag to drain. (Paper towels will work, but large brown bags are better.) Do not cover. Cook the rest of the batch and serve hot on a large platter. Help yourself. I'll take the back, the liver, and one of the wings, to start with.

Fried chicken goes best with mashed potatoes and gravy, peas and other vegetables, and hot biscuits or rolls.

# GULLAH MAA'SH HEN

Hunting marsh hens (usually clapper rails) and other coastal birds has long been a Low Country specialty. At one time, a number of species could be taken for the table, such as the delicious limpkin and the beautiful purple gallinule, but these days the legal bounty is restricted. Other small birds such as snipe and mourning doves can be used in this recipe, but check the latest game laws before working up an appetite.

| | |
|---|---|
| **8 marsh hens or snipe** | **flour** |
| **1 chopped onion** | **salt** |
| **1 cup vinegar** | **red pepper flakes** |
| **cooking oil** | |

Skin the marsh hens to help remove any fishy taste. Draw and soak them in about a quart of clean saltwater, using either ocean water or fresh water with salt added. Change the saltwater, add the vinegar, and let sit in a cool place overnight.

When you are ready to cook, drain the birds, sprinkle with salt, and dredge in flour. Fry them in about ½ inch of hot oil in a large skillet until nicely browned on both sides. Pour off most of the oil, then add the onion and red pepper flakes. Stir in a cup of fresh water, cover the pan, and simmer on very low heat until the birds are tender.

Serve with rice and steamed young okra pods (another Gullah specialty) or vegetables of your choice.

# SMOTHER-FRIED QUAIL

Non-hunters will find market quail, usually frozen, to be quite tasty, and sometimes fresh quail can be purchased from local producers. You'll need a skillet large enough to hold all the birds at one time instead of cooking in batches. I prefer a red wine for this recipe, but white might be the more proper choice. Any good mushroom will do for the gravy, but wild morels are perfect. Chanterelles or shiitakes are also great. Note also that about 2 ounces of dried mushrooms, properly reconstituted, are also very good in this recipe.

| | |
|---|---|
| 8 quail | 2 cups dry red wine |
| buttermilk | 1 cup chopped scallions with part of green tops |
| 16 ounces fresh morels or shiitakes | |
| peanut oil for frying | flour |
| 2 cups chicken broth | salt and black pepper |

Rinse the dressed quail, put them into a nonmetallic container, and cover with buttermilk. Refrigerate for several hours in the refrigerator, turning a time or two.

When you are ready to cook, drain the birds and pat dry with paper towels. Heat about ¾ inch of peanut oil in a skillet to about 350°F. Sprinkle each bird inside and out with salt and black pepper, then shake in a bag with flour, working one bird at a time. Shake off the excess flour and arrange the birds in the skillet, breast-side down. Cook for 4 or 5 minutes, then turn the birds on their backs. Cook until the birds are nicely browned, then put them aside to drain on a brown bag.

Pour off the oil and pour a little of the wine into the hot skillet, stirring it about and scraping any grimilles off the bottom. Add the rest of the wine, the chicken broth, mushrooms, and green onions, along with a little more salt and pepper, if desired. Add the quail back to the skillet, cover, reduce the heat, and simmer for about 30 minutes. Remove the cover, stir the birds about, and cook until the liquid reduces down to a gravy. Be careful not to burn the bottoms of the birds.

Serve hot with wild rice, steamed vegetables, and a chewy sopping bread. Servings? Allow 2 quail per person. One will do if you will fit in a chicken finger or two.

# MUSHROOM SMOTHERED CHICKEN

This is essentially a fried chicken with a mushroom and butter sauce poured over it during the last stage of cooking. I've included a list of ingredients, but it's easy to come up with your own ways and means for this one. Cut the chicken into legs, thighs, split breast, wings, back, neck, and bony pieces. The back and bony pieces can be saved for chicken soup or stock—but remember, these make for good gnawing at the table. The recipe works best with two skillets, as indicated below, but one skillet will do if you cook the mushrooms first and set them aside until needed.

| | |
|---|---|
| 1 fryer, cut into pieces | peanut oil for skillet frying |
| 12 ounces mushrooms, sliced | all-purpose flour |
| 1 cup butter | salt and freshly ground black pepper |
| ½ cup red wine | warm water |

Salt and pepper the chicken pieces. Put some flour into a bag and shake the chicken a few pieces at a time until nicely coated. Shake off the excess flour piece by piece and set aside.

Heat about an inch of peanut oil in a 10-inch or larger skillet. Fry the chicken, a few pieces at a time, on medium-high heat until the chicken is nicely browned all around. Drain on a brown bag.

While the chicken cooks, melt the butter in another skillet and sauté the mushrooms on medium heat for 10 minutes or so. When all the chicken has been fried, pour off the grease and deglaze the skillet with the red wine. Put the chicken pieces back into the skillet. Add the rest of the red wine and enough water to almost cover the chicken. Bring to a boil, reduce the heat to low, and add the sautéed mushrooms and butter from the second skillet. Sprinkle with a little salt and pepper. Cover and simmer for 20 minutes or so, stirring a time or two.

Serve hot, along with rice or mashed potatoes, baby peas, and so on.

# FAMILY CHICKEN

The measures in this simple recipe depend on how many folks you've got to feed. Usually, a fryer of normal size will satisfy a family of four. But my method considerably reduces the volume of a chicken, and, since the meat is boneless, more is eaten. If you've got heavy eaters, you may need two fryers for a family of four. I might add that a person's size isn't always an indication of appetite. Our daughter, thin as a rail, has always eaten as much fried chicken or fish as a normal lumberjack.

| | |
|---|---|
| **chicken (fryers)** | **salt** |
| **peanut oil** | **pepper** |
| **flour (all-purpose)** | |

Apart from leading to tasty fried chicken, the above list is important not for what it contains but for what it leaves out. The recipe obviously doesn't have twenty-two secret spices to mess with. More importantly, it doesn't have egg or buttermilk and thick batter ingredients, such as bread crumbs. My thinking is that eliminating the skin and thick batter does away with grease traps. But a batter, or bread-like coating of some sort, is needed simply because, if properly used on high heat, it prevents the meat from absorbing so much cooking oil.

I allow that I am fond of fried chicken skin and all, and, of course, my recipe will work with that method. For low-fat results, however, it's best to skin the chicken, keep the batter to a minimum, and fry it in a good vegetable oil. (Animal fat, such as beef suet or lard, contains lots of cholesterol.)

Skinned chicken seems to fry better if you bone it before frying. Boning the meat reduces the cooking time, makes for smaller pieces, and lowers the odds of inexperienced cooks putting chicken on the table that is brown on the outside and raw on the inside, as can (and does) happen with large pieces of bone-in breast. In fact, I usually cut the breast into fingers.

So, skin your chicken and bone it. Wash the meat. Salt and pepper each piece to taste. Roll each piece lightly in flour, or shake the batch in a small brown bag with flour. At this point, many cooks and cookbook writers recommended that the chicken be left out for a few minutes so that the batter will stick to the chicken. At one time, I did this, but I have changed my mind and find that I like the results better if the chicken is cooked almost immediately after flouring. Handle it carefully, however, during and after cooking so that the light coating of flour won't flake off.

If you are using an ordinary skillet, put about ½ to ¾ inch of peanut oil in it and bring it to heat before you start. I usually test the oil by touching a piece of floured chicken to it. If it sizzles nicely, I put several pieces into the skillet, then reduce the heat to medium. It's best to cook in several batches instead of overcrowding your frying pan. It's also important that each piece of chicken be drained properly before serving. This is best accomplished by laying each piece out on an ordinary brown paper bag. Spread the pieces out and avoid making a pile.

I always cook my chicken in an *uncovered* skillet, but many people do cover it up. A cover will reduce oil splatter, but, even so, I still don't recommend it. I don't want to be pinned down on this, but I'm certain that the sound and strength of the sizzle is an important part to sensing when the chicken is ready to turn or to take up. Also, I feel that covered chicken is partly steamed—which takes some of the crunch out of the fried batter. But this is just one man's opinion.

Another matter of opinion: Cast-iron skillets cook better chicken than deep fryers, and can cook chicken in a way that is difficult to duplicate with other techniques. The trick is to use just enough oil to cover about half of the chicken. In other words, each piece of chicken ought to touch the bottom of the cast-iron skillet, while the top of the piece ought to stick up out of the cooking oil. When the bottom is nicely browned, the piece is turned over and the other side is browned. Ideally, the chicken is turned only once. If all goes well, both the top and bottom of each piece of chicken will be browner than the sides simply because they were in direct contact with the cast iron. Thus, each piece of skillet-fried chicken offers a different crunch on top, bottom, and sides.

But cooking in a skillet is slow, and deep-frying is really better suited for feeding lots of people. To be sure, toothsome chicken can be deep-fried in a cast-iron pot of suitable depth, or in a Dutch oven. There is even a piece of cast-iron cookware called a chicken fryer. These are usually about 3 inches deep, as compared with 1½ or 2 inches for a frying pan, or 4 or 5 inches for a Dutch oven. There are also some cast-iron stew pots, fish fryers, and "french fry" pieces with a basket. All these can, of course, be used to fry chicken, and cast-iron washpots or other vats can be used at large outdoor cooking events. Indoors or out, however, large batch or small, I'll stick by the recipe above.

Just a few days after I had written the above text, one of my sons came in with a large wild turkey. We cut the breast into fingers, marinated it overnight in buttermilk, and then used the Turkey Fingers recipe to cook it. Nothing was left. Two days later, we used the rest of the bird to make a gumbo. It was delicious.

# TURKEY FINGERS

Although the breast from domestic turkey will work just fine, this recipe should be remembered as the perfect way to cook wild turkey for those who think they might not like the "wild" part. Truth is, the breast from a wild jake is tenderer and more moist than the typical market turkey. It can also have more flavor, depending in part on what it has been feeding on. Here's what you'll need:

turkey fingers (cut from the breast lengthwise)

buttermilk

flour

cooking oil

salt

pepper

Rinse the turkey fingers, put them into a glass container, cover with buttermilk, and refrigerate for several hours or overnight. When you are ready to start cooking, drain the turkey fingers, salt and pepper them to taste, and shake them in a bag with some flour. Heat ½ inch of cooking oil in a skillet. Fry all the fingers a few at a time on medium-high heat, turning once, and put them onto a brown grocery bag to drain. Use more than one brown bag if necessary to avoid piling the fingers atop each other. Eat while hot.

The breast from a fully grown wild turkey will usually feed 5 or 6. But wild turkey can be delicious, and if you've done a proper job of field dressing and cooking, your squeamish guest can eat more than expected.

*Note: This recipe also comes in handy for cooking chicken tenders, which don't need long soaking in buttermilk, and pheasant fingers, which should be soaked a little longer. Pheasant breast tends to be quite dry, so do not overcook it. As a rule, a young pheasant or a hen will fry up better than a tough old rooster—which also holds true for chickens.*

# SKILLET DOVES

I have eaten more doves than any other kind of game bird, partly because I like the rich dark meat—which I find even better than breast of duck. There are several types, such as mourning doves and white-wings, but most are similar except for a little variation in size. Pigeons are larger and should not be cooked by this recipe. Ground doves are smaller and are protected by law these days.

Whoever dresses the birds has a good deal of control over the quality of the final product and often does the wrong thing because it is easier than doing the right thing. If your wife always dresses the birds, tell her that doves ought to be dry-plucked. Skinning them (as too many people do) will make them drier and tougher. Breasting the birds is widely accepted, but I really can't in good conscience endorse the practice unless the bony parts will be used, along with the giblets, to make a giblet gravy. Cooking the birds whole in a skillet isn't the best way to go either. For best results, pluck and draw the birds, then halve them lengthwise, cutting close to the breastbone. Use no marinade if you want to savor the flavor of my favorite game bird.

| doves, halved | flour |
|---|---|
| peanut oil | salt and freshly ground black pepper |

Sprinkle the bird halves with salt and pepper, dredge with flour, and shake off the excess. Set aside while you heat an inch of peanut oil in a skillet. When the oil starts to quiver with heat, cook the birds 2 or 3 pieces at a time until browned nicely on both sides. Drain and cook another batch, repeating until all the birds are done.

Serve hot with mashed potatoes, gravy, vegetables, and a good bread. Eat the birds with your hands. First, gnaw off a few bites of the breast meat. Then gnaw on the bony pieces as best you can, nibbling and pulling with your fingers. Allow at least 2 doves per person. I'll take 3 or 4 if available, or nibbling rights to whatever bony pieces the others diners leave.

*Note: Snipe, woodcock, and other small birds can be cooked by the same recipe, but remember that doves are grain eaters that do not have a strong off-flavor. Other birds may require a marinade of some sort, as in the marsh hen recipe above.*

# SKILLET DUCK WITH MUSCADINE JELLY

*The Tabasco Cookbook* includes a recipe for venison chops with muscadine jelly, calling the result Marchand de Muscadine. A sidebar also sets forth an old recipe for cooking skillet duck with muscadines, a large, tasty grape that grows wild over most of the South. You simply fillet out the breasts of teal or wood ducks (saving the rest of the birds for duck and andouille gumbo). Dip each breast in melted butter and cook in a skillet for about 3½ minutes on each side, or until medium rare. (Be careful. Much depends on the heat of the skillet and the thickness of the fillets. In any case, the breasts should be medium rare.) Salt and pepper each fillet and smear lightly with muscadine jelly. Serve hot with wild rice.

The muscadine jelly can be ordered from Callaway Gardens in Georgia (404-663-5100). It's also easy enough to make your own, if you have the muscadines and the time. If you must, substitute guava or red currant jelly.

My copy of *The Tabasco Cookbook* sports an attractive cover, designed with the title fitted into the familiar Tabasco brand diamond, suggestive of the bottle. With taste buds atingle, I was unprepared for a typographical shock when I first opened my copy, naturally holding it with the cover right-side up. Astoundingly, the last page of the text was at the front—and all the pages were upside down! Maybe Tabasco sauce fans are expected to invert the book and shake out the contents.

# SMITH ISLAND DUCK

Chesapeake Bay's Smith Island was slowly sinking or being inundated even before global warming figured much into our thinking. I'm glad I stumbled upon this old recipe in *Mrs. Kitching's Smith Island Cookbook* before the landmass disappears! The recipe can be used with fatty critters like duck or possum or armadillo, and it might well be the best possible way to cook country sausage links or pork chops.

In braising, you see, the cook sautés the meat and then simmers it in a liquid until quite tender. In this method—which I consider to be of major culinary importance for the jackleg cook who has plenty of time to cook—the process is reversed. The meat is long simmered in water, during which time most of the fat cooks out of the meat. When all the water boils off and the meat is fork tender, the heat is turned up and the duck is fried in its own fat until nicely browned on both sides. It's very, very tasty. The whole duck can be disjoined and cooked, but I think skin-on duck breasts work much better in a skillet. Save the frames for soup or perhaps duck and oyster gumbo.

To begin, simply put the duck breasts skin-side down into a hot cast-iron skillet. Cover with water and maybe add some chopped onions. Cook down slowly until the duck is very tender and the water has evaporated. Turn up the heat and brown the breasts in their own fat until the skin is crispy.

That's it. All manner of easy variations are possible if you want to coin a "recipe." Try sprinkling on a little lemon-pepper seasoning salt during the browning phase. What could be easier? What better? It's a great method for camp cooking, because you don't have to tote in a jug of grease.

Be sure to try the technique to cook a couple of extra-fatty, well-marbled rib eye beefsteaks. Also note that this technique may be ideal for those people among us who love well-marbled rib eyes but, for reasons of safety or peace of mind, want all their meat cooked until well done.

# SKILLET GOOSE NUGGETS

Here's a recipe from Bob Stearns, a noted angling and boating writer, adapted here from *Angler Profiles*. It calls for using only the breast of the goose, leaving the rest for soup or gumbo. The recipe works for both wild and domestic geese, as well as for ducklings and the larger wild ducks such as mallards.

| | |
|---|---|
| goose breasts | 1 to 2 chicken eggs |
| milk | seasoned Italian bread crumbs |
| orange juice | olive oil |

Fillet out the breasts and cut them into bite-size pieces. Put these into a glass or plastic container of suitable size and marinate in milk for 12 to 14 hours in a refrigerator. Then rinse and marinate them in orange juice for 3 or 4 hours. Drain the orange juice and mix in a whisked egg or two. Sprinkle with bread crumbs, coating all sides lightly.

Heat a little olive oil in a skillet and sauté the pieces for 2 or 3 minutes on each side. Do not overcook. Servings? An average wild goose breast will serve 2 average people.

# CHAPTER

## 5

# Venison and Other Game

**V**enison and most other game can be very good eating—or almost inedible. Sometimes the same animal can fulfill either extreme, depending on how it was killed, dressed, and cooked. Usually, game purchased from a game farm or commercial market will be satisfactory—but a lazy or irresponsible hunter is often to blame for gamy-tasting meat being put on the table. As a rule, a young but mature animal will be better eating than a tough old buck, but the real culprit of that gamy taste is improper field dressing. I don't want to preach here, but I'll have more on this subject at the end of the chapter.

Most of the recipes here are for whitetail venison simply because whitetail deer are so plentiful in most parts of the country, but mule deer, elk, moose, caribou, and similar animals can also be used. Buffalo (bison) is especially good. The first few recipes in this chapter can be cooked in the home kitchen or on the patio, but they are also ideal for deer camp cookery after a successful hunt. This chapter also contains recipes for squirrel and rabbit. (For cooking such critters as coons and possums, see my *Complete Fish & Game Cookbook*.) Wild birds are discussed separately (chapter 4), and a few other game recipes appear here and there throughout the book.

# CHICKEN-FRIED LOIN CHOPS WITH SOPTION

Dump a cup or so of flour into a small brown bag, along with a little salt and pepper. Shake the chops in the bag, remove, and gently shake off any excess flour.

Pour ½ inch of peanut oil into the skillet and heat it to about 350°F. Fry the loin slices for 2 or 3 minutes, turning once, or until lightly browned on either side. Drain the slices on a brown bag. (Note: If the loin slices prove to be too tough for easy chewing—probably because you have cooked them too long—abort this recipe here at the draining stage and resort to Step B of the next recipe.)

Quickly pour off most of the oil and scrape up any bottom dredgings—the grimilles. Sprinkle a little flour into the skillet and cook for several minutes, stirring with a wooden spoon, until the flour browns. Add a little water, stirring constantly, and bring to a bubble. Sprinkle with some salt and pepper, and simmer, stirring until the gravy thickens to your liking.

Serve the gravy over rice, mashed potatoes, or biscuit halves along with the fried chops.

# BACKSTRAP CHOPS WITH RED WINE

*Note: No grease or breading is required for this recipe, making it a good choice for camp cooking, if you have the butter. If wild onions are available, try a few of these (½ cup) instead of the scallions.*

| | |
|---|---|
| backstrap chops for two | 1 tablespoon butter |
| 1 cup dry red wine | ½ teaspoon dry mustard |
| 1 cup minced scallions, including part of the green tops | salt and freshly ground black pepper to taste |

Melt the butter in a saucepan. Sauté the scallions until tender and lightly browned. Then stir in the mustard and wine. Set the sauce aside and keep warm.

Heat a cast-iron skillet over hot coals, or on high heat if using a kitchen stove. Sear the chops for 2 minutes on each side. Carefully pour the sauce around the chops in the hot skillet. Add a little salt and pepper. Lower the heat and cook for 2 minutes.

Serve hot, topped with the pan juices, with wild rice and vegetables of your choice, along with some chewy French bread and the rest of the red wine.

# A TENDERLOIN SAUTÉ

This recipe works with venison tenderloin of any sort and with most loins. The tenderloins are great for camp cooking after a successful hunt because they can be removed from within the body cavity during the field-dressing operation—before the deer is skinned (see "The Hunter's Responsibility" at the end of this chapter).

| | |
|---|---|
| 1 set whitetail tenderloins, sliced ½ inch thick | 3 tablespoons chopped green onions with part of tops |
| 3 tablespoons butter (divided) | salt and freshly ground black pepper |

Rub some ground pepper into each side of the tenderloin slices. Heat 2 tablespoons of the butter in a skillet. Sauté the tenderloins for 6 minutes for medium rare, turning once to brown both sides. Sprinkle with salt and set aside to drain on a brown bag.

Add the rest of the butter to the skillet, then sauté the onions for 4 or 5 minutes, stirring as you go. Spoon the onion mixture over the meat rounds. Feeds two hunters—maybe more if you have plenty of rice.

# DEER CAMP VENISON LIVER

Fresh venison liver is very tasty, unless you find all liver off-putting. I like it cooked with onions and a little port wine. As Cy Littlebee's *Guide to Cooking Fish & Game* put it, the port "not only improves the taste, but the smell is sure to bring in any lost hunters that might be near-by and down-wind." I agree—but the real olfactory magic here is onions sautéing in butter.

Note that other liver, such as calf or chicken, can be used. (See the turtle liver recipe, Higado de Tortuga, in chapter 7.) Note also that venison liver has no gallbladder attached to it, so that you don't have to worry about it during the field-dressing operation. I like to slice the liver about ½ inch thick. The onion should be halved lengthwise and then cut crosswise into half-rings.

| | |
|---|---|
| venison liver | port wine |
| bacon | flour |
| onion half-rings | salt and freshly ground black pepper |
| sliced mushrooms | |

Pour yourself a glass of the port to sip while cooking. Sprinkle the liver with salt, black pepper, and flour. Cook the bacon in a cast-iron skillet until crispy. Drain and set aside.

Sauté the onion rings in the bacon drippings until they start to brown around the edges. (If you burn them a little and have city folks seated at the table, change the name of the recipe to Venison Liver with Caramelized Onions.) Add the mushrooms and cook for a few minutes, stirring a time or two. Remove the onions and mushrooms and set aside. Add a little more bacon drippings (or cooking oil) to the skillet if needed. Fry the liver on medium-high heat for 2 or 3 minutes, or until medium rare. (If in doubt, cut into a slice of the liver for a visual test; it should be brown on the outside but pink on the inside.) Pour some port into the skillet around the liver. Add the onions and mushrooms. Cover and simmer for a minute or two.

Serve hot with the pan gravy, along with rice, vegetables of your choice, and a good crusty bread. Finish off with scuppernong hull pie (or maybe rhubarb pie) and the rest of the port.

# SAFARI STEAKS

Used by Kenyan hunters, this recipe specifies eland steaks, but it also works with steaks or chops of antelope, zebra, beef, veal, or buffalo. Any good American deer can be used. In any case, use only tender cuts of meat for this one—and do not overcook them.

2 pounds eland steaks, ½ inch thick

1½ pounds mashed potatoes (precooked)

1 pound mashed sweet potatoes (precooked)

½ cup dry red wine

½ cup sweet white wine

½ cup tomato sauce

2 tablespoons olive oil (maybe more)

2 tablespoons butter

2 cloves garlic, minced

salt and pepper to taste

chopped fresh parsley (for garnish)

Heat the oil and butter in a skillet almost to the smoke point. Add a small batch of the steaks and cook for 3 minutes on each side. (Do not overcrowd the meat.) Cook the rest of the steaks, using more oil if needed. Salt and pepper the steaks and set aside on a warm platter.

On lower heat now, add the wines and deglaze the skillet, stirring and scraping up the bottom grimilles with a wooden spatula. Add the garlic. Stir in the tomato sauce and simmer, stirring constantly, until the sauce thickens. Keep the sauce warm.

In a suitable bowln mix the mashed potatoes and sweet potatoes, adding a little salt and pepper to taste. Spread the potatoes over a serving platter. Top with the steaks and pour the sauce over all. Serve hot, garnished perhaps with chopped parsley.

# BIG SCRUB VENISON

Marjorie Kinnan Rawlings, the author of *The Yearling*, offered a good Florida Cracker recipe for frying venison in *Cross Creek Cookery*, a work that has been in print since 1941. I have used the recipe several times with butterflied tenderloin as well as with top loin chops.

| | |
|---|---|
| venison chops, ¾ inch thick | Crisco or vegetable oil |
| lemon halves | flour |
| butter | salt and pepper |

Rub the chops with half a lemon, squeezing on a little juice as you go. Dust each chop with flour and fry it in a cast-iron skillet on medium-high heat, using about 1 tablespoon of butter and 1 tablespoon of Crisco or vegetable oil for medium-size skillets. (In camp, try bacon drippings leftover from breakfast.) Fry the venison for 5 or 6 minutes, turning once. Season with salt and pepper to taste and serve hot.

# OLD WARSAW STUFFED VENISON CUTLETS

This recipe works with cutlets from venison loin, or from cutlets made from the muscles in the deer's leg. Cut them to about ½ inch thickness, then pound them down with a meat mallet to ¼ inch. The ground meat can be from the shoulder of the animal, or from other tasty cuts. I have adapted the recipe from Rysia's *Old Warsaw Cookbook*, taking the liberty to add a little bacon to the ground meat. Also, the original didn't spell out what to do with the flour—and I have chosen to beat it into the meat. You'll need a cover for your skillet to finish this recipe. An electric skillet will do just fine.

2 pounds venison cutlets
1 pound venison shoulder, for grinding
4 strips bacon (divided)
1 medium onion, minced
4 mushrooms, minced
½ cup good red wine
½ cup meat stock

1 bouillon cube, dissolved in a little water
butter (preferably clarified)
2 tablespoons flour
2 tablespoons dry bread crumbs
1 teaspoon Worcestershire sauce
salt and freshly ground black pepper

Sprinkle the venison cutlets with flour and pound them with the toothed side of a meat mallet. Turn the mallet and use the smooth side to pound the cutlets down to a thickness of ¼ inch. Set aside.

Cut the venison shoulder into chunks. Dice two strips of the bacon. Mix the venison shoulder and bacon and run it through a sausage mill, using a small wheel (⅛ to 3/16 size). Set the ground meat aside.

Fry the other two strips of bacon in a large skillet. In the hot drippings, sauté the onion and mushrooms until they start to brown. Stir in the ground meat and bread crumbs, along with a little salt and pepper. Spoon some of the stuffing onto each cutlet, roll, and secure with a toothpick.

Heat some butter in the skillet and sauté the venison rolls until browned on two sides, turning once. Add the wine, Worcestershire sauce, bouillon water, and meat stock. Bring to a boil, reduce the heat to very low, cover, and simmer until the venison is done and tender.

Serve hot with steamed cabbage sprinkled with crumbled bacon, boiled new potatoes sprinkled with a little dill weed, and plenty of crusty homemade bread.

# FOOLPROOF FRIED VENISON

Here's a good recipe and cooking method for camp or kitchen. The recipe will work with either loin (top backstrap) or tenderloin (bottom backstrap), and the foolproof cooking method can be used with other meats, fish, and fowl.

2 large white onions, thinly sliced

1 venison loin or tenderloin

1 cup flour

1 tablespoon each of cayenne, mild paprika, and salt

Lard or cooking oil for deep frying

Heat a casserole dish to about 150°F, add the onion rings, and keep warm. Slice the venison into rounds ⅛ inch thick. (Partially frozen meat will be easier to slice.) In a shake-bag, mix the flour, cayenne, paprika, and salt. Shake the venison rounds, a few at a time, to coat all around. Set aside while you rig for deep-frying in at least 3 inches of oil. When the oil reaches 350°F to 375°F, carefully drop in a few pieces of venison loin. When the pieces float, they are cooked enough to eat. Let them brown for another minute or so, then drain them quickly and place them atop the onions in the casserole dish. Toss, cover, and let stand for about 15 minutes. Serve warm with the onions or without. It's the onion flavor that counts.

Perhaps more important, the "when it floats" rule should be applied by those cooks among us, some perhaps close at hand, who overcook wild game simply because it is wild. Of course, the rule applies to fried fish as well as to venison, chicken, and other meats. You may need to bend the rule just a little to let the meat brown properly. But watch it like a hawk. If cooked too much, even tenderloin will be tough and chewy.

# EASY BIG-GAME STIR-FRY

The accomplished stir-fry chef will mix his own sauces and marinades, but most of us can usually get by with a commercial mix. Almost always, soy sauce is the base for a good stir-fry sauce, flavored with ginger root and sake. Several good frozen stir-fry vegetable mixes are available in supermarkets and other outlets. I lean toward Oriental mixes, which usually contain snow peas. In addition to those packages with "stir-fry" printed on them, look over the dozens of other mixes available, such as the San Francisco blend. The meat? I like loin or tenderloin, but shoulder or rump can also be used, cut across the grain.

| | |
|---|---|
| 1 pound tender big-game meat | Mongolian Fire Oil (optional) |
| 1 pound frozen stir-fry vegetables | Asian sesame oil (optional) |
| stir-fry sauce | cornstarch paste |
| peanut oil | rice (cooked separately) |

Trim the meat and cut it into strips about ½ inch wide and 3 inches long. Put the meat into a nonmetallic container, pour in some stir-fry sauce, toss to coat all sides, and marinate for several hours in a cool place. (How much sauce you use in the marinade isn't critical, but you don't need to completely cover the meat in liquid.)

When you are ready to cook, heat about 2 tablespoons of peanut oil in a cast-iron skillet. When the oil is very hot, quickly brown the meat in two or three batches, setting it aside to drain on a brown bag.

Add a little more oil if needed and stir-fry the vegetables for a few minutes. Put the meat back into the skillet, then add a little of the stir-fry sauce (or use the leftover marinade if you don't object to the blood), a few drops of Mongolian Fire Oil, and some sesame oil to taste. (Be sure to use the Oriental dark toasted-seed sesame oil used for flavoring, not the lighter sesame cooking oil.) Stir in the cornstarch paste, cover, and simmer for about 10 minutes, or until the vegetables are tender. Serve hot with rice.

# CARIBOU STROGANOFF

I was surprised to learn from Kira Petrovskaya's *Russian Cookbook* that the purists among Russian cooks would never add mushrooms or tomato paste to their Stroganoff. Although I like the mushrooms and think the tomato paste lends a nice color to the dish, I must confess that the true Russian way is very good, cooked as follows with caribou or tender venison of any sort. Bear, bison, or beef loin will work nicely.

1½ pounds caribou loin or tenderloin

1 cup meat stock or water

½ cup sour cream

1 medium to large onion, chopped

2 tablespoons whole wheat flour

2 to 3 tablespoons clarified butter

1 strip of dry crust from a slice of pumpernickel bread

salt and pepper to taste

egg noodles, cooked separately

Cut the meat into thin strips. Heat most of the butter in a skillet. Roll the strips of meat in flour, then quickly brown them, a few at a time, in hot butter.

In a separate pan, sauté the chopped onion in a little butter. Add the onions to the meat pan along with the stock, bread crust, salt, and pepper. Simmer until the meat is very tender. Add the sour cream, then bring almost to a boil, stirring as you go to prevent the bottom from sticking. Add a little more stock or water if needed. Serve hot with noodles.

*Variation:* If you have some edible wild mushrooms, as I often have, slice and sauté them along with the onions and stir them into the meat. If the Russians don't like it, they can pick the mushroom slices out with their fork.

# SQUAYRILL STOO

The little book *Bittle en' T'ing': Gullah Cooking with Maum Chrish'*, written by Virginia Mixson Geraty, is the best example of an authentic soul food cookbook that I have ever perused. The book contains only simple recipes, calling for a few basic ingredients.

Until modern times, the Gullah lived for the most part off the land, in the Carolina and Georgia Low Country, using wild plants as well as garden fare and making do with a minimum of staples that could be stored for long periods of time. Since the Gullah ate lots of wild game and seafood, the book should be of interest to hunters, fishers, and camp cooks, who must often make do with limited "puhwishun" (as provisions are called in the Gullah tongue).

In this recipe, Maum says to skin the squirrel carefully and nail the hide up to dry for use as a collar. Give the tail to a young man to sport on his hat. Maum also says that one squirrel will make enough stew for four people, which indicates to me that she disremembered (as we say here in rural Florida) how small a squirrel is or that maybe she has been influenced by modern cookbook servings. I stick to one gray squirrel for the recipe below—then I eat the whole thing myself. Note that the fox squirrel, a species that is now protected in some areas, is much larger and will do for two. The authors and editors of many fish and game cookbooks don't seem to know the difference.

| | |
|:---:|:---:|
| **1 gray squirrel** | **bacon drippings** |
| **1 medium to large onion, diced** | **salt and pepper** |
| **flour** | |

Sprinkle the squirrel pieces with salt and pepper. Shake them in a bag with flour. Heat the bacon drippings in a skillet and brown the squirrel pieces on both sides.

Remove the squirrel and sauté the onion until the edges start to brown. Put the squirrel pieces back into the skillet. Barely cover them with hot water. Bring to a light boil, reduce the heat, and simmer until the meat is tender and the gravy thick. Add more water and turn the squirrel from time to time if needed. (Be warned that an old boar squirrel with credentials will be very tough and needs long simmering.)

Serve with rice or biscuits.

# SKILLET SQUIRREL WITH DRIED MORELS

Any good mushroom will work with this recipe, but dried morels are hard to beat. Also try dried portobellos, oyster mushrooms, shiitakes, chanterelles, and so on. For cooking this dish to perfection, a heavy skillet is recommended. I use a cast-iron skillet, 10-inch diameter or larger.

| | |
|---|---|
| 2 gray squirrels, cut into pieces | flour |
| 10 dried morels | water |
| cooking oil | salt and pepper |

Soak the dried mushrooms in water for 40 minutes or longer. Drain and slice the mushrooms, retaining the water. Salt and pepper the squirrel pieces, then shake them in a bag with a little flour.

Heat about ½ inch of oil in a skillet. Brown the squirrel pieces on both sides. It's best to have the oil quite hot so that the squirrel browns nicely and shows darker spots, almost to the burn stage, where it was in direct contact with the skillet. Drain the squirrel pieces.

Sauté the sliced morels in the skillet for a few minutes. Pour off most of the cooking oil. Using a wooden spoon, stir in a little flour. Cook for several minutes, stirring until you have a brown paste. Slowly stir in enough of the mushroom water to make a thin gravy, adding a little plain water if needed. Stir in some salt and pepper.

Fit the fried squirrel pieces in the skillet, cover tightly, and simmer (do not boil) on very low heat for about 1 hour, or until the squirrel is fork tender. Turn the squirrel pieces and add more water from time to time if needed. Serve hot, spooning the gravy over rice or biscuit halves. This dish is just too good.

*Variation:* Try cottontail rabbit or young muskrat instead of squirrel.

# CROSS CREEK SQUIRREL

Marjorie Kinnan Rawlings, author of *The Yearling*, lived on Cross Creek, which connects Orange Lake and Lake Lockloosa in central Florida. She cooked on a woodstove and made good use of butter from her cow, Dora, instead of using store-bought cooking oil or shortening. Miss Rawlings's squirrel recipe, which also works for rabbit, quail, and dove, can be made with ordinary supermarket butter. Be warned that an old squirrel is usually very tough and requires long, slow simmering; otherwise, you can't stick a fork in the gravy, as the saying goes. For that reason, it's best to use young squirrels the first time you try this recipe.

| | |
|---|---|
| **young gray squirrels** | **salt and pepper to taste** |
| **butter** | **boiling spring water** |
| **flour** | |

Skin, draw, and disjoint the squirrels, cutting them into 7 pieces as follows: 2 hind legs, saddle, rib section, 2 front legs, and head. Salt and pepper the pieces and roll them in flour, shaking off the excess.

Heat ¼ inch of butter in a deep skillet or Dutch oven. Brown the squirrel pieces on both sides. If you have to cook in more than one batch, add more butter as needed. Barely cover the squirrel pieces with boiling water. Cover the skillet tightly and simmer until the meat is very tender—an hour or more. Turn the pieces from time to time and add more water if needed to prevent scorching on the bottom.

Remove the squirrel pieces to a serving platter. Dissolve a little flour into the water and use it to thicken the gravy, stirring as you go and adding a little more salt and black pepper as needed. Serve the gravy over the squirrels, or put it into a gravy boat and serve it on the side. Squirrel gravy is great when spooned over rice or mashed potatoes.

*Note: Be warned that some people in the Ozarks came down with something like mad cow disease, and all had been eating squirrel brains. Don't laugh. Squirrel heads were once a delicacy in rural areas, prized for their cheeks as well as the brains. They are still a good deal better than chicken heads. Still, I can't in good conscience recommend that you eat squirrel brains until the mad cow situation is better understood. So, forget the brains and content yourself with some good gnawing around the head. If you choose to live dangerously, however, or simply cannot resist squirrel brains, first gnaw the meat off the head, then cup it in your left hand and whop it with the back side of the spoon to crack the cranium so that you can get at the good stuff. It is not good manners, however, to suck the brains out at the table—at least not at my house. In camp, it's every man for himself.*

# AZTEC RABBIT

The Aztecs were fond of rabbits, and modern-day Mexicans of the central highlands share their enthusiasm. Here's a recipe suitable for cooking two cottontails or one large market rabbit in a large skillet.

2 cottontails, dressed (or 1 market rabbit)

1 jar medium-hot tomato-based salsa (16-ounce size)

1 cup pulque or perhaps hard cider

1 cup chicken stock (or rabbit stock)

¼ cup ground walnuts or ground roasted peanuts

juice of ½ lemon or lime

2 tablespoons butter

2 tablespoons olive oil or bacon drippings

1 tablespoon chopped fresh cilantro

water as needed

After your wife dresses the rabbits, set aside the hind legs and saddles, telling her to save the bony pieces (front legs, neck, and rib cage) for another recipe or to make a stock to use herein. (To make a stock, cover the bony pieces with water in a pot; add some chopped celery, carrot, and onion. Bring to a boil, reduce the heat, cover, and simmer for about 2 or 3 hours, adding more water if needed. Strain out the bones. Pull some of the easy meat off the front legs, mince it finely, and add it to the liquid in the pot. Reduce the liquid over medium heat until you have about 1 cup of stock. Substitute for the chicken stock in this recipe.)

Heat the butter and olive oil in a large skillet that has a lid. Brown the rabbit pieces, turning a time or two. Set aside. Add the cilantro, salsa, stock, and pulque to the skillet. Stir for a minute or so, then add the browned rabbit pieces. Cover tightly and simmer for 3 hours; add more water from time to time as needed and turn the pieces to keep them from burning.

Just before serving time, stir in the ground nuts and lemon juice. Simmer for 5 minutes. Serve hot, along with soft rolled tortillas for sopping. Feeds 2 to 4.

# THE HUNTER'S RESPONSIBILITY

Many hunters find it convenient to haul their deer to a professional meat processor for butchering. There's nothing wrong with this practice, but the hunter should realize that putting prime venison on the table usually requires prompt field dressing. Omitting this step can be an irreversible mistake. Nothing in the butcher's bag of tricks can make neglected meat taste as good as it should. Venison gone bad won't even make acceptable sausage. In the kitchen, even the best cooks can't salvage gamy meat with secret marinades, fancy recipes, French sauces—or even country gravy.

What makes some venison taste gamy? Many people believe that blood is the culprit and will beseech the hunter to bleed the animal as soon as possible. They are probably wrong. Bleeding isn't necessary and may not help at all, except in cases where a queasy partaker has blood on the saddle and blood on the mind. For all practical purposes, you can forget about the blood during the field-dressing operation, unless you want to collect it for making French gravy. Trying to bleed the animal just makes a mess and takes up time that could be put to better use. While on the subject, however, I might add that merely slitting the animal's throat won't drain out much blood simply because the jugular connects only the heart and brain. To bleed properly (if you feel that you must), the animal should be hoisted up by its hind legs, or otherwise positioned with the head and shoulders downhill, and "stuck." That is, a stout knife blade is inserted through the breast and severs the aorta where it connects to the heart. (You'll know by the gush when you hit it.) But all this is simply not necessary. Besides, a good lung shot with modern ammo along with prompt field dressing does a pretty good job of bleeding deer.

Other people believe it's the intestines and bladders that cause the gamy taste. Although gut shots or improper field-dressing techniques can indeed cause some problems, the tainted meat is usually quite localized. As a rule, the guts, as such, really don't hurt anything—up to a point. (Of course, any discolored or "blood shot" meat should be cut out during the butchering phase.)

Yet, the innards should be removed from a dead animal as soon as possible—not for their own sake, but because of the heat they contain. That's right. Heat. It's as simple as that. This is especially true for large grazing animals, which tend to have lots of innards in terms of bulk, and for rabbits and hares. In short, removing the innards promptly after the kill takes away a good part of the animal's total heat and opens up the body cavity for ventilation and quick cooling. In addition to maintaining the quality of the meat, cooling discourages the growth of *E. coli* and perhaps other harmful bacteria that may be present.

There are several books and videos on how to field dress a deer or other animal, but the process is really easy, especially for animals the size of whitetails and smaller. You simply roll the deer on its back, slit it open without cutting into the guts, turn it on its side, and dump the contents onto the ground. On a cool day, you'll feel the heat rising from the pile of innards.

Of course, the hotter the day, the more urgent field dressing becomes. In the extremely cold weather of the far north, however, it may even be better to delay the field dressing awhile. But usually, quicker is better, and a cold day certainly doesn't give the hunter license to abuse the meat. Stuffing the deer into a closed car trunk or displaying it across the engine-heated hood of a pickup truck is a culinary sin.

Be warned, however, that prompt field dressing really can't salvage the meat from a deer, bear, or boar that has been chased all over the country with dogs before the kill. (Even a domestic hog so riled would taste gamy, and some farmers have been known to "scratch a hog down" with a corncob before dispatching it with a well-placed blow of a ball-peen hammer.) It also helps to drop the deer or other animal quickly with a well-placed shot.

Thankfully, prompt field dressing yields some ready meat for the camp cook. The tenderloin requires no aging, and the liver and other innards are best when fresh. The liver is especially perishable, whereas the heart and kidneys can be kept longer or frozen. Although fresh venison liver is one of my favorite wild-game foods (quickly sautéed with onions in some bacon drippings, along with a few good edible wild mushrooms, if available), some people simply don't want liver of any sort at any time—and especially not after field dressing the animal.

Note that some hunters and cooks mistake the venison loins for the tenderloins. The two loins run along the top of the backbone, one on either side. To get at them, the animal must be skinned, which often makes them inconvenient for deer camp cookery. The tenderloins, on the other hand, are smaller and run underneath the backbone, one on either side. They are clearly visible in the body cavity after the animal has been gutted, and they can be cut out easily with a pocket knife. I have known people who saved only the hind legs and loins from the deer, thereby throwing away the ribs, shoulders, and neck as well as the tenderloins—the filet mignon of the deer.

For a visual cross section of the loins and tenderloins, imagine two twin T-bone steaks or center-cut pork chops jutted back to back, with the bones fitted together at the saw line. The two larger top rounds will be the loins. The smaller bottom rounds, the tenderloins. Both are sometimes called "backstraps."

In closing, I might say to the hunter that giving gamy meat away, or expecting the butcher and cook to do the impossible, merely passes the buck. If the hunter shoots the animal, taking care of the meat is his responsibility. Or hers.

# CHAPTER

# Fish and Shellfish

**M**ost lean fish cook rather fast, about 10 minutes per inch of thickness, making the skillet a sensible way to prepare a mess for a few people. The skillet recipes below, both old and new, should whet the appetite for skillet fish and shellfish, with some emphasis on fried and sautéed fare, and a few other recipes appear here and there throughout the book.

## DAN WEBSTER'S STIR-FRIED SHRIMP

"If you've got a good cast-iron skillet, you don't need a damned wok to stir-fry shrimp," Dan said, shaking a long wooden spoon at me as he spoke. "And you don't need soy stuff and monosodium glutamate, either."

Well, I quit arguing when I tasted the proof of the recipe.

|                    |              |
| ------------------ | ------------ |
| **fresh shrimp**   | lemons       |
| **butter**         | garlic       |

Juice the lemons, peel and crush the garlic, and melt the butter in a skillet. Mix lemon juice and garlic into the warm butter and put it aside while you peel the shrimp. When you are ready to cook, bring the butter mixture in the skillet to a medium-high heat. Add the shrimp and stir them with a wooden spoon for 3 or 4 minutes; 5 or 6 minutes may be required for jumbo size. If you've got more than a pound of shrimp, cook them in separate batches. Do not overcook. Serve while hot. No sauce is required, but I like to use the pan drippings.

I asked Dan how much butter, garlic, and lemon juice he used per pound of shrimp. "Use as much as you need," he said.

**Note:** *Stir-fry fans will be delighted to know that a cast-iron wok is now being manufactured in this country. See page 202.*

# FLORIDA HASH

One of my favorites, Florida hash, is best made with a large frying pan (about 14 inches wide). With smaller pans, cook the recipe in two batches.

| | |
|---|---|
| 2 cups cooked fish flakes | 1 teaspoon salt |
| 4 cups diced potatoes | ½ teaspoon pepper |
| 1 cup chopped onion | ½ tablespoon vinegar |
| 4 slices bacon | |

If you are using fresh fish, boil or steam it for a few minutes, until it flakes easily. (Left-over fish can also be used.) Flake 2 cups and set aside. Dice 4 cups of peeled potatoes, boil until tender, drain, and set aside. Dice 4 slices of bacon. In a large frying pan, cook the bacon until it is almost done. Add the chopped onion and cook until the onion and bacon start to brown. While the bacon and onion cook, mix the fish, potatoes, salt, and pepper. Turn this mixture into the frying pan and spread evenly. On medium heat, cook until the bottom of the hash browns. Carefully turn the hash over and brown the other side. Sprinkle lightly with vinegar and serve. This dish goes nicely with a large salad or lots of sliced tomatoes for lunch or a light dinner. It also makes a hearty breakfast. Serves 4 to 6.

# CHEROKEE MARY'S LEFTOVER FISH SCRAMBLE

The complete sporting cook will have a recipe or two for serving leftover fish. Here's an old family favorite of mine, often made by my father with salt mullet that we purchased off the rolling store. I loved the dish and still do, but salt mullet may be a little strong for modern breakfasts. So the sportsman might consider a similar dish made with any precooked fish with flaky mild flesh. Leftovers will do just fine. I don't use exact measures for the dish, but it's hard to go wrong.

| | |
|---|---|
| sliced bacon | cold sliced tomato |
| chicken eggs | freshly ground sea salt and black pepper |
| minced scallion with part of green tops | toast or biscuit halves |
| flaked fish, precooked | |

For each partaker, fry a couple strips of bacon in a skillet and set aside to drain. Lightly whisk the eggs in a bowl. Sauté the minced scallion in the skillet until lightly browned. Add the fish flakes and heat through. Serve at once, flanked by the bacon, a big slice of cold tomato, and toast or biscuit halves. A twist or two of sea salt and black pepper completes the treat.

*Note: A really good tomato is essential to this dish. I am fond of a reddish purple Cherokee heirloom variety, which adds a little of the unexpected to the presentation and establishes my lineage in this old family dish.*

# SKILLET FISH GRAVY

If you don't have enough leftovers to make Cherokee Mary's Leftover Fish Scramble, save what you have and set the skillet aside overnight. The next morning, pour most of the cooking oil out of the skillet. Heat the skillet and about 1 tablespoon of the oil along with any little brown bits in the bottom. Slowly stir in a little flour with a wooden spoon until you have a light brown roux. Add a little coffee or water, stirring as you do so, until a nice gravy forms. Stir in the leftover fish flakes and serve hot over biscuit halves.

This old fish gravy makes a very good breakfast, so don't ever throw out the makings. If someone objects to a skillet of grease sitting on the stove all night, hide it in the refrigerator until morning.

# THE REDUCED-FAT FISH FRY

Fried catfish is a tradition in the South, and the dish is fast catching on in other parts of the country. While river-run channel cats are highly prized by many anglers and connoisseurs, most of the market fish are raised in ponds these days. In the rural South, small cats of about 7 inches in length are the favorites for frying, but fillets from larger fish are usually more popular in urban areas of the South as well as in other parts of the country. Either kind will do for frying, but steaks from very large fish (cut across the backbone) are usually best when grilled or baked.

These days, fried fish are frowned upon by many health-conscious people simply because they contain lots of fat. Yet, the fat absorbed by the fish during cooking can be reduced, as shown in the how-to details in this recipe. Even more important, the traditional menu can be altered to reduce the overall fat intake. The British fish 'n' chips, for example, is simply fried fish and french fries. The latter usually soak up more cooking oil than the fish, especially if cooked by the twice-fried gourmet recipes, in addition to the fat-producing carbohydrates in the potatoes. In the South, the traditional fish fry menu usually calls for hush puppies, which are nothing but fried corn pone, along with the fried fish and the twice-fried french fries. So, give some thought to the menu if you want to reduce the fat at a fish fry, or take a tip or two from the serving suggestions following this recipe, based on a contribution this ol' country boy made to a book called *One Fish, Two Fish, Crawfish, Bluefish: The Smithsonian Sustainable Seafood Cookbook*, published by the Smithsonian Institution in 2004, a work put together for the most part with recipes by famous chefs. (I knew that I, a self-proclaimed jackleg, would stick out like a sore thumb, but I did it anyhow, mostly because I felt that an unprissified recipe for farmed cats would leave more river-run fish for those of us in the know.) I have also published several versions of the recipe in other cookbooks and magazine pieces, and I can only assert that recent thinking makes it better or at least more practical for modern times.

| | |
|---|---|
| **catfish fillets or small whole fish** | **salt and black pepper** |
| **lots of peanut oil for deep-frying** | **Tabasco sauce (optional)** |
| **fine white cornmeal** | |

Rig for deep-frying in a cast-iron skillet, heating an inch of oil to 375°F. When the oil is almost hot enough, sprinkle the fish lightly on both sides with salt and pepper, along with a little Tabasco sauce, if wanted. Put about a cup of cornmeal into a small brown bag or a suitable container. (If you can't obtain fine stone-ground meal made from whole-kernel corn, use ordinary wheat flour.) Place a few fillets into the bag and shake it, coating all sides of the fish. Shake off the excess meal.

When the oil is hot, put a few fillets into the skillet. Do not overcrowd. Cook for a few minutes. The fillets are done when they float, but let them brown for another half minute or so. Carefully pick up the smallest fillet (larger ones take the longest to cook) with tongs and hold it over the skillet to drain some of the oil. Then place the fillet on a large brown bag. Drain the rest, one by one. Do not pile on or overlap the fillets, using more than one bag if necessary. (This brown bag will soak up a lot of grease from the fish. Several thicknesses of paper towel can be used, but brown bags really work better. Also, I usually serve the fish on the brown bag at informal feeds.) When the first batch of fish is done, let the oil heat back to 375°F and cook another batch, and so on. Serve hot with the serving suggestions below.

To recap: If you want to reduce the grease in the fried fish without losing flavor, be sure to follow the above steps closely, for these reasons: (1) A light coating of meal or flour will not soak up much oil, whereas some of the thick batters are grease traps. (2) Cooking the fish at a high temperature (and peanut oil can be heated quite hot before it starts smoking) tends to seal the surface of fish, keeping the pieces from soaking up oil. (3) Proper dripping over the skillet and draining on the brown bags will minimize the oil that you actually consume with the fish. This last step is more important than most people realize. Merely taking the fish up in a wire basket and piling them onto a serving platter can result in noticeably greasy fish—especially those on the bottom of the pile.

# TROUT HEMINGWAY

I once started browsing about in *The Hemingway Cookbook* by Craig Boreth, enjoying Roast Duckling from the Harry's Bar, lunch with John Dos Passos, an Alice B. Toklas recipe or two (which seemed only tenuously connected to Ernest), Woodcock Flambé in Armagnac, and a few Algerian wines, which have an unusually high alcoholic content (owing to the hot summers, I learned). By chance, I happened upon an early and less pretentious recipe for trout, first published by the young Hemingway in his outdoors column for the *Toronto Star*, long before he moved to France and fished the streams of Spain. He didn't specify the size of the trout, but they would have to be small enough to fit into a skillet. Granted, we can use a large skillet and cook the fish one or two at a time, but small trout in a 12-inch skillet work just right.

|  |  |
|---|---|
| **4 whole trout** | **1 cup cornmeal** |
| **8 strips bacon** | **1 cup Crisco** |

Build a good wood campfire, letting it burn down to coals. Pull out a sparse bed of coals and melt the Crisco in the skillet. Cook the bacon on medium heat until it is almost done but not yet brown. Dust the fish with cornmeal. Place the fish in the skillet and cook for 5 minutes. Turn and top each fish with 2 strips of the partly cooked bacon. Cook for about 10 minutes, or longer for larger trout. If cooked to perfection, Hemingway says, "The trout are crisp outside and firm and pink inside and the bacon is well done—but not too done."

# CATALONIAN FISH WITH GARLIC

Here's an old fisherman's dish from the Mediterranean coast of Spain. Like so many other distinctive recipes, this one requires only a few ingredients. Don't be put off by the amount of garlic, unless you simply can't stand the stuff, in which case you probably wouldn't have gotten past the title of the recipe. The trick to the recipe is to cook the garlic until it is "burnt" or, as modern chefs say, well caramelized. I usually cook the dish in a cast-iron skillet large enough to hold the fillets in a single layer, but other skillets, including an electric skillet, will work fine. Any good, mild fish will work for this recipe. Try fillets of walleye or black sea bass.

| | |
|---|---|
| 1 to 1½ pounds fish fillets | olive oil |
| 20 large cloves garlic | 2 cups water |
| 1 very large ripe tomato | ½ teaspoon sea salt |

Peel the garlic cloves and slice them thinly lengthwise. Cut the tomato into wedges (unpeeled) and remove the seeds. Then finely chop what's left of the tomato.

Heat the oil in the skillet, add the garlic, and stir with a wooden spatula for 10 to 15 minutes, or until the garlic has turned dark brown. Add the chopped tomatoes. Cook over low to medium heat, stirring with the wooden spatula, until you have a rather dry paste. Stir in 2 cups of water, bring to a boil, and cook until the sauce is reduced by half.

Sprinkle the fillets with sea salt, then place them in the skillet without overlapping them. On medium heat, cook the fillets from 3 to 5 minutes on each side, turning only once, or until the flesh flakes easily when tested with a fork. (The general rule applies: Cook for a total of 10 minutes per inch of thickness.)

Serve hot, spooning the sauce over each fillet. The sauce is also good over rice.

# VIETNAMESE PERCH WITH NUOC CHAM

A condiment called nuoc cham (with some tricky accent marks) is essential to this dish, and Vietnamese fish sauce is essential to nuoc cham. Substitute Thai or Indonesian fish sauce if you must. In any case, nuoc cham is served with just about every meal in Vietnam, north or south, and is best prepared fresh for each meal, made with the aid of a mortar and pestle. It goes nicely with fried seafood. I normally use a fresh red cayenne pepper or Tabasco sauce for the recipe, but any fresh red chile will do.

As compared with the Chinese deep-fry, the Vietnamese use only a small amount of oil and do not often use a batter or flour coating. For this recipe, any good fish of about ½ pound can be used, preferably scaled. I list white perch, but also try bluegill or even crappie.

### Nuoc Cham

| | |
|---|---|
| 2 tablespoons Vietnamese or Thai fish sauce | ½ hot red chile pepper (fresh) or to taste |
| 2 teaspoons light brown sugar | ⅛ lime (wedge) |
| 1 clove garlic | water to taste |

Seed and mince the pepper, carefully removing the inner pith as well as the seeds. Peel and mince the garlic. Put the pepper and garlic into a mortar, along with the sugar. Grind into a paste. Squeeze the juice of the lime into the mortar, then remove the lime pulp with a baby spoon or small knife and work it into the mixture with the pestle. Add the fish sauce, blending well. Slowly stir in the water to taste. (Note that the strength of the sauce depends on how much water you use; so, taste it as you go.) Pour the sauce into a small bowl and put it on the table, warning your guests that it is addictive.

### The Fish

| | |
|---|---|
| 4 freshly caught white perch or similar fish | ½ cup peanut oil |

Scale and draw the fish, leaving the heads intact. Cut a shallow X on either side of each fish, just slitting the skin. Heat the oil in a skillet, getting it quite hot. Dry each fish with a paper towel and fry it quickly until both sides are nicely brown, turning once. Do not overcrowd the fish, frying in more than one batch if necessary.

Put the fish on a heated serving platter or directly onto each diner's plate. Spoon on a little sauce and serve with vegetables and breads of your choice. Remember that the Vietnamese eat lots of raw vegetables, so serve accordingly.

# SKILLET FILLETS WITH SOY

This skillet dish can be made with any mild, white fish fillets of reasonable size. Bass, walleye, or channel catfish of about 1 pound each are ideal and will yield boneless and skinless fillets of about ¼ pound each. Allow two fillets per person. I like to cook the fillets in an electric skillet or a square cast-iron skillet.

| | |
|---|---|
| 4 fish fillets, boneless and skinned | 2 tablespoons soy sauce |
| 1 medium onion, finely chopped | 2 tablespoons sake or dry vermouth |
| ½ red bell pepper, seeded and finely chopped | 1 tablespoon peanut oil (maybe more) |
| ½ green bell pepper, seeded and finely chopped | ½ tablespoon light brown sugar |
| | salt and freshly ground black pepper to taste |

Heat the oil in a large skillet. Sauté the fillets for 3 or 4 minutes, turning once. Carefully put the fillets onto a platter with the aid of spatulas.

Sauté the onion and peppers for 4 or 5 minutes, adding a little more oil if needed. Mix the soy sauce, sake or vermouth, and brown sugar. Stir the mixture into the skillet contents. Carefully place the fillets back into the skillet and spoon some of the sauce over the tops. Sprinkle lightly with freshly ground black pepper and more salt, if needed. (Remember that the soy sauce is quite salty.) Cover the skillet and simmer for about 10 minutes.

Serve the fillets and skillet sauce with rice, steamed vegetables or raw salad, and a crusty bread.

# A NASSAU FISH STEAM

Here's an old Conch dish that has been traced back to the slaves who worked the cane fields in the Bahamas. There are many variations, such as this one adapted from *The Florida Cookbook*. Essentially, it's a method of steaming fish in a large covered skillet, and in the lower Keys, it is called a "fish steam." I find that an 11- or 12-inch square electric skillet works great for these measures.

The recipe calls for cooked grits, which can be prepared easily from supermarket grits, following the directions on the package; for best results, however, the cooked grits should not contain lumps and should be cooked slowly and stirred with tender loving care. I might add that grits are often served with fried fish in Florida, especially at a Cracker breakfast.

The Old Sour asked for in the recipe is a popular condiment in the Florida Keys. It is made by mixing salt into freshly squeezed lime juice and fermenting for a couple of weeks. See the note below.

| | |
|---|---|
| **1½ pounds boneless fish fillets** | **salt and pepper to taste** |
| **3 cups hot grits (cooked separately)** | **water as needed, about 2 cups** |
| **2 medium Bermuda onions** | **fresh lime wedges** |
| **2 Key or Persian limes** | **hot pepper sauce such as Tabasco** |
| **¼ cup butter** | **Old Sour served in a cruet** |

Slice the onions and layer them in a large heated skillet. Cut the unpeeled limes into thin slices and layer over the onions. Add enough water to barely top the onions, cover the skillet, and simmer for 20 minutes.

Divide the fillets into at least 4 servings. Carefully place the fillets into the skillet, using tongs to pull some onions and lime slices over them. Add enough boiling water to almost cover the fish. Put a dab of butter over each fillet (saving about half the butter for the end) and sprinkle with salt (easy on the salt if you plan to use lots of Old Sour as a condiment) and freshly ground black pepper. Cover and simmer for 5 minutes, then spoon some of the pan juice over the fillets. Cover and simmer for another 4 or 5 minutes, or until the fish flakes easily when tested with a fork.

Serve in individual bowls or deep soup plates, with soup spoons. Put a large spoonful of grits in each bowl and top with a serving of fish, garnished with a little butter, onion, and lime slices. Each mouthful should contain some fish, some grits, and some broth. Have at hand plenty of lime wedges, Old Sour, and perhaps a hot sauce such as Jamaican Pickapeppa or Dat'l Do-it (made from the Florida datil peppers), if wanted.

*Note: To make a batch of Old Sour, sterilize a wide-mouth fruit jar (Mason jar) in boiling water. When the jar cools, add 2 cups freshly squeezed lime juice and 1 tablespoon sea salt. Shake to dissolve the salt. Put a clean square of cheesecloth over the top and tie with cotton twine or secure with a rubber band. Put the jar in a dark closet or cupboard for 6 to 8 weeks. Strain the juice with a piece of doubled cheesecloth and funnel it into sterilized serving bottles. (Old Conchs like to keep it in brown-colored Old Crow whiskey bottles.) Cork or cap the bottles and save until needed. Store in a dark place at room temperature. Old Sour is especially good at the raw bar or as a condiment for fish dishes and conch salad.*

# A. D.'S CYPRESS TROUT

The ingredients list for this dish calls for a pound of stir-fry vegetables. For convenience, I often use a frozen mix, but most good, fresh vegetables will do. Try diced potatoes, Jerusalem artichokes, squash, onions, snow peas, cauliflower, and so on. As for the tsukeyaki (sukiyaki) sauce, I use Chef Myron Becker's, available in some gourmet shops. If you can't find any such sauce locally, try mixing to taste a little soy sauce, sake, grated ginger, honey, a touch of lemon juice or lemon zest, and freshly ground black pepper. I designed this recipe to help cook the bowfin, also known as grinnel, mudfish, blackfish, cypress trout (my favorite), and countless unprintable names. Although acknowledged for its fighting ability on light tackle, the bowfin is generally regarded as a trash fish and presents the cook with a culinary challenge. If you can't catch a cypress trout, try using fillets from yellow bullheads or, better, a firm-fleshed fish such as sheepshead.

| | |
|---|---|
| **½ pound diced skinless fillets** | **tsukeyaki (sukiyaki) sauce** |
| **olive oil** | **rice (cooked separately)** |
| **1 pound stir-fry vegetables** | **cornstarch mixed with a little water** |

Cut the fillets into ½- to ¾-inch dice, cover with tsukeyaki sauce in a nonmetallic container, and marinate for 30 minutes.

Heat the olive oil in a cast-iron skillet. Drain the fish chunks and stir-fry on high heat for 2 minutes. Remove the fish with a slotted spoon or wire strainer. Drain.

Stir-fry the vegetables for a few minutes, adding a little more oil if needed. Put the fish back into the skillet, then add a little fresh tsukeyaki sauce. Cover and simmer for a few minutes, until all the vegetables are done.

Spoon some of the mix onto heated plates, along with some cooked rice. Quickly add some cornstarch paste to the remaining liquid in the skillet, stirring until the sauce thickens. Spoon a little sauce over the stir-fry and rice. Serve hot, along with crusty bread.

# SALMON PATTIES

Salmon patties are made in a skillet with only a small amount of oil. The mixture should be rather thin so that it will flatten out easily. A salmon croquette, by comparison, is made with a stiffer mixture, coated with egg, dipped in bread crumbs, and fried in deep fat. It is easy to adapt this recipe to croquettes, if you so desire. (See also the next recipe.)

| | |
|---|---|
| 1 can salmon (24-ounce size) | 1 tablespoon minced fresh parsley |
| 3 medium to large chicken eggs | salt and black pepper to taste |
| ¼ cup clarified butter | |

Drain and flake the salmon, retaining the juice from the can. Whisk the eggs lightly in a bowl. Add the salmon, parsley, salt, and black pepper. Mix well with your hands, and add a little of the reserved salmon juice, if needed. Heat the butter in a skillet. Shape the salmon mixture into patties about the size of your hand (sizing them so that only 2 or 3 fit into the skillet, unless you have to use a very large one).

Using a spatula, slip the patties into the hot butter and fry until golden brown on both sides, carefully turning once. Serve warm.

*Note: Use vegetable oil if you prefer, and feel free to reduce the amount of the oil, using just enough to keep the patties from sticking.*

# CAMP CROQUETTES

My mother often cooked salmon croquettes, but it never occurred to me to ask for her recipe. I'm certain that the ingredients list would call for chicken eggs, and I have watched her roll the formed croquettes in freshly crushed cracker crumbs. I haven't tried here to duplicate her results, but I have had occasion to cook my own creation in camp, where fresh eggs are likely to get broken.

The French definition for a croquette, on the other hand, calls for a cream sauce mixed in with the meat or fish, and I find that American canned cream soup works fine—just perfect for the camp cook. My recipe is simple enough, but cooking the croquettes to perfection requires some doing. I won't say the method requires skill, but a little practice will help. In short, if the mix is too mushy, the croquettes will flatten out in the skillet. If this happens, you can get yourself off the hook by calling the result salmon patties instead of croquettes. But the croquette-shaped ovals are more toothsome, being, if cooked perfectly in rather hot oil, crispy on the outside and creamy inside.

| | |
|---|---|
| 2 cans pink salmon (14¾-ounce size) | 1 medium onion, minced |
| 1 can cream of celery soup (10¾-ounce size) | butter or olive oil |
| 1 sleeve saltines (about 40 crackers) | salt and pepper to taste |

Drain the salmon and dump both cans into a mixing bowl. Stir in the soup and minced onions. Crush the saltines (while still in the sleeve if need be) into a fine meal and pour about three-quarters of this into the salmon bowl. Mix well, adding a little salt and black pepper.

Pour the rest of the cracker meal into a plate or onto a flat surface and spread it out. Shape the salmon mixture into croquettes about 1 inch in diameter and 3 inches long. As you go, carefully roll each croquette in cracker meal and line them up, side by side, on a plate or platter. (If you have a refrigerator or ice at hand, it's best to chill the croquettes for half an hour or so. This makes them easier to handle without tearing up or flattening out.)

Heat about 2 tablespoons of the butter or oil in a 10-inch skillet. Using a spatula, place several croquettes into the hot skillet one at a time; do not overcrowd. Cook them for several minutes, turning only once, until nicely browned on both sides. (Note that gently rolling the croquettes over, using the spatula and a spoon, is better than flipping them.) Serve hot with wild rice and vegetables of your choice.

This recipe will feed from 4 to 6 people. I recently tried the recipe with half measures, thinking that I could easily consume a can of salmon. I had more croquettes than I wanted to eat at one sitting, but my dog Nosher was eager to help out. She now claims that these salmon croquettes are even better than my hush puppies.

# EASTERN SHORE CRAB CAKES

Too many recipes for crab cakes have too much breading in the mix and not enough crab. The breading, of course, along with chicken egg, helps make a goo to hold the cake together. Reducing the breading makes a richer cake but also makes it harder to turn and serve the cake without breaking it apart. I recommend that you gamble a little by cutting back considerably on the breading and increasing the crab meat. If things fall apart at the end of the cooking, go ahead and break it all up and call it Scrambled Crab or Crab Norfolk. Note also that soft bread crumbs are specified in this recipe instead of the hard, gritty kind. These produce a better texture in the cake.

Anyone interested in crab cookery ought to take a look at *Mrs. Kitching's Smith Island Cookbook*, a delightful little volume full of such terms as the highly regarded jimmy crabs (mature males), sooks (mature females), and sponges (pregnant sooks). Buckrams, not normally available commercially, are soft-shell crabs (usually eaten whole, fried, or sautéed) that have hardened back to a delightful, crinkly, paper-thin shell.

| | |
|---|---|
| ½ cup soft bread crumbs | ½ red bell pepper, finely chopped |
| ¼ cup mayonnaise | 1 teaspoon Worcestershire sauce |
| 1 large chicken egg, whisked | ¾ teaspoon Old Bay seasoning |
| 1 tablespoon Dijon mustard | salt and freshly ground black pepper to taste |
| 2 scallions, finely chopped with part of green tops | 1 pound lump crab meat |
| | peanut oil |

Mix half the bread crumbs with the mayonnaise, chicken egg, mustard, scallions, bell pepper, Worcestershire sauce, Old Bay, salt, and pepper. Wet your hands and mix in the crab meat. Shape into six cakes about 2½ inches wide and at least 1 inch thick. Put the rest of the bread crumbs on a plate and gently coat the cakes on both sides, one by one. Set aside.

Heat ½ inch of peanut oil in a skillet on medium high. Carefully cook the crab cakes two or three at a time, turning once. (The quintessential crab cake should be nicely browned and crisp on the outside and quite moist inside.) Serve hot with a good tartar sauce.

# SAUTÉED BAY SCALLOPS

Small bay scallops, including the calico, are sweet and tender but firm if they are shucked and cooked shortly after capture. (The much larger sea scallops have a stronger flavor.) Market scallops are usually soaked in water, puffing them up. The bay scallops can be fried, broiled, or cooked in a number of ways, but they are really not large enough for kabobs. If you can't obtain fresh bay scallops, try the flash-frozen kind. In my neck of the woods, where the St. Joe Bay is home to an annual scallop festival, I can purchase flash-frozen eyes in 20-pound bags, with each one separate from the other so that I can take out what I want. My favorite way to cook them is hardly a recipe, but I'll list the ingredients anyhow just to make my point.

**fresh bay scallops in the shell**          **salted butter**

Shuck the scallops into a bowl, but do not wash off the saltwater. Heat some butter in a skillet and, on medium heat, sauté the scallops a few at a time. Drain on a brown paper bag.

If you are dining informally, serve the scallops on the brown bag, along with salad, steamed vegetables, and lots of chewy French bread. Enjoy. Go and catch some more scallops! If you catch only a few, however, and need to stretch the menu while experiencing a rather daring new culinary adventure, see the following recipe.

# A. D.'S WHOLE SCALLOP FRY

Our thinking about scallops has been greatly influenced by what's available in our commercial markets, on restaurant menus, and in recipes, which invariably limit the choice to the bay (or calico) and sea scallops that grow along the Eastern Seaboard, ignoring West Coast species.

I suppose that properly equipped frogmen can dive for their own sea scallops, but most of the recreational scalloping is for the small bay or calico species. These can sometimes be taken in very shallow water, often around eelgrass beds, by wading. The scallops can be caught with a small net, or simply picked up by hand. A snorkel, mask, and swim fins may come in handy, and sometimes diving a few feet will be quite productive. Of course, conditions vary from one good scalloping spot to another, so it's always best to check with local sportsmen and tackle shops before wading in. Note also that scalloping is highly regulated in most areas these days, with seasons and bag limits. From time to time, certain waters may be closed owing to low reproduction rates, which can swing wildly from one season to the next—or because contamination of some sort makes the shellfish unsafe for human consumption.

Happily, frozen farmed scallops are now available, and it's even possible these days for landlubbers to purchase live (unshucked) farmed scallops with overnight delivery. For openers, check with www.farm-2-market.com—or roll your trousers and go Googling. Oh, 'tis a brave new world for culinary sports, and now is the time to take a hard look at eating the whole scallop, not just the white adductor muscle, which is the only part that is commonly eaten in America. In other parts of the world, the whole scallop is often consumed, but those books and magazine articles that mention eating the whole thing are a little short on details. I know why. Anyone who has shucked a bay scallop and examined the insides up close will not be too enthusiastic about eating what he sees. Don't be put off. Just remember that from this ugly mess arose Aphrodite, and try this method of making the whole scallop prettier to see and easier to swallow. The trick is to fry the scallop in the half shell, following a method sometimes used in Alaska to fry butter clams.

**whole bay scallops, freshly gathered**                                    **peanut oil for frying**
**flour, cracker crumbs, or finely**
**ground white cornmeal**

Heat about an inch of peanut oil in a deep skillet. While the oil is heating, partly shuck some of the scallops, removing the top part of the shell but leaving the bottom part attached by the adductor muscle. Do not clean out the insides or spill out the juice.

Spread some flour or other breading onto a plate. Going one by one, set the scallop into the flour shell-side down. Sprinkle some of the flour generously onto the open scallop. Carefully dump out the excess flour. (This will leave some breading mixed with the natural juices of the scallop. Be warned that hot grease and water mix violently, so make sure all the juice is absorbed and won't spill out into the skillet.) Repeat until you have enough breaded scallops to fit loosely into the skillet.

When the oil is hot, carefully set each scallop into the skillet shell-side down. (I use a slotted kitchen spoon, with scalloped tongs at hand if needed.) Fry for a couple of minutes, until the inside of the scallop shrinks a little. Turn the scallops over, meat-side down now, and fry two or three minutes, or until nicely browned. Remove the scallops, draining with a slotted spoon, and place them shell-side down on a serving platter or plate. These make an attractive presentation.

To eat, scoop out the scallop with a regular table spoon, dislodging the adductor muscle and good stuff as you go. All the innards will have pulled into a solid mass, and the whole stays together for a one-bit experience. The breading, soaked with scallop juice and fried, makes for a flavorful crunch. The sensation is not unlike eating a fried oyster, with a crusty outside and a juicy inside—but with the added chewiness of the adductor muscle. It's a toothsome morsel.

*Note: This technique can also be used on some clams as well as small mussels or even well-scrubbed small oysters.*

# SHRIMP MOSCA

Some of the best Italian-American cooking comes from the New Orleans area—and here's a world-class surprise. The recipe was named for Nick Mosca, a chef at the old Elmwood Plantation near New Orleans. It has been adapted here from *The New Orleans Italian Cookbook*, a committee venture put together by the Italian-American Society of Jefferson Auxiliary.

Note that the dish must be cooked with unpeeled shrimp, preferably with the heads intact. You can reduce the measure and use beheaded shrimp if you must—but they must be unpeeled. Peeled shrimp simply won't work the magic.

| | |
|---|---|
| 4 tablespoons olive oil | 1 teaspoon dry Italian oregano |
| 6 toes garlic, crushed | 1 teaspoon rosemary |
| 1 tablespoon salt | 3 pounds head-on shrimp |
| 1 teaspoon freshly ground black pepper | 2 tablespoons sauterne |
| 2 bay leaves | |

Heat the olive oil in a large cast-iron skillet. Sauté the garlic for a couple of minutes. Add the seasonings and continue sautéing for a few minutes. Add the shrimp and cook 5 minutes, turning the shrimp once. Add the wine and cook for a few more minutes. Let it coast while you set the table and slice some good chewy Italian bread. Serve with lemon wedges and a few sprigs of parsley for a little color.

*Note: Most Shrimp Mosca recipes will specify a longer cooking time. Be warned that overly cooked shrimp are difficult to shuck and a little tough to chew. Ideally, the shrimp texture and juices should sort of burst in your mouth, and, of course, the seasonings and olive oil come from contact with the peelings. So hunker down. It's truly an Italian flavor, needing no Tabasco sauce or Cajun dust.*

# SKILLET SHRIMP WITH SWEET PEPPERS

Here's an old recipe from coastal Georgia and the Low Country in South Carolina, where shrimp like to run up the tidal creeks. Small or medium shrimp work best, boiled in salted water for only 2 or 3 minutes, until they are nicely pink. Cooking the shrimp longer makes them tough and difficult to peel. An electric skillet works just fine for this recipe.

| | |
|---|---|
| 2 cups peeled boiled shrimp | 2 cloves garlic, minced |
| 2 cups chopped tomato | ½ teaspoon red pepper flakes |
| 2 bell peppers, seeded and cut into strips | salt and freshly ground black pepper to taste |
| 6 slices bacon | white rice (precooked) |

In a large skillet, fry the bacon until it is crisp. Remove the bacon and set aside, leaving the drippings in the skillet. Add the bell pepper strips and cook for a few minutes, stirring a time or two. Add the garlic, chopped tomato, and red pepper flakes. Cover and cook very slowly for about half an hour, stirring frequently. Add a little water if needed.

Add the shrimp along with some salt and freshly ground black pepper. Cook for about 5 minutes. Serve on a bed of rice, with a green salad topped with crumbled bacon on the side.

# LOBSTER NORFOLK

This old recipe from the Chesapeake Bay area can also be cooked with lump crabmeat. Be sure to use regular butter, not unsalted. I allow half a pound of meat per person. That's quite a bit, but it's so good that you'll be looking for seconds. Try this one with spiny lobster (sometimes called crawfish in Florida) or the smaller bulldozers (shovel lobsters).

| | |
|---|---|
| 1 pound lobster meat, uncooked | 1 cup butter |

Warm two serving ramekins in an oven on low heat. Cut the lobster meat into bite-size servings. Melt the butter in a cast-iron skillet. Add the lobster meat and increase the heat to high. Cook for 3 or 4 minutes, stirring with a wooden spoon. Reduce the heat to low and cook for 4 or 5 minutes, stirring and tilting the skillet in a circular motion.

Spoon the lobster into the warmed ramekins and pour the butter left in the skillet equally over each serving. Serve in the ramekins, along with plenty of chewy bread and lots of pretty salad.

# EASY CAMP CHOWDER

New Englanders claim that good fish chowder can't be made without chowder crackers, a regional staple that no doubt evolved from the old sailor's hardtack. Well, here's a camp chowder that may violate New England sensibilities—but taste it before you start writing nasty letters and accuse me of trying to start the Civil War again.

½ to 1 pound fish fillets

1 can cream of clam chowder (10¾-ounce size)

1 pound small red potatoes, sliced

1 medium to large onion, chopped

several strips of salt pork (or bacon if need be)

salt and freshly ground black pepper

oyster crackers, saltines, or chewy French bread

Dice the salt pork and fry it in a 12-inch skillet until the oil is cooked out. Drain the cracklings and set aside. In the drippings, sauté the onion for a few minutes, stirring as you go. Layer on the sliced potatoes and add the fish chunks. Sprinkle lightly with salt and pepper. Dump in the can of clam chowder. Rinse out the can with water, pouring the contents into the skillet to add more moisture. Cook on reduced heat for about 12 minutes. Don't stir while cooking, but check with a spoon to make sure the bottom isn't about to scorch.

If all goes well, the chowder can be removed in layers, almost like a slice of pie. If you want it more soupy, simply add a little water and serve along with the French bread for sopping, or serve topped with either oyster crackers or saltines for crunch. In either case, sprinkle each bowl of the finished chowder with the cracklings before digging in.

# SKILLET SOFTCRAWS

Most anglers know that soft-shelled crawfish make better live bait than hardcraws. Few realize, however, that softcraws can also be much better additions to the camp skillet and can, in fact, save the day.

The problem with crawfish cookery in general is that the tail end is small in relation to the head, and the delicious white meat gets even smaller when you shuck it out for frying. If the crawfish are small to start with (and few of the 200 species that grow around the country will measure up to the Louisiana reds), then Livingston's Law of Futile Foraging sets in. Roughly stated: The energy expended in catching, dressing, cooking, and eating the prey is more than that derived from its consumption.

Still, in Mid-America every country boy's dream is to get up enough crawfish to feed the whole family. A culinary breakthrough down in Cajun country can make this task much easier. If you are lucky enough to catch a softcraw, you can fry and eat the whole thing—almost. This shortens the preparation time, simplifies the eating, and reduces the energy expended on catching the food, simply because a few softcraws can go a long way.

Like crabs, crawfish molt from time to time, usually in spring or summer. After shedding the old shell, the crawfish quickly grows a new one, drawing from two balls of calcium that have been built up inside its head. These look like pearly BBs. Although the new shell grows surprisingly fast, the molting crawfish is left with a soft shell for a few hours. There will be an optimum stage of softness for eating purposes, but the hungry sportsman probably won't even notice a little crunch.

The idea of eating soft-shelled crustaceans whole is really not new. Along the East Coast and the Gulf of Mexico, old salts and adventurous vacationers have long since taken advantage of the soft-shelled blue crabs. At market, these were expensive and not always available. In time, commercial holding tanks were developed, enabling the crabber to have more control over nature. At present, both fried and broiled soft-shells are not unusual items on the menu of coastal eating houses.

The holding-tank idea can also be applied to crawfish. The process is relatively new, however, and how widely available softcraws become remains to be seen. There are marketing problems even with hard crawfish, which are often precooked before they reach the consumer. In any case, Googling "crawfish cookery" on the Internet will keep you up to date.

Fortunately, the sportsman and wild foods forager doesn't have to wait for a soft-craw market to develop. Just about every lake, pond, stream, and wet-water ditch in the country will hold plenty of live crawfish, free for the taking. Further, the smaller species of crawfish may be even better, culinarily speaking, than the larger commercial varieties. A small softcraw properly fried makes a nice bite, at once crispy and succulent.

You can cook this recipe with all softcraws, if you have them, or you can fill in with peeled tails from hardcraws. This approach will enable the forager to use a mixed bag. If you can't get up a combined mess of soft- and hardcraws, add a few small fish to fill in. Hornyheads or any perch will do. If gashed and crisply fried, these can be eaten bones and all.

**2 dozen live soft-shelled crawfish or substitutes**

**peanut oil for deep-frying**

**2 chicken eggs whisked with a little milk**

**flour**

**fine bread crumbs**

**salt and cayenne to taste**

To prepare the live softcraws for frying, rinse them and snip off the front part of the head, cutting in right behind the eyes with kitchen shears. Squeeze the head a little and watch for the balls of calcium to come out of the cut. Remove these and discard the pointed part of the head. Be warned that both calcium balls should be accounted for; these things are as hard as steel bird shot and simply must be removed, lest one of your guests breaks a tooth at the table.

To proceed, heat 3 or 4 inches of peanut oil to 350°F or 375°F in a suitable pot or fish fryer. Put the flour into a small brown bag, along with some salt and cayenne pepper. Put the bread crumbs into a separate bag. Dip the crawfish one at a time in the whisked egg, drop it into the flour bag, and shake it. Dip the dusted crawfish in the egg again, then shake in the bread crumbs. Fry the breaded crawfish, a few at a time, for 2 or 3 minutes, or until golden brown. Drain on brown bags. Serve hot.

**Note:** *Fried softshells are wonderful in sandwiches slathered with mayonnaise.*

# GROUPER STACKS

This sandwich has become a favorite lunch in family eateries around the Gulf of Mexico. A plump fillet about an inch thick and large enough to stick out over the bread is the key to the stack. Bread the grouper fillets and fry until golden brown and crispy, but soft and moist inside. Slather the insides of two slices of thick sandwich bread with mayonnaise, tartar sauce, or some such "twangy" white spread. Sandwich with a fried fillet, followed by a slice of red-ripe tomato, salt, pepper, and a little lettuce, either sliced or shredded. A thin slice of mild onion or a few onion rings can also be added, if wanted. Serve with twice-fried shoestring potatoes and dill pickle spear on the side. A wedge of lemon adds a little color.

*Note: Many commercial eateries give the customer the choice of fried, grilled, or blackened fillets for building a grouper stack. I suspect that many of the "grilled" fillets are simply sautéed, but some might well be cooked over hot coals. In any case, I prefer to have mine crisply fried (unless I am doing the grilling over real coals) instead of soggy—but I certainly won't turn down any well-laid grouper stack. Note also that most mild fish with flaky white meat can be used in this recipe. Fillets of black bass are perfect.*

# SUMAC TROUT

I claim bragging rights to this recipe, which I published in a previous book. Try it the next time you see bunches of sumac berries growing along a stream or shoreline. That's right. Sumac. All of the American sumacs with red berries (genus *Rhus*) can be used; these include staghorn sumac, scarlet sumac, squawbush, smooth sumac, and others. The berries are covered with tiny hairs, which in turn are coated with a substance called malic acid. This stuff has a pleasing, tart flavor. In the Middle East, sumac berries are used to make a spice, and ancient recipes from Apicus (the Roman culinary sport) call for Syrian sumac.

A pleasing drink, sometimes called Indian lemonade, can be made from the sumac berries and a little sugar. Usually, the drink is made by sloshing some berries around in cold water. The berries don't have to be crushed, since most of the flavor is on the tiny hairs that grow on the surface. The liquid is then strained through a double thickness of cloth to get rid of the spent berries and the fine hairs that shed off. (Note that washing the berries in the stream will rob them of flavor; note also that a strong rain can wash the flavor from the berries, so that it's best to get them during dry weather.)

In addition to making Indian lemonade, the early American settlers used a sumac infusion as a substitute for lemon juice, which is what gave me the idea for this recipe. To make what I call sumac concentrate, boil some of the juice (unsweetened) until it is reduced enough to suit your taste.

If you like the flavor of sumac, remember that the berries grow in large bunches and are very easy to gather. So, fill your canoe before the rains come. The berries can be stored in a dry place for winter use, or you can freeze the juice. Make a little extra concentrate and try it in recipes that call for lemon juice, just as the early American settlers did. Then you can smile the next time you price a lemon in the supermarket.

| | |
|---|---|
| **1 or 2 small trout, less than 1 pound** | **sumac concentrate** |
| **2 or 3 tablespoons butter** | **salt to taste** |
| **flour** | |

Dress the trout with or without heads, depending on the relative size of your skillet, and sprinkle inside and out with salt. Dust the trout lightly with flour. Melt the butter in the skillet. Sauté the trout until done on both sides, turning once. Remove the trout to drain. Add a little sumac concentrate to the skillet, stirring and shaking the pan for a few minutes. Taste and add more sumac, or more butter, if needed. Pour the sauce over the trout and eat hot.

# CHAPTER
## 7

## Exotic Meats

**I**nternet marketing, flash-freezing techniques, and overnight shipping have made it a brave new world for culinary sports across the land. Slowly, American tastes are evolving, helping us appreciate the incredibly wide range of foods eaten around the world and now available to the modern epicure. A short chapter in a short book like this can't possibly do justice to this new cookery, but maybe the few recipes below will inspire us to go Googling for new tastes and exotic flavors. More important, perhaps the new cuisine and fusion cookery will cause us to take a closer look at what is available in our own backyards or at the local bait shop.

### CHICKEN-FRIED GATOR

Alligators always get attention, whether on TV, golf courses, in the wild, or, these days, on the menu of some upscale restaurants from Dallas to New York City. They have always been welcome table fare for old Florida Crackers and Louisiana swamp dwellers. Even when on the endangered species list a few years back, gators were farm raised for profit and were poached illegally for hides and meat. These days, gators are legal game in some areas, "harvested" by state-run lottery permit and strict regulations. Many of the regular hunters, at least here in Florida, recoup part or all of the fees and expenses of the hunt by selling the hides. Some even show a good profit, in spite of high permit fees.

The hunts are all right, I guess, but legally, you can't simply go out and shoot a gator the way you would a deer or a turkey. The many rules and regulations for the hunts are available on the Internet, along with butchering procedure, hide care, outfitters, guides, and so on. For openers, try www.wildflorida.org/gators/public.htm, or perhaps search for alligator meat on Google. If your main interest in the gator is culinary, you may decide to purchase some meat from one of the many suppliers, or from a professional hunter who "rescues" the "nuisance" gators in several states. Names and addresses are also available on the Internet.

In any case, remember that most of the gator meat on the market is from large specimens, partly because the hide is more valuable than the meat. Large gators tend to be tough. In many cases, the meat sold on the market has been "cubed." That is, it has been tenderized with a machine, making it similar to the cubed beef and pork sold at supermarkets. The same effect can be achieved by pounding the meat with the cubing side of a hand-held meat mallet. If you want the meat at its best, catch yourself a yearling of 4 or 5 feet—and field dress it as soon as practical.

In any case, here's a recipe that works best with market meat that has been run through a meat-tenderizing machine. If you butcher your own gator, use a meat mallet to flatten the meat to about ⅜ inch thickness. Servings? I allow at least half a pound of gator per person. More is better, within reason. The measures below can be modified to suit your needs or your appetite.

<table>
<tr><td>2 pounds cubed gator</td><td>¼ cup half-and-half</td></tr>
<tr><td>juice of two lemons (plus one for Plan B, if needed)</td><td>1 tablespoon salt</td></tr>
<tr><td>2 cups all-purpose flour</td><td>2 teaspoons finely ground black pepper</td></tr>
<tr><td>1 medium onion, minced</td><td>1 teaspoon cayenne</td></tr>
<tr><td></td><td>peanut oil</td></tr>
</table>

Put the meat into a plastic zip bag and add the lemon juice, turning about to coat all sides. Refrigerate for several hours. When you are ready to cook, drain the meat and heat ½ inch of peanut oil in a cast-iron skillet. Mix the salt, black pepper, and cayenne into the flour and put it into a medium-size brown bag. Shake the meat, a few pieces at a time, in the bag and set aside, retaining the seasoned flour.

Fry the meat a few pieces at a time on high heat for a couple of minutes on each side, until nicely browned. Drain the meat on a brown bag. Take a bite. If it is too tough to chew, resort to Plan B below. If it is tender, proceed as follows: Pour off most of the skillet oil, leaving about 1½ tablespoons. Sauté the minced onion. Sprinkle a little of the reserved flour into the skillet, stirring as you go, until you have a light roux. Slowly stir in the half-and-half until the gravy is as thin as you like it.

Serve the steaks on individual plates, topping each one with some of the gravy, along with rice and vegetables of your choice. Swamp cabbage (heart of palm) always goes nicely with gator.

Plan B: If the meat is too tough to chew after frying, set it aside and pour most of the grease out of the skillet. Put the browned meat back into the skillet and sprinkle with a little of the reserved flour. Add the juice of another lemon, along with enough water to cover the meat. Bring to a boil, reduce the heat to very low, cover tightly, and simmer for 2 hours or longer—until the meat is tender. Stir and add more water as needed.

# ISLAND FROGS

The legs of crapauds, also known as mountain chickens, the large frogs found in Dominica and Montserrat, are considered to be gourmet fare in island circles. The recipe also works nicely for the legs of large stateside bullfrogs. The marinade helps the texture of the meat in addition to adding flavor.

| | |
|---|---|
| 2 pounds large frog legs | 1 tablespoon rum |
| 1 medium onion, grated | 1 teaspoon salt |
| 3 cloves garlic, crushed | ½ teaspoon white pepper |
| cooking oil | ½ teaspoon freshly ground allspice |
| flour | lime wedges for garnish |
| 1 tablespoon red wine vinegar | |

Mix the wine vinegar, rum, onion, garlic, allspice, salt, and white pepper in a nonmetallic container. Add the frog legs, toss about to coat all sides, and marinate for an hour or so, turning from time to time.

When you are ready to cook, heat the oil in a skillet. Drain the frog legs and shake them in a bag of flour. Shake off the excess flour, then fry the frog legs a few at a time in the skillet for about 5 minutes on each side, turning once. Brown nicely but do not overcook. Drain the frog legs on a brown bag and serve hot, along with lime wedges.

# FROGS STURDIVANT

Large American bullfrog legs tend to be a little stringy when fried like chicken. In this regard, legs from the smaller leopard frogs, once harvested commercially in the Florida Everglades, are better than big ol' speckled-belly river swamp bulls. Also note that commercial frogs, some pond-raised in Asia, are available in several sizes. Medium or small are better for frying, although some people think that large is better.

The whole frog can also be cooked, and, I'll submit, the front legs are a little better in that they have a shorter muscle fiber. In spite of numerous "eyewitnesses," dead frogs of any size don't jump out of the skillet. In any case, here is a recipe, adapted from *Game Cookery* by E. N. and Edith Sturdivant, that tames frog legs considerably and improves the texture on the big ones. Note that the frog legs are lightly parboiled before they hit the hot skillet.

| | |
|---|---|
| **8 pairs frog legs** | **salt and freshly ground black pepper to taste** |
| **½ cup lemon juice** | **cooking oil** |
| **1 chicken egg** | **water for poaching** |
| **cracker crumbs** | |

Bring some water to a boil and add the lemon juice and a little salt. Simmer the frog legs for 2 minutes. Drain.

Beat the chicken egg in a bowl and place some cracker crumbs in a plate. Sprinkle the legs with salt and pepper, dip them one at a time in the egg, and roll them in the cracker crumbs. Heat about an inch of oil in a skillet and fry about half the legs until golden brown, usually from 3 to 5 minutes, depending on the size of the legs. Drain the legs on a brown bag and cook the rest.

Serve hot, along with rice, a green vegetable, and hot biscuits.

*Note:* *For very large legs from those old speckled-belly frogs, you may want to marinate in lemon juice before parboiling.*

# TURTLE STEW WITH ACORN GRAVY

Some of the best eating often comes from a sparse cupboard supplemented with plenty of good wild foods. Once, while living in the country, I needed to feed a couple of hungry college boys on short notice. Looking around in the freezer, I found a piece of snapping turtle that I had been saving—actually, it was from a large turtle my younger son had caught from our cypress pond. Tough, yes, I knew it would be tough, partly because we had already eaten about 10 pounds of the meat. The remaining pound or two was from a leg quarter—one of the toughest parts. Consequently, I knew that long cooking would be in order.

In the freezer, I found a package of tough oyster mushrooms that I had gathered one morning from the trunk of an ancient oak near the cypress pond. These were the last of about 2 gallons of beautiful mushrooms, and I knew from experience that they hold up to long cooking. In the freezer, I also found a few pods of okra that I had been saving for a gumbo, along with a small package of frozen wild onions with part of the green tops. In the cupboard was a can of tomatoes. We had plenty of rice.

My first thoughts pointed toward a turtle-and-okra gumbo, but I changed my mind while considering a pile of sweet live oak acorns on my countertop. A turtle-and-acorn stew with tomato and wild onions would be in order (real Indian chow), served up over a bed of steamed rice. Vegetables? Across the fence from the pond grew a field of soybeans. The stalks were planted thick, and each stalk was loaded with pods. These were still in the green stage, and I had always wanted to try them cooked like green field peas—one of my favorite Southern dishes. I had previously shelled a few pods and put the green beans into a vegetable soup. The okra pods could be cooked right in with the soybeans, a combination that was at one time quite popular in the rural South.

Some of the soybeans were quite mature and had to be cooked for about 40 minutes. They were delicious and held their texture and green color better than field peas. Since America grows countless tons of soybeans each year, I don't understand why we don't eat more of them while they are still green. In addition to being very good, they are loaded with protein. These are merely simmered for 30 or 40 minutes in water, preferably seasoned with a little salt pork or ham hock.

Anyhow, here's the recipe for the turtle stew with acorn gravy. I published a version of the recipe in my column for *Gray's Sporting Journal*. Since then, I have doubled the measure of mushrooms.

| | |
|---|---|
| 1 pound turtle meat | wild onions with part of green tops |
| ¼ to ½ pound oyster mushrooms | water |
| 1 can tomatoes (14½-ounce size) | salt and freshly ground black pepper |
| acorn meal | rice (cooked separately) |
| cooking oil | |

Cut the turtle meat into small cubes. (The meat can be stringy, so small pieces are easier to eat.) Heat a little cooking oil in a large skillet, then brown the turtle meat and the wild onions. Add the can of tomatoes, along with the liquid from the can, and the oyster mushrooms. (The mushrooms should be cut into slices.) Add about two tomato cans of water. Bring to a boil, reduce the heat, cover tightly, and simmer for 2 or 3 hours. Add more water from time to time as needed. It's best to barely simmer the meat instead of boiling it.

When the meat is very tender, add some salt and freshly ground black pepper. Sprinkle on a little acorn meal, stirring and cooking as you go, until you have a gravy. I don't use exact measurements, but about a tablespoon of acorn meal will be about right. Add more water if needed.

Cook and stir, cook and stir, until the dish acquires a deep, dark brown color. (Acorn meal tends to turn quite dark when cooked.) The acorns add to the flavor, and the color makes the stew go nicely over a bed of white rice. Serve with cooked soybeans or other vegetables and a crusty bread. Sop the gravy.

**Note:** *Substitute mushrooms of your choice for the oyster mushrooms, but remember that some of these will have to be cooked for the whole time. Also, sun-dried tomatoes work nicely in this recipe.*

*Warning:* Make sure that you have sweet acorns for this recipe. Bitter acorns, usually of a black oak variety, require special handling and much soaking in water to get out the bitter tannin. When I first published this recipe in *Gray's Sporting Journal*, a schoolteacher from Georgia sent me an acorn recipe book put together by her students. One recipe for acorn soup called for 2 gallons of macaroni and 1 acorn. Clearly, the boy got hold of a bitter acorn for testing purposes.

# HIGADO DE TORTUGA

To Peru we go. The whole country has wonderful food, including about fifty kinds of potato, one of which is actually freeze-dried in the high Andes by an ancient procedure. The coastal areas have seafood in great plenty and the people in the mountains still eat alpaca and guinea pigs, but my favorite recipes come from the east of the Andes—a vast Amazonian expanse, which the Spanish conquistadors failed to conquer. In addition to the regional game and fish, a large species of soft-shell turtle plies the Amazon, similar to the big cooter that lives in the lakes of central Florida. These things can weigh 30 pounds or better, have a neck as long as your arm, and can strike as fast as a snake. They have a large, flat liver, which I have more than once proclaimed to be excellent eating. But I also want to point out that this simple recipe (adapted here from Marks's *The Exotic Kitchens of Peru*) can also be cooked with fresh venison liver. So, be sure to take along a pinch or two of freshly ground cumin the next time you head for camp. It makes a difference.

**1 pound turtle liver (or whitetail liver)**
**2 teaspoons salt**

**¼ teaspoon ground cumin**
**cooking oil**

Slice the liver into thin pieces, about ¼ inch. Sprinkle with salt and cumin. Heat a little cooking oil in a skillet and fry the liver strips over rather low heat for 2 or 3 minutes, turning a time or two.

Serve hot, perhaps along with steamed quinoa (or rice), baked plantains, sautéed onion rings, and corn pone, topped off with tropical fruits. In camp, sautéed onion rings and mushrooms will do, perhaps cooked in the skillet along with the liver.

# NEWFIE COD TONGUES

The heads of Atlantic cod are sometimes cut in two, sprinkled with salt and pepper, dusted with flour, and fried until golden brown on both sides. More often, the best parts of the cod heads—the cheeks and the tongues—are removed and fried separately, sometimes along with the sounds (air bladders). These parts are usually marketed separately (available in some seafood markets and on the Internet). In Newfoundland, the tongues are fried in freshly rendered pork fat and served along with the cracklings, which are called scrunchions, I understand.

| | |
|---|---|
| **16 medium cod tongues** | **1 teaspoon salt** |
| **½ pound salt pork (or more)** | **½ teaspoon black pepper** |
| **1½ cups flour** | |

Cut the salt pork into ½-inch cubes. Fry these in a skillet until the oil is cooked out and what's left of the salt pork cubes are brown and crisp. Drain the browned pork cubes (scrunchions now), leaving the drippings in the skillet. Mix the flour, salt, and pepper in a bag. Shake the cod tongues in the seasoned flour, a few at a time, and lightly panfry, also a few at a time, until lightly browned. Serve with mashed potatoes and green peas, along with the scrunchions. Servings? Allow 8 medium cod tongues per person.

For specific information regarding the anatomy of codfish, I stand in debt to James R. Babb, editor of *Gray's Sporting Journal*, and to the culinary sports at Myron's Fine Food, who have a camp in Newfoundland. Further reading on the cookery of Newfoundland and Labrador can be found in the book *Fat-Back & Molasses*, edited by Ivan F. Jesperson, St. Johns. For a more historical approach, be sure to read *Cod: A Biography of the Fish That Changed the World*, by Mark Kurlansky. In the spirit of that text, I point out that the director of the National Library of Iceland once wrote a treatise on the social values of eating cod heads: Among other virtues, the practice teaches forbearance and, according to old Icelandic lore, increases intelligence.

# A. D.'S CRICKET CRISPS

Most fish bait shops sell light brownish-gray crickets that fry up nicely. These can be purchased from wholesalers in bulk, or from local dealers who price them by the hundred—and at very affordable prices, I might add. Crickets are also easy to raise in large wooden boxes heated with a light bulb. In the wilds, we find other species, including a black field cricket. These too are edible, along with the leaf cricket that rolls itself up in something like a sleeping bag, zippered together with silk threads.

In all cases, it's best to keep the crickets alive until the last moment, and most people do not feed them for a day or so prior to the feast in order to clean them out, so to speak. There are several commercial bait containers, usually a wire cage with a funnel mouth designed to dispense crickets, but these are not ideal for cooking purposes. If you have to catch and add them cricket by cricket, the first ones will be done before you get all of them into the pot. I prefer to use an empty Quaker Oats container, making it easy to dump the whole batch directly into the hot oil.

| | |
|---|---|
| 100 crickets | parsley or watercress (optional) |
| peanut oil for deep-frying | Asian dipping sauce |
| fine sea salt | |

Heat about ¾ inch of oil in a cast-iron skillet to 375°F. Dump in the crickets a few at a time and fry until they are crisp—only a minute or two. Remove the crickets from the skillet with a strainer and drain on brown bags, sprinkling them lightly with a little salt. Garnish with parsley or freshly snipped watercress.

It's best to eat these crickets with the fingers, picking up each one by the hind legs, which tend to stick straight up when fried in hot oil. Dip the cricket into a suitable dipping sauce, preferably homemade Vietnamese nuoc cham (see recipe in chapter 6), and bite it off at the legs. If you are feeding snooty or squeamish folk, you might break off and discard the legs before serving and give each guest a round toothpick for dipping and eating the delicacies. The legs are edible, I might add, but the lower part sometimes lodges between the teeth or feels annoyingly like a tiny fishbone or hair hook stuck in the throat.

# RAT

G. Gordon Liddy of Watergate fame said he once cooked and ate a rat to help overcome an inordinate fear of the rodents. I don't know what sort of rat the tough guy chewed on, but my guess is that it was either a common black rat (which is often brown) or the Norway rat, both of which originated in Asia and moved into Europe and other parts of the world by land and sea. These used to be called "wharf rats." During the long voyages of sailing ship days, they were highly prized by the crew and were purchased from the ship's official rat catcher.

Although Europeans are known to have eaten these rats during times of famine, recipes are hard to come by. But during the siege of Paris in 1870, coopers at large wineries in France marinated skinned rats in a mixture of olive oil and chopped shallots. Then they grilled the rats over wood fires made with disjointed wine barrels. These were called "Cooper's Entrecote," according to the French culinary tome *Larousse Gastronomique.*

Rats are commonly eaten in Asia, and in China they are sometimes called household deer. A restaurant in Canton once prepared rat cooked seventeen different ways, including "golden rat," which is a whole rat marinated in a diluted soy sauce and then deep-fried. When duly garnished with a few sprigs of green stuff, the properly cooked golden rat plates nicely.

While the common rat is too closely associated with diseases to be widely consumed in the United States, our North American muskrat is surely one of the cleanest of all rodents, owing to its water habitat and strictly vegetarian diet. Although muskrats grow over most of the United States and are taken by trappers for their fur, the meat is commonly consumed only in Delaware, parts of New Jersey, and Louisiana, where it is sometimes marketed as "marsh hare."

Most of the recipes for muskrats call for soaking the meat overnight in a solution of salt and water, or soda and water (about 1 tablespoon of salt per quart of water). They also strongly advise us to remove the glands on the small of the rat's back and under the forelegs. I didn't know all this when I first started eating muskrats years ago, and I have always ignored the warnings. (During my youth, we caught our rats not with steel traps but with wire fish baskets baited with peanut cake, the residue left after the oil is expressed from peanuts.) But if the marinade and denuding helps you get the "musk" and "rat" off your mind, then by all means have at it. You might also remember to sever the scaly tail if you are feeding squeamish folks. In any case, here's my standard recipe for rat.

| | |
|---|---|
| 1 young muskrat, skinned and disjointed | bacon drippings |
| 1 medium large onion, diced | ½ cup flour |
| salt and pepper | good red wine |

Put the meat, onion, and a little salt and pepper in a pot. Cover with water, bring to a boil, reduce the heat, and simmer for an hour or so, or until the meat is tender. Remove from the pot and drain. In a skillet, heat the bacon drippings almost to the smoke point and sizzle the rat pieces until browned. Add the cooked onions. Reduce the heat, add a little red wine, cover, and cook for half an hour, turning from time to time to keep from burning. Remove the cover, increase the heat, and cook for another few minutes, being careful not to burn. Serve hot with rice and vegetables of your choice. I like rats with young cattail shoots—sometimes called Cossack asparagus—on which the muskrat feeds.

# CHAPTER

# Vegetables and Fruits

**O**n first thought, the skillet seems to be an unlikely utensil for cooking most vegetables. The pot, the stovetop Dutch oven, the steamer, or the oven-bound casserole dish would get top billing in any honest competition for the indispensable utensil, and these days even the grill would get a few votes. Still, the skillet can produce some very good eating and should be used more often even by vegans and vegetarians. In addition to cooking the vegetables, the uncovered skillet can produce a wonderful aroma for the cook to enjoy, as, for example, when browning a few chopped onions in butter. Anyhow, here are a few recipes to try.

# SAUTÉED CHANTERELLES

Sliced mushrooms are delicious when sautéed in a little butter or olive oil. These are good when served by themselves, or as a topping for steaks, pasta, omelets, and so on. Often the pan drippings—butter and mushroom juices—are also served. Sautéed mushrooms freeze nicely, making this a good recipe for preserving big batches of wild mushrooms such as chanterelles, which are often found in large numbers, or market mushrooms on half-price sale at the supermarket. Note also that mushrooms to be added to soups and stews are better when first sautéed and then added to the main dish, along with the pan juices.

| | |
|---|---|
| chanterelles | salt and freshly ground black pepper |
| butter | |

Cut the chanterelles across the gills into thin slices. Sauté a handful at a time in butter on medium heat in an open cast-iron skillet, stirring as you go with a wooden spoon and adding salt and pepper to taste. Cook until tender—usually about 5 minutes. (Some wild mushrooms are a little tougher, however, and will require longer simmering in a covered skillet.) Serve as needed—and find a use for the pan drippings.

*Note: Parsley, minced garlic, and so on can be added to the recipe, if these fit the intended use of the mushrooms. For freezing, however, I prefer to stick to the basic stuff. Other ingredients can be added after the mushrooms thaw.*

# WILD MUSHROOM FRITTERS

I owe Euell Gibbons, author of *Stalking the Wild Asparagus*, for this recipe. I have, however, added half a red bell pepper for color and some minced scallions to the fritter. I have also cooked it with elderberry blow. It's a versatile recipe, so suit yourself.

| | |
|---|---|
| 1 pound mushrooms, chopped | ¼ cup butter |
| ½ red bell pepper, finely chopped | 2 teaspoons baking powder |
| ½ cup scallions, finely chopped | 1 teaspoon monosodium glutamate |
| 2 chicken eggs, lightly whisked | salt and freshly ground black pepper |
| 1½ cups flour | cooking oil for frying |

In a 10-inch skillet, sauté the mushrooms, bell pepper, and scallion in the butter until lightly done. Pour the mixture and the skillet juice into a bowl along with the eggs. Sift the dry ingredients together in a mixing bowl. Stir into the mushroom and egg mixture, making a batter.

Heat about ¹⁄₁₆ inch of oil in the skillet on medium-high heat. Drop the batter by large spoonfuls into the skillet, as when making pancakes. Fry until nicely browned on the bottom, about 1½ minutes. Turn the fritters and brown the other side. Serve hot.

# ONION RINGS

Skillets work just fine for fried onion rings, using about ¾ inch of oil on medium-high heat. Any large onion will work, but white Vidalias are perfect. Smaller onions can be used, of course, but the large rings get more respect at the table. If you can't get the right kind of cornmeal (fine and soft, not hard and gritty), use the flour twice. Many people will have a favorite recipe for dipping the rings in a liquid batter instead of a dry coating before frying. Suit yourself, but remember that a thick batter tends to soak up lots of grease from the skillet. Note also that cooking a large batch of these rings takes some time. For feeding a crowd, a Dutch oven or deep fryer works quicker.

| | |
|---|---|
| 2 or 3 large white onions | buttermilk |
| 2 cups white stone-ground cornmeal, fine | peanut oil for frying |
| 1 cup all-purpose flour | salt and freshly ground black pepper to taste |
| 2 chicken eggs | cayenne (optional) |

After peeling, slice the onions ¼ inch thick, separate into rings, and place in a bowl. Cover with buttermilk and set aside for 2 or 3 hours. Then drain the rings, retaining the buttermilk.

Add a little salt, black pepper, and cayenne (if wanted) to both the flour and the cornmeal, putting each mixture into separate shallow dishes. Whisk the eggs together with ½ cup of the reserved buttermilk. Dip a few of the onion rings into the flour. Shake off excess flour and dip into the egg bath. Finally, dip into the cornmeal and shake off the excess. After putting about ⅝ inch of oil in a skillet and turning on the heat, bread the rest of the onions.

When the oil is heated to about 350°F, fry a few of the rings for 2 or 3 minutes, until golden brown, turning once with tongs. Remove to drain with tongs and fry a few more, being careful not to overload the skillet. Serve hot.

*Note: These are usually eaten out of hand at the table with the rest of a meal, but also try them on burgers, po'boys, and such. Many outdoor grills have an auxiliary burner for skillet cooking, making this recipe fit right in with a cookout.*

# SAUTÉED ONIONS

Some modern chefs and even jackleg cooks are calling these "caramelized" onions. It's a ten-dollar vogue word for a very old recipe. In addition to being tasty as a burger topping or a side dish, the onions fill the kitchen with a wonderful aroma, especially when cooked in butter. Note that a large cast-iron skillet works best for this recipe. If you don't have a large skillet, cook it in two or three batches in an 8-incher.

| | |
|---|---|
| **2 pounds large onions** | **salt and freshly ground black pepper to taste** |
| **¼ cup butter** | **balsamic vinegar (if needed)** |
| **¼ cup olive oil** | |

Peel the onions, cut in half lengthwise, and slice into half-rings. Heat the butter and oil in a 12-inch skillet. Add the onions, cover, and cook for 10 minutes on medium-low heat. Uncover, sprinkle with salt and pepper, and cook on medium heat for another 10 minutes, stirring from time to time with a wooden spoon. Watching carefully, cook for a few more minutes, until the onions are golden brown. If you burn them a little around the edges, fine. Just add a squirt or two of expensive balsamic vinegar and tell your guests that the onions are caramelized.

# FRIED GREEN TOMATO SANDWICHES

I've seen dozens of recipes for fried green tomatoes, and some are unnecessarily complicated. One book on cast-iron cooking sets forth a recipe calling for ten ingredients, including Sauce Rémoulade (which itself requires eight ingredients). The instructions tell us to core the tomatoes! In any case, here's a simple recipe for frying green tomatoes (almost mature but not yet ripe) and using them to make a sandwich. The idea for the sandwich came to me from the Busy Bee Café in DeFuniak Springs, Florida, which serves a po'boy or hoagie made with fried green tomatoes. My recipe is a little different, made with regular white sandwich bread. If you don't want to make a sandwich, fry the tomatoes and serve them separately.

| | |
|---|---|
| 2 green tomatoes | fine white cornmeal (freshly stone-ground) |
| 4 slices bacon | mayonnaise |
| peanut oil | salt and pepper |
| buttermilk | sandwich bread |

Slice the tomatoes and soak in buttermilk for an hour or so. Cook the bacon in a skillet until it is crispy. Drain and set aside.

Add enough peanut oil to the bacon drippings to measure about ½ inch. Heat on medium-high. Drain the green tomato slices, sprinkle with salt and pepper, and dredge in cornmeal, shaking off the excess. Fry the slices a few at a time until golden brown on both sides, turning once.

Smear the mayonnaise on 2 slices of sandwich bread. Top each slice with 2 pieces of bacon. Sandwich with slices of fried green tomatoes. Slice in half and serve at once. Go ahead. Take a bite right out of the middle.

# TURKISH EGGPLANT

The Turks like to fry vegetables, serving them cold or warm and, sometimes, in a sandwich. Eggplant is especially good fried, although it does soak up lots of grease. Happily, the Turks lean toward olive oil for frying and use no batter or breading on the eggplant.

2 large eggplants
olive oil
1 cup yogurt
2 cloves garlic, crushed

½ teaspoon caraway seeds
salt and pepper
fresh dill (optional garnish)

Slice the unpeeled eggplants into ½-inch rings. Salt the slices on both sides and place them side by side on a brown bag. Let drain for 30 minutes. Rinse the slices and dry with absorbent paper or towel.

Heat ¾ inch of olive oil in a large skillet. In a single layer, fry the eggplant slices 2 or 3 at a time until golden, turning once. Drain on brown bags.

Mix the yogurt, crushed garlic, caraway seeds, salt, and pepper in a serving bowl. Place the fried eggplant slices on a heated platter, pour the yogurt sauce over them, and garnish with sprigs of fresh dill around the outside. Serve with grilled meats or kabobs.

# FRIED JAPANESE EGGPLANT

There are several configurations for the eggplant fry. Regular eggplant can be cut into slices, or it can be reduced to fingers similar to french-fried potatoes. My favorite is to use the small elongated Japanese eggplant, cut into ½-inch wheels, with the skin left on. These rounds make a nice bite and don't seem as mushy as the larger slices of regular eggplant.

Japanese eggplants

chicken egg, lightly whisked

flour

bread crumbs

peanut oil

salt and pepper to taste

water

Slice the eggplants into wheels ½ inch thick. (Or, for french-fried eggplant, slice length-wise and then cut the slices into fingers.) Soak the slices in salted cold water for an hour or so. Rinse in fresh water and drain.

Heat ½ inch of peanut oil in a large skillet. Sprinkle the eggplant with salt and pepper. Dip in flour, shake, dip in egg, roll in bread crumbs, and fry a few at a time until nicely browned. Drain on a brown bag. Serve hot.

# SKILLET CABBAGE

Boiled cabbage is good, steamed is better, and sautéed is perfect, especially when cooking for only two or three people.

fresh cabbage

butter or bacon drippings

salt and freshly ground black pepper

Heat the butter or bacon drippings in a large skillet on medium-high heat. Shred the cabbage and put a double handful into the skillet. Cook uncovered for a few minutes, stirring with a wooden spoon and sprinkling with salt and pepper. Continue cooking and stirring, cooking and stirring, uncovered, until the cabbage is done to your liking, about 20 minutes. Serve hot.

# EAST AFRICAN STUFFED OKRA

Okra probably originated in Africa, and the early slaves brought it to the New World. In Africa, the pods are eaten either fresh or dried—often with a combination in a single recipe. The flowers are also edible. Here's a recipe from East Africa (maybe by way of India) that calls for sautéing whole okra pods, more or less stuffed. It's an interesting variation on Southern fried okra, suitable for serving in New York or San Francisco.

| | |
|---|---|
| **a dozen or so 4-inch pods fresh okra** | **2 teaspoons turmeric** |
| **¼ cup lemon juice** | **2 cloves garlic, minced and crushed** |
| **¼ cup peanut oil** | **salt and cayenne red pepper to taste** |
| **2 teaspoons curry powder** | |

Starting at the tip, cut the pods of okra in half lengthwise, down to but not through the stem end. Hinge the pods open. Mix all the other ingredients except the peanut oil into a paste. Spread the paste onto one side of the split okra. Close the pods and press lightly to stick the sides together.

Heat the peanut oil in a skillet to about 325°F and sauté the okra pods until lightly browned. Serve hot with rice, fried fish, and a green salad, or with meats and vegetables of your choice.

*Note:* This recipe was adapted from Harva Hachten's very interesting book, Best of Regional African Cooking. *Another recipe for okra, Pombo, called for the addition of chile pepper and dried shrimp or dried crayfish. If you like the strong flavor of dried shrimp, try adding a little dried shrimp paste to your stuffing for split okra. Or try your own combinations, leaving out the lemon juice. Try a little dried shrimp mixed into a tomato-based salsa.*

# PURSLANE FRIES

Although generally considered a weed, purslane, which probably originated in Persia, has been cultivated for food and fodder in such places as Burma (now Myanmar) and Yemen for centuries. The early settlers brought it to America, where it was used mostly by the Indians and the French. (According to Sturtevant's *Notes on Edible Plants*, "In 1604, Champlain says the Indians along the Maine coast brought him purslane, which grows in large quantities among the Indian corn.") In any case, purslane now grows wild just about everywhere in the Americas, free for the picking from southern Alaska to northern Tierra del Fuego. It can be raised from seeds in the home garden, and it is even available commercially in some markets, especially in Mexico. I have even seen store-bought purslane on a recent television cooking show or two. Ironically, some people who plant the seeds in their home gardens may be surprised to learn it's the same stuff they have been pulling up as weeds for years!

Anyone interested in wild foods or adventurous eating can easily pick a mess of purslane in late summer or early autumn, a time when other such wild greens are in decline. This was nicely put by Paula Wolfert in her book *The Cooking of the Eastern Mediterranean*: "In late summer, when all wild mustards, nasturtiums, sorrels, amaranths, dandelions, and lamb's-quarters have withered, turned tough and bitter, and gone to seed, there is still one wild green left to enjoy—purslane. Its soft, thick leaves stay fresh even under the hottest sun."

Look for wild purslane along the edges of woods and fields and gardens. Once a stand is located, it's easy to pull a mess. A good plant can cover a square foot, and in heavy stands, the plants will interlock. You can pull the whole plant, but you don't have to do so. The tips of the stems (which make the best eating, I think) can easily be pinched off in the field, and they will regenerate. Remember also that you don't have to pick very much purslane to have enough for a mess. It doesn't cook away as drastically as spinach, turnip tops, kale, or other greens.

The whole plant is edible, including the small flowers. The tiny seeds form on the end of the tips in small pods, and Native Americans ground them for use in breads. The thick leaves, which grow up to 2 inches long and ¾ inch wide, can be cooked separately, saving the stems for stir-fry or pickles. The tender tips can be enjoyed raw in a mixed salad, or they can be boiled or steamed like other greens. I prefer them fried, as in this recipe.

Being a little mucilaginous, purslane makes a purely excellent addition to gumbo as a substitute for okra. Also like okra, it is delicious when fried. So, pull a few tips or leaves for camp. Use your favorite recipe for fried okra, or try the following.

| | |
|---|---|
| **purslane tips or large leaves** | **cracker crumbs (crushed saltines)** |
| **chicken egg, lightly whisked** | **cooking oil** |
| **flour** | **salt** |

Rig for frying in ½ inch of oil at 350°F. Wash the purslane tips carefully and drain but do not dry completely. Sprinkle the tips with salt, then shake in a brown bag with flour. Roll them one by one first in the beaten egg and then in cracker crumbs. Fry a few at a time until golden brown, turning a time or two. Drain on a brown bag and serve hot.

# FRIED POTATO ROUNDS

These potatoes are easier to slice into rounds than they are to french-cut, making them a better choice for the camp cook. They should be between ⅛ and ¼ inch thick—or exactly ³⁄₁₆ if you have a precision slicer. I don't peel these, but suit yourself. Any good potato can be cooked by this method. Use the roundish medium size, if you have a choice, thereby saving the long ones for french fries. Note that these fried sliced potatoes require only a small amount of oil, whereas french fries work better when deep-fried.

| | |
|---|---|
| **medium raw potatoes, sliced** | **salt to taste** |
| **peanut oil for frying** | **Hungarian paprika** |

Heat about ¼ inch of peanut oil in a skillet to medium high. Fry a handful of sliced potatoes for a few minutes on each side, until nicely browned. (The slices should not overlap; so figure on cooking in several batches.) Spread the potatoes on a brown bag to drain, again being careful not to overlap the slices. Sprinkle with salt and Hungarian paprika. Serve hot.

# GARDEN MEDLEY IN THE SKILLET

Here's a recipe that I adapted from the *Progressive Farmer*. Being rather frugal, I use the whole cauliflower, including part of the stem.

| | |
|---|---|
| 1 small head of cauliflower | ¼ cup butter |
| 2 medium zucchini | 2 tablespoons freshly grated Parmesan |
| 1 bell pepper | 1 teaspoon dried basil |
| 1 small to medium onion | 1 teaspoon dried oregano |
| 2 vine-ripened tomatoes | salt and freshly ground black pepper to taste |
| 1 large toe garlic, peeled and crushed | more freshly grated Parmesan |

Separate the cauliflower into pieces. Trim the end off the inner core and slice it into wheels along with the zucchini. (I also cut a few slices off the tender part of the cauliflower leaves.) Seed the bell pepper and cut it into strips. Peel and slice the onion.

Heat the butter in a large skillet. Add the onions and slices of cauliflower core. Cook for 5 minutes, stirring as you go. Add the cauliflower pieces, zucchini, garlic, and bell pepper. Cook for a few minutes, stirring a time or two, and add the tomatoes, basil, oregano, salt, and pepper, along with 2 tablespoons of Parmesan. Cook for about a minute, tossing a time or two.

Transfer the mix to a serving dish, sprinkle with Parmesan, and serve hot. These measures should feed 6 folks, if you have plenty of good bread.

*Variations:* I really prefer to cut back on the zucchini simply because it is not one of my favorite vegetables. I also add other vegetables if I have them in the garden. Try diced rutabaga, for example. If fresh herbs are available, use them to taste, minced, instead of the dried basil and oregano.

# A. D.'S GREASY SUMMER SQUASH

Many people like yellow squash and zucchini sliced into wheels and sautéed in butter or perhaps olive oil and cooked for only a few minutes, until tender. These are edible, but I seldom ask for seconds. Adding a little parsley or basil doesn't help much. The slices can also be deep-fried, but these aren't any better. Mixing the two together won't help. Truth is, quickly sautéed squash isn't much more than water and won't have much taste.

Cooking them for a long time, on the other hand, will reduce the bulk and concentrate the flavor. Yeah, yeah. I know that some people will say that long cooking will drive out the vitamins. Maybe it will—but you'll end up eating ten times as much squash, thereby getting more of the good stuff. Note that this method can be cooked with a skillet, but larger batches work best with a cast-iron pot or a deep "chicken fryer" skillet.

lots of crookneck yellow squash

3 strips of bacon

salt to taste

Fry a little bacon in a 12-inch cast-iron skillet until it is crisp. Drain and set aside. Cut the squash into wheels about ½ inch thick. (If the squash are young, it will not be necessary to remove the seeds. If old, cut them in half lengthwise, and remove the seeds and center pith with a spoon. Slice into half-rounds.)

Heat the bacon drippings and fill the skillet with squash. Cook, stirring from time to time, until the squash slices reduce a little. Cover and simmer for 20 minutes or so, stirring a time or two. Remove the lid, stir, and sprinkle with a little salt. Continue to cook and stir, cook and stir, until the squash slices break apart, cook down to a mush, and—careful now—turn brownish. Do not burn, but push the cooking to the limit, stirring as you go with a wooden spoon. Servings? I don't know—but I can eat the whole skilletful for lunch along with the fried bacon and a little corn pone.

*Note: This is one of those recipes to which ingredients should not be added whimsically. Too much rosemary and such stuff may destroy the true flavor and essence and goodness of summer squash—which many of your guests will never have experienced before.*

# EASY SKILLET BEANS

I love really good Boston baked beans cooked slowly for 8 hours or longer. But I can get by with ordinary canned pork and beans, helped along a little. My best advice is to use the unrefined Mexican cone sugar, called piloncillo, which is increasingly available in upscale supermarkets and by mail. (Ordinary supermarket brown sugar has been refined and molasses added to give it color and taste.) The piloncillo comes in 8-ounce cones and the cook has to shave off what is needed with a knife. If necessary, use dark brown sugar.

| | |
|---|---|
| 2 cans pork and beans (16-ounce size) | 1 medium to large onion, finely diced |
| cured bacon | 1 teaspoon dry mustard |
| ¾ cup lightly packed piloncillo, divided | ½ teaspoon powdered sea salt |

Preheat the oven to 350°F. Fry 2 pieces of bacon until crisp in a 12-inch cast-iron skillet. Drain the bacon. Sauté the onion in the bacon drippings until brown around the edges. Set aside.

Mix the beans, ½ cup of the piloncillo, onions, crumbled bacon, sea salt, and dry mustard in a bowl, then turn out into the skillet. Cover with strips of bacon and sprinkle with the rest of the piloncillo. Bake in the center of the oven for about 30 minutes, or until the bacon is crispy on top.

Serve hot with barbecued pork and a crusty white bread, or with fried fish and hush puppies.

# SKILLET-FRIED CORN

This delicious dish can be cooked plain, using only the corn fried in a little butter, or together with finely chopped spring onion with part of the green tops and half a diced red bell pepper. In either case, the fresh corn is shucked, silked, and cut from the cob with a sharp knife. Then the cob is scraped with the back of the knife to get more of the good stuff.

| | |
|---|---|
| 4 cups fresh corn | ¼ cup butter |
| ½ cup chopped scallions | 2 chicken eggs, lightly whisked |
| ½ cup chopped red bell pepper | salt and pepper to taste |

Melt the butter in a 12-inch skillet. Add the corn, scallions, and red bell pepper. Cook on medium-high heat for 5 or 6 minutes, stirring frequently. Sprinkle with salt and pepper to taste. Stir in the chicken eggs and cook for another minute. Turn out into a serving bowl. Serve hot.

*Note: If you want creamed corn, omit the scallions, bell pepper, and chicken eggs. Cook the corn for about 5 minutes, stirring from time to time. Add 1 cup of whipping cream. Cook on medium heat for about 10 minutes, stirring as you go to keep the mixture from sticking to the skillet or forming lumps. Salt and pepper to taste, stir again, and turn out into a serving bowl. Serve hot.*

# ELDER BLOW PATTIES

Here's a dish that I like to cook in camp when the elderberry is in bloom, forming large white umbels. The fish flakes can be made from leftovers, but it's really best to poach fresh fish for about 10 minutes, then flake the meat with a fork. Almost any good fish will work. Black bass flake nicely and are ideal. Use freshly picked elder blossoms. The cornmeal should be stone-ground from whole kernels; if this isn't available, use all flour.

| | |
|---|---|
| 2 cups fresh elder blossoms | ¼ cup flour |
| 2 cups cooked fish flakes | ¼ cup milk |
| 1 large chicken egg, whisked | cooking oil |
| ½ cup fine white cornmeal | salt and pepper |

Mix the fish flakes, milk, flour, cornmeal, eggs, elder blossoms, salt, and pepper. Heat a little oil in a skillet. Shape the mixture into patties. Carefully fry the patties on medium heat until each one is nicely browned on both sides, turning once with a spatula. Serve hot. Feeds 2 hungry campers. Increase or decrease the measures as needed.

# FRIED APPLE SLICES

I got this idea from *The Alice B. Toklas Cookbook*, which in turn got it from a lady in London. Miss Toklas, sidekick to Gertrude Stein, says the dish goes nicely with a pork roast that has been cooked in a half bottle of cider or more, basted frequently. I find that the apples also go with barbecued ribs and other feeds.

| | |
|---|---|
| apples | sugar |
| bacon drippings | cinnamon |

Core and slice the apples into ½-inch wheels. Heat about ¼ inch of bacon drippings in a skillet. Fry the apples until nicely colored on the bottom. Turn, sprinkle the top with sugar, and cook until the other side is nicely colored. Turn and sprinkle with sugar. Cook for half a minute, then turn and cook for another half a minute. Remove from the skillet to drain, sprinkle lightly with cinnamon, and serve warm with roast pork or other meat.

# FRIED FIGS

Here's an old recipe that I found in *Gulf City Cook Book*, published by The Ladies of the St. Francis Street Methodist Episcopal Church, Mobile, Alabama, in 1878—perhaps the first of the American committee cookbooks! I have two nice, very productive fig trees in my garden, so I was especially eager to try this recipe. I wasn't disappointed.

| | |
|---|---|
| large ripe figs | brown sugar |
| butter | |

Peel the figs and cut them in half lengthwise. Heat some butter in a skillet. Sauté the figs a few at a time in the butter until light brown. Place on a serving platter or plate, then sprinkle lightly with brown sugar. Eat warm. Try these for breakfast, topped with a little heavy cream.

# ROASTED CHESTNUTS

I regret not having ordered a special chestnut roasting pan from a mail-order catalog I received some time ago. Still, my trusty cast-iron skillet does a pretty good job on coals from the campfire or at the hearth in my den.

To proceed, cut an X into the flat side of each chestnut. (Special chestnut knives with short, hawk-beaked blades are available, but a regular knife with a short, stout blade will do.) Heat a cast-iron skillet, completely dry, on coals from the fire or on the stove. Fill the skillet with chestnuts, but do not overcrowd. Roast in the fire for 4 or 5 minutes, shaking the skillet a few times, until the shell of the nuts browns a little and the X opens up. Remove the skillet from the heat but leave the chestnuts in it to stay warm. To eat, first peel off the shell and the inner skin.

# CHAPTER

# Bread, Corn Bread, and Biscuits

**M**ost good chefs, North and South, will agree that the best corn breads are cooked in cast iron. But that's about as far as the regional accord goes. The real culprit is the cornmeal itself. In the past few decades, most of the white cornmeals were marketed only in parts of the South and in Rhode Island. These are usually ground by small local millers from whole-grain white corn by a slow stone-grinding process. This meal does not have a long shelf life and will develop a strong, rancid taste. When fresh, however, it has a pleasing earthy flavor and makes a bread that is not as dry and crumbly as most yellow-meal breads. Storing this whole-kernel white meal in the refrigerator or freezer at home helps extend its life, and I have even seen it in the refrigerated dairy section of small country stores.

For the most part, the yellow meals on the market have been milled by a high-speed, heat-producing process for corn robbed of the germ and its essential oils. This product has a long shelf life, but it tends to be dry, crumbly, and relatively tasteless, in my opinion. It should be used only in bread recipes that call for chicken eggs and other goo to stick the works together, not with the pure stuff consisting only of meal, water, and a little salt.

Along with a few other writers, I have argued, sometimes hotly, about the loss of good white cornmeal from the American pantry. The large millers are beginning to pay attention, and some have added a stone-ground yellow meal to their line. Well, this doesn't mean very much, unless they use the whole kernel, including the germ and its oils, in the product. The result is simply not the same as stone-ground whole-kernel white cornmeal.

There are thousands of recipes for corn bread made with yellow meal and even blue meal. Some of these are quite good, suitable for serving at the table as well as for stuffings and dressings. But what I resent is the fact that the large millers, supermarkets, recipe writers, and publishers have squeezed white meal out of the mainstream of American cookery—and pretty much out of our cookbooks. Thus, we have almost lost a very good thing. I can only hope that this modest book and a few other enlightened works will help show the way back. It is with this agenda in play that I have given more recipes in this book to white cornmeal than to yellow. If I have pushed too hard here and there, I have done so in good conscience. For a different point of view—and for forty-four cornbread recipes—see Sheila Buff's *Corn Cookery* and the Yankee Corn Bread recipe in chapter 17.

Of course, biscuits and other breads can also be cooked in a skillet, and some of these recipes are also included in this chapter. But it's corn bread that makes the old black skillet shine.

# JOHNNYCAKES

The New England colonists made very good use of the corn that they got from the American Indians. Cornmeal johnnycakes, buttered and eaten with maple syrup, became traditional fare. Actually, they were first called journeycakes, simply because they rode well and were standard fare on a trip before motels and fast-food outlets lined our trails. There are a thousand variations, but here's a good basic recipe:

| | |
|---|---|
| 2½ cups yellow cornmeal, fine | 1 cup whole milk |
| 2 large chicken eggs | 1 cup water |
| 2 tablespoons lard (or other shortening) | 1 teaspoon salt |

In a bowl, beat the eggs slightly, then stir in the water and milk. Mix in the cornmeal. In a 10-inch cast-iron skillet, melt the lard, pour it into the bowl, and stir in well with the cornmeal mixture and salt. (Leave a little lard in the skillet, spreading it to cover all the bottom and sides.) Heat the greased skillet, then pour ¼ cup of cornmeal mixture into it. Spread it thin, like a pancake. The thickness should be about ¼ inch. Cook the johnnycake for 3 or 4 minutes. Turn and cook the other side for 3 minutes. Repeat until all the batter is used up. Serve the bread with a meal, or butter each johnnycake and top it with maple syrup.

A similar bread, sometimes called hoecake, became traditional in parts of the South. It was often made with white meal mixed with water and a little salt. Thick cane syrup was usually eaten with it instead of maple syrup, and of course many farms had their own cane mills. If you want hoecakes instead of johnnycakes, use my recipe for griddle bread (below). Butter the bread and eat it with sugarcane syrup. I might add that there is much confusion about what's what, and some people call corn pone hoecake, partly because the pones are about the size of your hand, just the right size for cooking on the blade of a hoe.

# CROSS CREEK CRACKLING BREAD

When I make crackling bread, I merely add a handful of cracklings to my simple corn pone or griddle bread recipe. But recipes abound, and you may want to try the one below, which I have adapted from Marjorie Kinnan Rawlings's Cross Creek Cookery. This recipe, she says, turns "po' folks' cornbread in the autumn into a delicacy unobtainable in high places." I agree. She set the recipe in the fall of the year because that is hog killing time in rural areas, when cracklings are rendered (as described under the next heading). Here's what you'll need:

2 cups fine white cornmeal, water-ground style

½ cup good cracklings

½ cup skim milk

½ cup water

1 chicken egg

3 tablespoons baking powder

1 teaspoon salt

Preheat the oven to 400 degrees and grease a 10-inch cast-iron skillet. Mix the cornmeal, baking powder, and salt in a bowl. Add the water and skim milk. Stir until you have a smooth mixture. Stir in the egg and cracklings. Put the mixture into the greased skillet and bake it for about 30 minutes.

The size of the cracklings makes a difference. As Mrs. Rawlings says, "If the cracklings are no larger than a pea, I stir them in whole. Otherwise, I break up the larger pieces. Some cooks crush the cracklings with a rolling pin, but this makes them too fine for my taste. There is no point in having cracklings, and then disguising them." Mrs. Rawlings also noted that crackling bread is a far cry from the "shortening bread" made famous by the song. Frankly, I'll have to admit that I don't really know what shortening bread is. I've never eaten anything that was called by that name by the cook who made it. According to Jessica B. Harris's *Iron Pots and Wooden Spoons*, shortening bread was made with butter, flour, brown sugar, and a little salt—and she lists it as a dessert, not a bread. Maybe that's why Mama's little baby loves shortenin' bread, shortenin' bread. I rest my case. For the time being.

# HOW TO MAKE CRACKLINGS

**M**any people, including some cookbook writers who ought to know better, believe that cracklings are pork skins, or rinds, that have been cooked down in the process of rendering lard. It's true that cracklings may contain some skin or rind, but it's also true that cracklings do not necessarily have to contain any skin at all. In fact, the best ones often don't. Too much skin, improperly handled, can ruin crackling bread, making it or part of it chewy, like greasy leather.

To make cracklings at hog-killing time, the fat is trimmed away from the various parts. Some of this fat has no skin attached to it; in fact, most of the hog's skin is left on the hams, shoulders, jowls, and slabs of bacon. What's left of the skin is sometimes cut up with chunks of fat and put into the lard pot. But it can also be cut off the fat and discarded or perhaps set aside for later use as fried "pork skins" or, maybe, for bass-fishing lures.

In any case, the fat is cut into chunks, with or without skin, before it is put into the lard pot. The best cracklings will result from small chunks no larger than an inch. Even smaller chunks are better—especially if they contain skin. The fat is then heated in a large pot, usually a cast-iron washpot, until the lard is rendered. The residue of each chunk of fat will float to the top. After further cooking, it will then sink to the bottom. It's best to get each crackling just before it sinks, but of course it's impossible to get the whole batch at exactly the right time. Larger pieces will take a little longer. Also, it's best to stir the pot with a paddle from time to time so that the bottom won't get ready before the middle. After the cracklings are skimmed from the lard, or strained out, they are spread on a table or other surface to drain. If all has gone well, each crackling will be about the size of a #1 buckshot, and will be crisp and dry. If the cracklings contain skin, it should be crunchy but not hard or leathery.

Cracklings are sometimes available in meat markets, but usually these are too large for making good bread. Break them up. If the skins are leathery, throw them out.

If you want to make some cracklings, but don't plan to kill hogs anytime soon, get 10 or 12 pounds of good pork fat from your butcher or meat processor. Tell him that you want it for rendering lard and making cracklings. Cut it into small pieces and cook it slowly in a cast-iron Dutch oven for several hours, stirring from time to time. Take up the cracklings when they are brown and crisp. Drain them on brown paper bags.

Save the lard. When it cools, put it into widemouth jars and store it in a cool place. Use it in old recipes that call for "shortening" or lard. I'm no bakery expert, but some good cooks say that pork lard is necessary for making some of our more dainty pastries.

I refrigerate cracklings (and lard), but, frankly, I don't think you'll have much of a storage problem if you'll make a batch of crackling bread. I've made two batches in one day, and, in fact, I can make a meal of it if I've got some good cold buttermilk. Call it soul food, joke about it as being "poor white trash cooking," or make a jingle about shortenin' bread—better yet, shut up and pass the platter my way!

# JALAPEÑO BREAD

Here's a tasty recipe that I like with Brunswick stew and somewhat bland casseroles made with whole-kernel corn.

**3 cups fine yellow cornmeal**

**2 cups buttermilk**

**6 or 8 fresh jalapeño peppers**

**1 large onion**

**3 chicken eggs**

**¼ cup peanut oil**

**1 teaspoon salt**

Grease a large, well-seasoned cast-iron skillet and preheat the oven to 375 degrees. Slice the jalapeño peppers in half lengthwise and remove the seeds. Then mince the peppers. (Many chefs will brown the peppers under a broiler or on a hot skillet first, then peel them. I don't do this, but suit yourself.) Peel the onion and grate it. When you get through crying, mix the meal, buttermilk, and oil. Break and whisk the chicken eggs, then mix them into the batter, along with the peppers, onion, and salt. Dump this mixture into a large cast-iron skillet. Pat the top with oil and then bake the bread in the center of the oven for 40 minutes, or until the surface is slightly browned. Turn the skillet over onto a plate, and the bread will come out without sticking every time.

This bread and similar yellow-meal breads are sometimes made in a special cast-iron pan with 6 or 8 pie-shaped cavities. These pans work fine, especially when you want neat pieces of bread that require no cutting and that hold together well. Usually, half the above recipe will fill one of these bread pans.

This cast-iron pan bakes bread in convenient pie-shaped pieces.

# LIVINGSTON PERFECT

I don't want to overwork skillet breads and other cornmeal products, but, on the other hand, I feel that I owe this recipe and technique to my readers simply because it's the best. I don't often make exact measures for corn bread, mixing, instead, by feel and adding either meal or water until I get the right consistency. Nonetheless, I worked out the meal-to-water measures below and added some finely diced salt pork. The results are outstanding. One word of caution, however. Ideal measures may depend in part on the kind of cornmeal you have, and whether it be extra-fine, medium, or whatnot. Adjustments in the meal may be necessary.

**2 cups fine-ground white cornmeal**  
**2½ cups boiling water**  
**1½ tablespoons peanut oil**

**¾ cup diced salt pork**  
**½ teaspoon salt**

Preheat the oven to 400 degrees. Finely dice some salt pork in a 10-inch skillet, then fry it until it is crisp. Cook enough to yield ¾ cup. Drain the diced pieces and discard the oil that cooked out of the salt pork. In a bowl, mix the meal, water, salt, and fried salt pork. Let sit for 15 minutes. Put 1½ tablespoons peanut oil in the skillet, coating the bottom and sides. Put the meal mixture into the skillet and place it into the center of the oven. Cook for 30 or 40 minutes, or until the corn bread has a crispy crust on the sides and on the top. During the last 10 minutes of cooking, brush the top of the bread with oil to help it brown properly.

# HUSH PUPPIES

Almost everyone will agree that an American fish fry is simply not complete without hush puppies. Hackles begin to rise, however, as soon as the ingredients are set forth. Some purists insist that real hush puppies contain only fine cornmeal, water, and salt, all of which must be mixed into a mush of exact consistency, shaped into patties of the proper shape and size, and fried to perfection in a cast-iron skillet. I have both feet in this camp. Most cookbook and recipe writers, however, seem to have a deep-seated need to amplify instead of simplify a list of ingredients, adding all manner of stuff, including chicken eggs and chopped onion and even beer.

Some jackleg chefs and cookbook writers use the coarse yellow cornmeal, and editors allow it. I've eaten hush puppies made from blue meal from the land of the Zuni, west of the Pecos. This stuff might be all right with those Yaqui catfish taken from the desert creeks of Arizona, but, in my opinion, it will ruin a mess of good Mississippi channel cats, Maine white perch, Minnesota walleye, or California grunion.

I won't get into a windy discussion, at this time, of what sort of fat or oil should be used for frying good hush puppies, but I'll have to say that bacon drippings are hard to beat for brute flavor. These days, however, many people will want to avoid animal fat altogether because it is high in cholesterol. Canola oil seems to be coming on strong these days, but I still prefer peanut oil. It has a high smoke point, it's tasteless, and it doesn't absorb much odor.

Measures? I've never seen a cook measure out the ingredients for making this kind of hush puppy or corn pone. Most of us go by the consistency of the batter. Exact measurements are not a good idea, really, because, it seems, each batch of meal is different. For starters, however, you may want to try the following:

**2 level cups of fine white stone-ground cornmeal**

**peanut oil**

**1⅞ cups hot water**

**salt**

Start by mixing white cornmeal in hot water and a little peanut oil until you have a mush that will drop nicely from a kitchen spoon, making a piece about the size of a chicken egg. Stir in a little salt, then let the mixture sit while you heat ⅞ inch of peanut oil in a cast-iron skillet. Spoon the batter into the hot peanut oil. If the mixture is just right, the batter will flatten slightly as it settles on the bottom of the skillet. Proceed until the pan is almost full of hush puppies. Cook the hush puppies on both sides over medium heat. When done, the outside of the hush puppy should be golden and crunchy, but the inside should be mushy when hot. When the pieces are done to your liking, take them up with a spatula or tongs and let them drain on a brown bag. As they cool off a little, the inside will firm up considerably.

Remember that the above combination of ingredients is guaranteed to produce the world's best hush puppies only if you have the right cornmeal. Substitute regular supermarket meal at your culinary peril. Most ordinary dogs will eat the hush puppies, but my dog Nosher says the stuff is unfit for canine consumption.

Yet, there are thousands upon thousands of recipes for this yellow-meal bread, calling for all manner of ingredients. For example, a well-known New York literary editor by the name of Angus Cameron, co-author of the *L.L. Bean Game & Fish Cookbook*, set forth a recipe for mixing yellow cornmeal, wheat flour, baking powder, milk, and chicken egg. This mix he called "corn pone" and said that he served it in the morning along with jam and jelly. Also in the believe-it-or-not category, George Leonard Herter said that he puts ammonia bicarbonate into his hush puppies—and eats them with mayonnaise.

It seems obvious to me that some very good people all over this great country of ours have been searching desperately for the right stuff, and that they have gone far astray. Trying to satisfy a yearning, they have added all manner of extraneous ingredients to hush puppies. They are going the wrong way, however, and should return to the basics. The classic unleavened corn pone mixture as set forth above is pure and simple—if you have the right kind of meal. If you can't find a local miller, consider buying yourself a kitchen grain mill.

# MAMA'S CRUSTY CORN PONE

My mother had a way of making hand-shaped pones with a crusty bottom and a wavy two-toned top. She didn't use a recipe, so I am proceeding cautiously. (The ingredients list looks almost identical to other corn bread recipes I have published, but the technique is different. This just goes to show that two people cooking the same recipe will be likely to come up with vastly different results.) You need, of course, finely ground whole-kernel white cornmeal and bacon drippings.

| | |
|---|---|
| **finely ground white cornmeal** | **hot water** |
| **bacon drippings** | **salt and pepper** |

Pour some cornmeal into a bowl and mix in some salt and pepper. Add enough hot water to make a stiff dough, mixing well. Stir in a small amount of bacon drippings. Let sit for 20 minutes or so, while the oven preheats to about 350°F. Add a little more water to the dough if needed and shape the dough into three hand-shaped pones, just large enough to fit into an 11- or 12-inch skillet. The pones should be about 1 inch thick.

Heat about 1/16 inch of bacon drippings in a skillet, saving a little of the bacon drippings at room temperature for later use. When it is hot, carefully add the corn pones one at a time. They should touch here and there but should not meld together. Using one hand, lightly dip the bottom of your fingers into the reserved bacon drippings. Then lightly pat the top of each pone, making a wavy surface.

Put the skillet into the oven and bake until the pones are lightly browned on top, with a few dark peaks. If all has gone well, the bread will have a crusty bottom and a tasty, attractive top. Serve as you would any other bread—or eat hot, slathered shamelessly with fresh butter.

# COWBOY BISCUITS

The original Dutch oven, sitting on short legs and fitted with a flanged lid, was ideal for hearthside cooking at the early homestead. On the go, a skillet was easier to manage.

| | |
|---|---|
| 2 cups flour | cooking oil |
| ¾ cup buttermilk or sour milk | 1 teaspoon baking soda |
| ¼ cup shortening or lard | 1 teaspoon salt |

Mix the flour, baking soda, and salt in a bowl. Cut in the shortening, working until the mixture has a texture similar to coarse bread crumbs. Make a hole in the mixture and pour in the buttermilk. Stir from the center outward until the dough sticks together. Do not overwork. Lightly flour a smooth surface and knead the dough 10 times.

Heat 1 inch of oil in a skillet to about 375°F. Pinch off pieces of the dough about the size of a golf ball, rolling them as you go. These will increase in size as they cook. Place the balls, a few at a time, into the hot oil. Fry for 2 minutes on each side, turning once. Drain on a brown bag and serve hot.

*Note: I usually used cultured buttermilk (the kind sold in modern supermarkets) for this recipe, but dried buttermilk, mixed as directed on the package, can be used in camp. Also, sour milk can be used instead of buttermilk.*

# SKILLET-BAKED BISCUITS

The best biscuits I ever ate were made during a local flood a few years ago here in Florida. My cabin on Dead Lakes was knee-deep in water, and for several nights, I stayed in a Red Cross shelter in the Community Center in Wewahitchka. My dog Nosher slept in the truck out front and was not allowed in the shelter. A local volunteer, a big and pleasingly plump woman, brought in some cast-iron skillets, and in these she cooked our breakfast—usually bacon, eggs, and biscuits. I don't have her recipe, but she gave all the credit to the cast-iron skillets, which she used to hold the biscuits like any other pan while they baked in the oven.

I always brought Nosher one or two of the biscuits when I came out in the morning, and she thought they were mighty fine. After two or three days, the floodwaters receded, and Nosher and I returned to our cabin, with fond memories of a plump country lady who liked to cook for homeless old men and their dogs.

Since then I have seen special cast-iron biscuit cookers with circular compartments to hold the biscuits, but I think the regular round skillets work better. It's best to place five or six biscuits along the perimeter, arranged so that they touch the cast iron on the outside and touch each other lightly on two sides. The cast-iron sides and bottom will put a nice crust on the biscuits, with a soft spot where two biscuits touched. The soft spot makes it easier to split the biscuits in half with your fingers, as biscuits are almost always eaten. The soft spot is also great if the kids want to wallow out a hole with a finger and pour in some honey or molasses.

Anyhow, try your favorite cast-iron skillet instead of a pan the next time you bake biscuits. Use your grandmother's recipe, starting from scratch, or perhaps use a biscuit mix, pretty much as follows.

| | |
|---|---|
| **2¼ cups Bisquick mix** | **salt to taste** |
| **⅔ cup milk** | **bacon drippings** |

Preheat the oven to 450°F and warm a 12-inch cast-iron skillet. Mix the Bisquick, milk, and salt until you have a soft dough. Do not overmix. Knead dough 10 times—no more. Dust a smooth board with Bisquick or flour and roll out the dough until it is about ½ inch thick. Cut into rounds with a 2½- or 3-inch cookie wheel.

Lightly grease the bottom and sides of the warmed skillet with bacon drippings. Fit the biscuits in the skillet, putting one in the middle. Pat a small amount of bacon drippings—not much—on the top of each biscuit with your fingers. Put into the center of the oven and bake for 8 to 10 minutes, or until the biscuits are nicely browned on top. Serve hot.

# AZTEC SUNFLOWER BREAD

The American Indian made very good use of sunflower seeds, either whole or ground into a meal for breads and as a soup thickener. In addition to using available wild sunflowers, they also planted the seeds as a crop. In fact, the first cultivated plants in North America were probably sunflowers, especially in the Southwest. These days, plants with very large seed heads are cultivated all around the world and are especially popular in Russia. The gardener can find a dozen varieties to grow, and the forager can still find plenty of wild sunflowers growing across the land from Canada to Mexico. Others can purchase whole seeds and ground meal from health food stores and by mail order, and, of course, snack packs of hulled seeds are sold as noshing fare. Even sunflower seed cooking oil is widely available these days.

2 cups hulled sunflower seeds       ¼ cup very fresh stone-ground cornmeal
2 cups water                        1 teaspoon salt
1 cup sunflower seed cooking oil

Put the seeds, water, and salt into a saucepan, bring to a boil, reduce the heat, cover tightly, and lightly simmer for an hour, stirring from time to time and adding a little more water if needed. Mash this mixture to a paste in mortar and pestle, or zap it in a modern blender or food processor. Stir in the cornmeal a little at a time, using just enough to make a dough. If the dough is too stiff, add a little more water. Heat the oil in a skillet until it's hot enough to spit back at you. Shape the dough into golf ball–size rounds, then flatten these with your hands into small patties. Fry a few at a time, turning once, until the patties are lightly browned on both sides. Serve hot.

# SEMINOLE PUMPKIN BREAD

The Seminole people of Florida prepared a bread with puréed pumpkin mixed with flour or meal, and, I'm sure, the authentic version of old called for some coontie or perhaps live oak acorns or the fine flour extracted from cattail roots. So, experiment with this one if you're into wild foods.

I've seen several recipes, some calling for baking powder and baking soda, but I have settled here for self-rising flour. Some recipes call for spices, especially cinnamon and nutmeg, as used in many recipes for pumpkin pie. I have substituted allspice, an American spice that has a similar taste. Suit yourself.

The pumpkin can be freshly cooked and mashed, if available. If not, canned pumpkin purée will do. The Seminoles of old probably used some sort of wild bird eggs whenever available (seabird eggs were gathered commercially from Florida islands in recent years for commercial baking purposes), but a chicken egg will do. For cooking oil, the resourceful Seminole might have used pig lard or perhaps rendered bear fat or manatee blubber. These days, the modern Native American is more likely to use vegetable oil.

**2 cups cooked pumpkin purée**

**2 cups self-rising flour, plus a little more if needed**

**1 large chicken egg**

**water**

**salt and pepper**

**1 teaspoon freshly ground allspice berries**

**cooking oil**

In a large bowl, mix the pumpkin, flour, chicken egg, spices, and enough water to make a soft dough. Divide the dough into balls about 2½ inches in diameter. Work each ball with your hands, kneading and pulling, kneading and pulling, until the dough is elastic. Continue working—patting and pulling—until you have flat rounds about ¼ inch thick.

Heat about ⅛ inch of cooking oil in a skillet. Fry the bread rounds for a few minutes on each side, until golden brown and crisp.

# CHAPATI

A number of flatbreads are made in Africa, India, and other far-flung places. These are called chapati, roti, and so on. Some are made with rice flour, millet four, or a mixed-grain flour. Here's a basic chapati recipe from Swahili, as set forth in *Best of Regional African Cooking* by Harva Hachten. Although the ingredients list is quite simple, the technique should be practiced.

| | |
|---|---|
| **2 cups all-purpose flour** | **a little oil** |
| **1 teaspoon salt** | **water** |

Mix the salt into the flour, then sift into a bowl. Stir in enough water to make a stiff dough and knead well. Plop the dough onto a lightly floured work surface and roll out into a thick circle. Brush with oil. Make a cut from the center of the circle to the edge. Then roll the dough into a cone. Press in both ends and form into another ball. Once again, roll out a thick circle, brush with oil, cut from the center to the edge, roll into a cone, fold in, and shape into a ball. Repeat twice more.

Divide the dough into 5 balls and roll these out into a thin circle. Heat the skillet, brush with oil, and cook each piece until golden brown on each side. Serve hot or cold.

# CARIBBEAN CASSAVA BREAD

Here's a recipe from Haiti, similar to several such breads made in the Caribbean and parts of South America. I tested it with cassava root (yucca) purchased in a supermarket. If you are buying cassava in South America or on the islands, make sure that it is not the poisonous sort that might require special handling.

| | |
|---|---|
| **1 pound cassava root** | **2 cloves garlic, minced** |
| **2 tablespoons butter (or bacon drippings)** | **salt** |

Peel the cassava, then grate it with a fine mesh. Put the cassava pulp into a piece of cheesecloth. Holding it over the sink, gather the corners of the cheesecloth and twist it, squeezing out the liquid. Remove as much of the liquid as you can. Shape the cassava pulp into thin patties, sprinkle them with salt, and cook them 2 or 3 at a time (do not overlap) in a cast-iron skillet until they are nicely browned on both sides.

When all the patties have been cooked, heat a little butter in a skillet and sauté the garlic. Return the patties to the hot skillet, turn quickly, and serve hot.

*Note: A similar bread is made without the garlic, oil, or even salt. Simply grate 2 pounds of cassava root, squeeze out the juice, and shape the pulp into a round cake about 5 or 6 inches in diameter and about ¾ inch thick. Cook the cake in a small skillet until it sets, turning once. This cake is sometimes moistened with a little milk and browned under a broiler, or fried in bacon drippings.*

# SINGING HINNIE

All manner of unleavened flatbreads, such as tortillas and roti, can be cooked in a cast-iron skillet. Here's a similar bread cooked on the thick side, adapted from my work *The Whole Grain Cookbook*. I use a 10-inch skillet for this recipe, cooking one piece at a time. Use a true whole-grain wheat flour, which includes the germ of the wheat kernel.

| | |
|---|---|
| 3 cups whole-grain wheat flour | ¼ cup lard or shortening |
| 1 cup buttermilk | 1 teaspoon sugar |
| ⅔ cup currants | 1 teaspoon salt |
| ¼ cup butter | 1 teaspoon cream of tartar |

Heat the skillet on the stovetop until it spits back at you. Cut the butter and lard into the flour, mixing in the sugar, salt, and cream of tartar. Slowly stir in enough buttermilk to make a soft dough. Add the currants. Roll the dough out into a round to fit the skillet.

Carefully place the round into the hot skillet, listening carefully for the song to start. Turn off the television. Be quiet. Put your ear in closer. Listen. Hear that! Cook for a few minutes, until the bottom starts to brown nicely. Turn with the spatula and cook the other side. Serve hot with butter.

# CAMP BANNOCK

Here's an easy bread for cooking in camp without an oven—and with only a few ingredients. I use an 8½- or 10-inch skillet. Longer recipes for bannock call for more ingredients, such as chicken eggs and milk, and the real stuff (Scottish) was made with barley meal and oatmeal. Suit yourself.

| | |
|---|---|
| 3 cups all-purpose flour | salt |
| 6 teaspoons baking powder | water |

Mix the flour, baking powder, and salt in a bowl or suitable container. Make a well in the middle and pour in a little water. Stir and pour, stir and pour, until you have a nice dough. Knead the dough for several minutes. Flatten it out to a shape to fit the skillet.

Cook on a mixture of hot coals and ashes until the bottom starts to brown. Test for doneness. If necessary, remove from the heat and let cook in the skillet for a while until the center of the bread is done.

*Note:* *If you have a suitable piece of iron at hand, such as a fire poker, heat it in the coals until red hot. Move the hot end about close over the bannock to brown the top as it cooks in the skillet. At one time, such metal rods, called salamanders, were widely used in hearthside cookery. Some modern cooks use a miniature blowtorch to brown crème brûlée and such. The salamander heat tastes better, methinks.*

# CROUTONS

These are simply crispy squares of bread, used in salads and soups. Store-bought croutons are all right, but freshly made ones are better, even if they are made from stale bread. Most any loaf bread will be suitable, but I like to use thickly sliced French or Italian loaves with the crust removed.

**6 slices bread, cut into cubes**
**¼ cup olive oil or butter**

**salt to taste (optional)**

On medium heat, cook the cubes in the oil or butter until they are nicely browned all around, turning and stirring about from time to time with a wooden spoon. I like to add a little finely ground sea salt toward the end of the cooking.

*Variation:* If you want garlic croutons, cook 4 to 6 peeled cloves in the oil or butter for a few minutes until the oil is flavored. Then remove the garlic and fry as usual. You can also start with garlic oil—that is, olive oil in which garlic has been steeped for several weeks.

# CHAPTER

## 10

# Gravy

**I**f you have the time, a classical French cookbook is the place to look for complex sauce recipes. Some of these have a list of ingredients as long as your leg, and often you'll have to make recipes of sauces A and B in order to complete sauce C. In short, most of these sauces are not practical for making at home and are out of the question for the jack-leg camp cook. Also, sauces are being used more and more as decoration these days, squirted onto the plate in thin strips and curlicues, and dribbled in dots around a little dab of meat and a few sprigs of green stuff. Some of these compositions are simply too pretty for a good man to eat.

Gravy is a less prissified concept, requiring only a few basic ingredients and not much artistic talent. Often the camp cook makes a mess of gravy in the same skillet or pot that cooked the rabbit or squirrel. Most country cooks over fifty years old know how to make good gravy, and sometimes the right stuff can be found in our rural restaurants. I remember a lunch special that I ate in The Bayou, a family eatery here in Wewahitchka, Florida, where I have lived for a few years. They actually served up two colors of gravy on the same plate! A white gravy topped the hamburger steak, and a dark brown gravy filled a large spoon cavity in the snow-white mashed potatoes, all flanked with fried okra and stewed yellow squash, with a little sopping bread on the side. In short, the plate was piled high and heaping over, leaving no room for art. It wasn't pretty. For brute flavor and a tight belly, however, nothing in Paris can top a two-gravy country plate.

Here are a few suggestions, all made in a skillet in camp or kitchen, along with the author's favorite barbecue soption for the patio. A number of other sauces and gravies are made with drippings from a meat cooked in the same skillet, such as steak au poivre.

# SOPCHOPPY TOMATO GRAVY

In Alabama and Middle Tennessee, a tomato gravy is really a sort of country breakfast dish. To make it, you split hot biscuits in half. Spoon stewed tomatoes, with a little salt added, over the biscuits. Pour hot cream gravy over all and enjoy. It's a very old recipe. In north Florida, however, a tomato gravy is quite different, although it is also often consumed at breakfast and is simple enough to be cooked in camp.

The version below has been adapted from Leslie Adam's recipe in *Angler Profiles*. Of this recipe, Les said, "Once you've served it on grits, you'll need no further proof of the existence of God, because only He could have created this fantastic gravy." He—Les—says the recipe originated in north Florida, and I like to place it within a 90-mile radius of Sopchoppy. In this area lies Bristol, Florida, a place of rare flora such as the torreya tree, on the banks of the Big River, as the Apalachicola is called hereabouts. Because of the unusual flora, a local doctor of scholarly bent once reckoned an area just north of Bristol to be the exact location of the original Garden of Eden.

Anyhow, for tomato gravy here's what you'll need:

**1 pound smoked bacon**

**1 can whole chopped tomatoes (28-ounce size)**

**2 small cans V-8 juice (5.5-ounce size)**

**flour (as much as needed)**

**Worcestershire sauce to taste**

**Tabasco sauce to taste**

**salt and pepper to taste**

**grits, biscuits, or rice**

Fry the bacon in a large cast-iron skillet until crisp. Remove it to drain on a brown bag. Measure (or estimate) the bacon drippings, pour them back into the skillet, heat on a medium-hot burner, and slowly stir in an equal amount of flour. Cook and stir with a wooden spoon until you have a dark brown roux. Lower the heat and add the tomatoes and the liquid from the can. Add also the V-8 juice, Worcestershire sauce, Tabasco, salt, and freshly ground black pepper. Simmer for a while, stirring occasionally. Serve hot on grits or polenta, biscuit halves, or rice, with the bacon on the side.

# ALASKAN DRIED MUSHROOM CAMP GRAVY

Dried mushrooms are even better than fresh ones for some recipes that require long, slow cooking in a liquid. They can be purchased in some supermarkets and from gourmet shops and mail-order outfits. I prefer dried morels or chanterelles, which I dry myself whenever I happen upon a bonanza in the wild. In any case, this recipe is made in a skillet in which venison chops have been fried in a small amount of bacon drippings. It's great for camp, where, presumably, the chops would be at hand. It can also be made with beef or pork.

2 or 3 tablespoons pan drippings from chops
1 ounce dried mushrooms
1 tablespoon minced dried onion
flour
1 cup milk
salt and freshly ground black pepper to taste
water

Put the mushrooms into a nonmetallic container, cover with water, and let soak for several hours, or overnight, turning a time or two and adding more water if needed. When it's time to cook, drain and chop the mushrooms. Save the soaking liquid.

Heat the pan drippings (adding a little cooking oil or bacon drippings if needed) and slowly add a little flour, stirring with a wooden spoon, until you have a light brown roux. Stir in the chopped mushrooms, dried onions, and a little of the soaking liquid. Cook and stir for about 10 minutes, making sure the mushrooms flavor the roux. Slowly add the milk, increase the heat, and stir briskly until the mixture boils. Salt and pepper to taste. Remove from the heat and check the texture. If it's too thick, stir in a little more of the milk or mushroom soaking liquid and reheat. Enjoy this gravy over halves of man-size sourdough biscuits.

# TENNESSEE REDEYE GRAVY

This old breakfast gravy is made by first frying a large slice of country-cured ham in a skillet. This kind of ham will be quite salty, and some cooks insist on soaking the slices overnight in fresh water, perhaps changing the water a time or two. Usually, the slices are about ½ inch thick. Serve a whole slice, and its gravy, to each partaker. Dividing the measures won't work, as I found out in a small Tennessee restaurant that served country ham and gravy. One night I asked for the gravy and biscuits without the ham, but the owner rather indignantly informed me that it took a whole slice of ham to make a serving of gravy.

| | |
|---|---|
| country ham slices | freshly ground black pepper |
| freshly brewed coffee, black and strong | bacon drippings |

When you are ready for breakfast, fry the ham for a few minutes in a cast-iron skillet greased with a small spoonful of bacon drippings. Turn and cook the other side. Remove the ham to drain. Into the hot skillet pour a little of the coffee, stirring with a wooden spatula or wooden spoon. This is called deglazing the pan. (Note that the skillet should be quite hot, causing the coffee to sizzle.) Stir in a little black pepper if wanted. If you have added a bit too much coffee, cook the gravy a little longer to reduce it, but remember that redeye is a thin gravy. Serve hot over biscuit halves, along with the country ham and eggs.

*Note: One television cooking show featuring Martha Stewart omitted the coffee, using only water for deglazing the skillet. There is some confusion about how the name redeye came about, but I subscribe to an association with moonshine whiskey, which is sometimes called red-eye, and to the bloodshot eyes at a breakfast after a drunken night. A reluctant cook on the Martha Stewart show garbled the issue, saying the name came from something about not shooting until you saw the red of their eyes. Stewart knew better, I'm sure, and ought to be put in jail. Other cooks allow the use of regular supermarket ham, the kind that has been pumped up with water and chemicals. It's best to stick to the real stuff, hard and salty. Still other cooks add a little flour to thicken the gravy. Suit yourself—but don't leave out the black coffee and country ham, if you want real redeye.*

# FOXFIRE GRAVY

The early settlers made extensive use of cornmeal simply because it was widely available before wheat became the dominant grain in the American kitchen. Cornmeal was sometimes called Indian meal. It's best to use fine stone-ground white meal. If you have only gritty yellow meal from the supermarket, you should pass on this recipe. (See my notes on cornmeal in chapter 9—and don't get me started on this subject again this late in the book.) In any case, I find this gravy to be a good one for camp cooking.

1 cup stone-ground white cornmeal                    milk
¼ cup bacon drippings                                water
salt and pepper to taste

Heat the bacon drippings in a skillet until quite hot. Mix in the cornmeal along with a little salt and pepper. Cook on medium-low heat, stirring with a wooden spoon, until the meal is nicely browned. Mix in a little water and a little milk, about half and half, stirring constantly, until the gravy is the consistency you like. Serve at breakfast over biscuit halves, or sop with corn pone.

# GIBLET GRAVY

This gravy is traditionally made from turkey giblets for the Thanksgiving dinner, served as a topping for the dressing or stuffing. I sometimes save the giblets from chickens and game birds (even small ones like quail or snipe) to make the gravy for serving over biscuit halves. The giblets properly include the heart, liver, gizzard, and neck from the bird. Even the feet can be used, especially if you're feeding French guests. (Note that if you are dressing your own birds, the gizzard should be split open with a knife, turned, emptied of its contents, and washing thoroughly.) Hens sometimes provide immature eggs, some of which should also be used in the gravy instead of boiled eggs.

| | |
|---|---|
| 1 set turkey giblets | 2 hard-boiled chicken eggs, sliced |
| 2 tablespoons flour | salt and black pepper to taste |
| 2 tablespoons bacon drippings or cooking oil | water |

Heat a little salted water in a saucepan and simmer the gizzard, heart, feet, and neck for an hour and a half, until tender. (The gizzard is especially tough.) Pull the meat off the neck (discarding the bones) and chop it along with the gizzard and heart. Discard the feet, unless you like to nibble on the toes. Put the chopped meats back into the saucepan, along with the liver. Cook for another 20 minutes or so, until the liver is tender.

While the liver cooks, heat the bacon drippings in a 10-inch skillet. Add the flour and cook, stirring as you go, until it browns nicely. Stir in about a cup of the liquid from the giblet boil. Chop the liver and add it to the gravy, along with the other giblets. Add some salt and pepper as needed. Carefully stir in the sliced boiled eggs. Serve warm in a gravy boat.

# A. D.'S BBQ SOPTION

Shame on the jackleg cook who stays up all night slow-cooking Boston butts or shoulder to perfection—only to pour store-bought sauce over the pulled pork. It's easy to come up with your own tomato-based sauce by mixing this product and that. (Every jackleg has a secret recipe, which probably changes a little on each batch.) For flavor and texture, however, I would recommend starting with a commercial tomato-based salsa—or use your own salsa recipe. The recipe below is based on one that I came up with and published in my book *Strictly Barbecue*. Use it as your own, or modify it to suit your fancy and available ingredients.

I might add that bottled salsa is now America's number one condiment, surpassing even catsup, I understand. Hundreds of variations are available in brand-name bottles from food conglomerates on down to kitchen-table creations sold locally in Mason jars. Since most of these salsas are made with tomatoes, onions, and chile peppers, they are ideal for making an easy barbecue sauce with a Southwestern touch. Of the several such barbecue sauces that I have formulated down through the years, this one is my favorite—partly because it's also easy to make.

| | |
|---|---|
| 1 jar medium-hot chunky salsa (16-ounce size) | ¼ cup Mexican brown sugar (also called piloncillo, or cone sugar) |
| 1 medium onion, minced | 2 tablespoons red wine vinegar |
| 4 cloves garlic, minced | 2 tablespoons soy sauce |
| | 1 tablespoon olive oil |

In a cast-iron skillet, heat the olive oil and brown the onion. Add the garlic, sugar, soy sauce, and red wine vinegar. Heat until the sugar is melted, stirring with a wooden spoon. Add the salsa. Simmer on very low heat for a few minutes, stirring constantly, until the sauce thickens to your liking. Do not burn. Excellent with pulled pork and barbecued ribs.

*Note: The Mexican sugar is available in cones, which must be shaved with a knife or grated.*

# NIGERIAN ATA SAUCE FOR BEEF OR VENISON

This Nigerian creation is only one of hundreds of sauces made in Africa, where several sorts of hot peppers are cultivated in great plenty. I have adapted the recipe from *Best of Regional African Cooking* by Harva Hachten, but similar recipes appear in other books. In my version, I roast the red peppers over a wood or charcoal fire before proceeding simply because I like the smoky flavor; the charred skin is peeled off before using. I also increased the number of tomatoes from two to three. The ground dried shrimp used in the recipe can be purchased in some Asian markets or can be made by pounding dried shrimp with mortar and pestle. Shrimp paste can also be used, if available. (I have also used dried salt mullet roe, grated, which makes a great seasoning.) The chile peppers can be varied according to taste and hotness. If in doubt, fresh jalapeño peppers will do.

3 red bell peppers, roasted, seeded, and peeled

3 large tomatoes, peeled and chopped

3 to 5 fresh green chile peppers, seeded and minced

1 large onion, minced

½ cup peanut oil or olive oil

1 teaspoon ground dried shrimp

salt to taste

Grind the roasted peppers, onion, green chile peppers, and tomatoes in a food mill. Heat the peanut oil in a large cast-iron skillet and sauté the ground vegetables for 5 or 6 minutes, stirring with a wooden spoon. Add the ground shrimp and a little salt. Reduce the heat to very low and simmer until the sauce starts to brown, stirring constantly to avoid burning. If needed, add a little more salt.

Serve the sauce as a topping for broiled or grilled venison backstrap cutlets, or similar cuts of beef, bison, or other good red meat. In Nigeria, the meat (often game) is sometimes simmered in a little water until tender, drained, browned quickly in very hot oil, and then cooked for a few more minutes in the sauce before serving, all of which can be accomplished in a camp skillet.

# ALMOST FOOLPROOF SKILLET GRAVY

This isn't really a recipe, and the gravy can be made in a skillet behind fried or sautéed venison chops, quail, game burgers, wild turkey fingers, and so on. Simply drain off most of the cooking oil, then deglaze the skillet with a little red wine or other liquid, being sure to scrape up any dredgings that may have stuck to the bottom. Add some cream of mushroom soup, stirring until you have a nice thick gravy. Serve the gravy with the meat, or use it to top rice, mashed potatoes, or biscuit halves. I also like to use the gravy to add a little moisture to venison burgers, which tend to be on the dry side.

Excellent gravy can be made from pan drippings from a roasted turkey or pot roast. We don't need a recipe. Just skim off some of that surface grease from the roasting pan (especially if it's a fat domestic bird), put the rest of the drippings into a cast-iron skillet on medium heat, and stir in some flour a little at a time, adding water or red wine as needed to make a gravy as thick as we want it. Stir. Taste. Stir. Taste again. Needs a twist or two of black pepper and a touch of salt. What could be easier? What better?

# CHAPTER

# Blackened Fish, Fowl, and Red Meat

**T**he popularity of "blackened redfish" years ago—almost a craze in some quarters—owed more to a radical cooking technique than to the fish itself. In fact, the redfish is nothing but an ordinary red drum. It's also called a channel bass, and small ones, less than 10 pounds, are sometimes called puppy drum.

Apparently, the original recipe for blackened redfish was created by professional chef Paul Prudhomme in Louisiana. My guess is that the dish was born of necessity when a cook accidentally burned somebody's order of pan-fried fish, which happened to be the last fillet in Prudhomme's place! In any case, the popularity of the dish put an inordinate demand on the Gulf Coast commercial and sport fishery in that it required redfish of a certain size. In order to blacken properly, a fish fillet has to be from ½ to ¾ inch thick. Ideally, fillets of this size must be taken from a relatively small redfish. This requirement for thin fillets, in turn, created a demand for these smaller fish, and helped spread the notion that larger redfish are not fit to eat. While it is true that large redfish (and they grow up to 80 pounds) are coarse and taste none too good, smaller fish, 15 pounds and under, are quite toothsome when cut into fingers and fried. (As always, the fish should be properly dressed and should be eaten fresh.) Many other kinds of fish are quite suitable for making "blackened redfish," including largemouth bass and walleyes. Even some rough fish can be blackened. A recent issue of *Outdoor Life* magazine, for example, set forth an article about a Texas couple who bagged alligator gar by bowfishing—and blackened the fillets.

Although much emphasis has been put on prepared Cajun "blackening" spice mixes, I think the real secret is of technique and specification. First, the cookware must be extremely hot, and cast iron is the only common cookware material that will withstand such temperatures. Second, the thickness of the fillet must be such that it will brown and form a crust on the outside while staying moist and succulent on the inside. Third, spices provide both flavor and crust, almost like a batter provides a crust in frying.

Be warned that true blackening produces clouds of smoke, and this rules out the kitchen stove. Even a stove with a powerful overhead vent may cause problems. Although I have blackened fish and meat successfully in a kitchen fireplace, I believe that it's best to take your blackening outside. But it is difficult to heat cast iron hot enough for true blackening, and remember that ordinary charcoal on a grill simply will not get hot enough to do the job. (Wood chips will help.) By far, the best bet for obtaining the required heat is from a gas-fired burner, such as those used for heating large fish fryers. Just any gas burner won't do. Some camp stoves, for example, won't put out enough heat. Also, a good deal depends on your cast-iron piece. In any case, cast-iron pieces will start turning white on the cooking surface when they are hot enough. Don't worry. It's hard to get cast iron too hot with normal cooking equipment.

Prudhomme used a large cast-iron skillet to illustrate the how-to pictures in one of his books. Another New Orleans sharp, Frank Davis, recommends (in *The Frank Davis Seafood Notebook*) that a cast-iron Dutch oven be used. I don't recommend either a skillet or a Dutch oven simply because the sides of these pieces are not needed for blackening and serve only as heat sinks. A cast-iron griddle is what you need, I say, and special "blackening" griddles of oval shape are now available. These are ideal.

An oval cast-iron griddle is ideal for cooking blackened redfish and similar dishes.

# BLACKENED REDFISH

Having said that technique and exactness are the keys to this recipe, I'll have to add that the spice mix can be varied quite a bit. I prefer to use the spices set forth in Chef Paul Prudhomme's *Louisiana Kitchen*, although I change the proportions from one batch to the next. Hotness aside, I feel that lots of paprika is needed to give the spice mix body. It is very important that a thick coat of spices cover the fish flesh, and I use lots of paprika as a sort of filler. (I also cut back on the cayenne.) I've also seen other mixes. Frank Davis, for example, adds 12 crushed bay leaves and some basil, although he calls the recipe "Paul Prudhomme's Blackened Redfish." Also, *The Official Louisiana Seafood & Wild Game Cookbook* listed fresh chopped parsley. (This work also specified fillets that are 1 inch thick, and said that a tablespoon of butter can be added to the hot skillet just ahead of the fish to prevent sticking. Be warned that a tablespoon of butter will smoke something awful and burn almost immediately. Also, I never had a problem with any blackened food sticking, if the cast iron was hot enough.) In most recipes, the trend is to add stuff to the original, and the ingredients list for blackened redfish, already quite long, will continue to grow. It wouldn't surprise me to see monosodium glutamate listed.

In any case, here is my recommendation for blackened fish:

fish fillets (½ to ¾ inch thick)

melted butter

1 tablespoon salt

1 tablespoon Hungarian sweet paprika

½ teaspoon ground red cayenne

1 teaspoon white pepper

1 teaspoon black pepper

1 teaspoon garlic powder

1 teaspoon onion powder

½ teaspoon crushed dried thyme leaves

½ teaspoon crushed dried oregano leaves

Mix the salt, spices, and herbs. Bring the fillets to room temperature. Melt the butter in a pan and coat each fillet on both sides. Sprinkle each fillet liberally with the spice mixture. Heat a griddle or skillet as hot as you can get it and warm some individual serving platters. Prepare bread, salad, cold drinks, et cetera, for serving. Get ready. Using tongs, hold a fillet by one end and lay it out on the super-hot griddle. Sizzle for 2 minutes. Using tongs, flip the fillet over and sizzle the other side for 2 minutes. (Fillets that are only ½ inch thick will require even less cooking, and fillets that are 1 inch thick will require longer cooking.) Pick the fillet up with tongs and place it on a heated serving platter. Serve with melted butter as a sauce.

*Alternative Method:* After turning the fillet, carefully spoon some melted butter onto the cooked side. Flop the fillet over when placing it on the serving platter, then spoon some butter onto the other side.

# BLACKENED BEEF

Following the popularity of blackened redfish, creative chefs and backyard jacklegs started blackening and burning other meats across the land, alarming local fire departments and polluting the atmosphere with smoke. My favorite spin-off recipe is for blackened beef, and I adapted it from an article in a special 1980s issue of *Life* magazine. The success of the recipe depends in large part, I think, on the seasoned gravy. To make the dish, I use a skillet for the gravy and a griddle for the blackened beef.

### Seasonings

1 tablespoon salt

1 tablespoon plus ¾ teaspoon black pepper

2½ teaspoons cayenne pepper

2½ teaspoons dry mustard

5 teaspoons fennel seeds

Crush the fennel seeds and mix all the ingredients. This seasoning will be used in the gravy and on the meat. I prepare the gravy first so that it will be ready when the meat is blackened.

### Gravy

1½ teaspoons blackening seasonings (from above)

⅓ cup cooking oil

⅔ cup flour

1 cup chopped green onion tops

4 cups beef or chicken stock

Heat the beef or chicken stock in a saucepan and keep it warm. (You can also use plain water or water with bouillon cubes. Also, I have used a diluted ham stock with great success.) In a large skillet, heat the cooking oil and gradually stir in the flour. Cook very slowly for about 5 minutes, stirring constantly, until you have a medium-brown roux. Remove the skillet from the heat and stir in the chopped green onion tops. Gradually stir in the warm stock and the seasonings. Put the skillet back on the heat, turn to high, and bring to a boil. Stir, reduce the heat, and simmer uncovered for 15 minutes. Stir once or twice. During these 15 minutes, get your meat ready to cook so that both meat and gravy will be hot in temperature as well as in seasoning.

### *The Meat*

| | |
|---|---|
| **choice beef, preferably tenderloin, ¾ inch thick** | **melted butter** |
| | **seasonings (from above)** |

Let the meat come to room temperature. Then dip each piece into melted butter. Sprinkle both sides of the meat generously with seasonings, and press some seasonings into the meat with your hands. Before cooking the meat, it's best to warm individual serving platters in an oven.

Heat an *ungreased* griddle (preferably oval) on very hot wood coals or on a gas burner, as directed above. When the griddle is very hot, put one or two pieces of seasoned meat on it. Sizzle for 2 or 3 minutes, or until a crust forms on the bottom. Turn the meat with tongs and sizzle the other side for 2 or 3 minutes. Using tongs, place the meat onto the serving platter. Spoon on some hot gravy and serve with lots of good bread, green salad, baked potato—and lots of ice water.

# BLACKENED HAMBURGER

Here's a spin-off dish that really doesn't belong in this section, so I'll keep it short. First, let me say that most ground beef contains too much fat to be properly blackened. The grease from the meat causes too much smoke and too much smell of burned grease. (If you insist on real blackened hamburger, buy some very lean beef, trim it carefully, and grind it yourself.) With most of the commercially available ground meat, it's best to form patties about ¾ inch thick, add some salt and pepper to the meat, and broil it in an oven, so that the heat from the top causes the grease to drip out the bottom. If the meat is placed about 2 inches from the heat source, it can be cooked medium rare on the inside and well browned on the outside in about 3 minutes to each side. Then, serve on a heated platter with plenty of spicy gravy. Make up your own gravy mixture, or use the one set forth above. With hamburger, I really prefer lots of chopped onions as well as onion tops in my gravy.

# BLACKENED CHICKEN

The regular blackening technique for fish and beef can also be used for chicken. Of course, the meat must be somewhat flattened and must not be too thick. Obviously, a blackened drumstick would be raw down next to the bone. By far, the best bet is to use boned chicken breasts; then, with the smooth side of a wooden meat mallet, beat them down between two pieces of waxed paper. For blackening, I like mine ½ inch thick.

A good spice mix for blackened chicken is available at supermarkets, and I usually use it instead of mixing my own. I do, however, sometimes blacken chicken with relatively tame spices, served for those who don't care for too much hot stuff. The trick here is to use lots of bright red Hungarian paprika. The secret of "blackened" meat depends, in part, upon having a crust of spices on both sides of the meat. Paprika can provide such a crust with only a small amount of hot pepper. However, I don't recommend that you start dumping the spice rack into a "blackened chicken" recipe, simply because some herbs don't work too well at such high temperatures. For openers, it's best to go with commercial blends or stick pretty much to hot pepper (black or white) and paprika, and maybe some powdered mustard. Red cayenne can also be used, but remember that it is very, very hot.

# BLACKENED DUCK AND GOOSE

Breast of domestic duck can be blackened quite successfully. It's best to skin the duck, fillet out both sides of the breast, trim off any fat, and cook in exactly the same way as set forth above for beef. I use the same spice mix, and often cook the duck and beef together, giving my guests a choice of meats. Usually, a fillet of duck breast will be the right thickness to yield a crusty surface with a medium-rare middle, which is ideal for both beef and duck, in my opinion.

Wild duck can be used successfully, but the breast fillets may not be quite thick enough for ideal blackening. Moreover, the meat of some wild ducks can be a bit strong for some tastes, in which case a 24-hour marinade of 1 tablespoon baking soda to 1 quart of water will help.

Breast fillets of wild and domestic geese can also be blackened. Fillets from large geese, however, may require flattening slightly with a wooden mallet. In fact, I've eaten some geese that could stand a bit of tenderizing with the toothed side of a meat mallet.

# BLACKENED TILAPIA

Many recipes for blackened fish make an issue of the amount of smoke the process generates, suggesting that maybe you ought to notify the local fire department before you start cooking. There is some smoke, but proper cooking technique will hold it to a minimum, while making a perfect blackened fillet: crisp and black on the outside, moist and white on the inside. Soggy blackened fish aren't the real stuff and were probably not cooked at high heat. How high? About as hot as you can get a cast-iron skillet or griddle on an electric stove, and hotter than some briquette-burning outdoor grills and camp stoves will afford. My favorite rig for blackening is a high-BTU outdoor gas burner used to heat large pots for boiling crawfish or frying a whole turkey. Of course, you use a cast-iron skillet or flat griddle instead of a big pot. Skillets of other materials will be in danger of warping or cracking under the heat.

There are several commercial blackening spice mixes on the market. Some of these are quite hot and, if you use my method set forth below, should be diluted with mild paprika or mild powder from ancho or New Mexican chile peppers (not to be confused with commercial chili powder blends loaded with cumin).

*Note: A number of recipes, some from Louisiana where the blackened redfish craze started a few decades ago, call for coating the bottom of the skillet or griddle with butter or oil before proceeding. Don't do it. That's where most of the smoke comes from. Don't worry. The fish won't stick if it is properly coated with the spice mix and the skillet is hot enough.*

The original blackened fish recipe called for redfish, as the Cajuns and Gulf Coast fishermen call the channel bass. The redfish in question had to be small simply because the fillets to be blackened must be thin. The demand soon overwhelmed the supply of small redfish, causing all manner of restrictions to be placed on the fish. Actually, any rather small fish with mild flavor can be used provided that the fillets are a little over ½ inch thick—¾ at the most. I prefer a fish with lean, white flesh. Farm-raised tilapia, sometimes marketed in my neck of the woods as Nile perch, are perfect. Fresh tilapia can be purchased in some markets, but I have taken to frozen fillets that have been vacuum-sealed in individual bags. This allows me to get out as many fillets as I need from the package without having to thaw the whole works.

If you purchase whole market tilapia, you'll have to fillet them. This isn't hard, but note that the tilapia has a row of short, odd bones on either side of the backbone, some-what like saw teeth. The ends of these stubby bones can be cut off during the filleting process, in which case they should be removed by cutting out a thin triangular strip of meat from the fillet.

Anyhow, the spices listed below can be varied quite a lot, and some of the Cajun recipes are as long as your leg, but I do insist on having real butter (not margarine) and a cast-iron skillet or griddle.

This recipe and preamble have been adapted from a contribution I made to *One Fish, Two Fish, Crawfish, Bluefish: The Smithsonian Sustainable Seafood Cookbook*, by Carole C. Baldwin and Julie H. Mounts. Let's start with the blackening seasoning.

### A. D.'s Cajun Dust

| | |
|---|---|
| ½ cup powdered ancho or New Mexico chile | 1 tablespoon finely ground white pepper |
| 1 tablespoon cayenne (or to taste) | 1 tablespoon finely ground sea salt |
| 1 tablespoon finely ground black pepper | 1 tablespoon onion powder |

Mix all the seasonings and set aside until you are ready to cook. Note that this mix contains more mild red pepper than most recipes or commercial blackening seasonings. I use it as a sort of filler, permitting me to make a rather thick coating on the fillet as compared to a mere sprinkle. The same effect can be achieved by adding quite a bit of mild paprika or ground chile powder to a commercial blackening mix. I might add that most other recipes also call for thyme, oregano, and other spices. Suit yourself. Experiment.

### The Fish

| | |
|---|---|
| tilapia fillets | melted butter |
| blackening dust (from above) | a cast-iron skillet or griddle |

Rig a hot fire or gas burner on the patio, or pull out some red-hot wood coals from a campfire. Heat the skillet until it is very hot. (Use a kitchen stove only if you have a good vent.) Melt the butter in a suitable container. Pour some of the blackening dust into an oblong container, a little larger than the fillets. Get ready. Dip a fillet into the melted butter to coat one side; turn to coat the other side. Shake off the excess butter, then place the fillet down on the spice mix; turn and coat the other side. Shake off the excess dust and carefully place the fillet on a platter or plate. Coat the rest of the fillets. Then look at each fillet again, starting with the first, and sprinkle on enough of the spice mix to cover any wet spots.

Now, take a deep breath and hold it. Using tongs, place a fillet onto the hot skillet. Let it sizzle for about 1½ minutes. Turn and sizzle the other side for the same length of time. (The cooking time should be varied according to the thickness of each fillet: 1¼ minutes for ½ inch thickness, 2 minutes for ¾ inch thickness.) You should now have a fillet that is dry and charred on the outside, but moist and white inside. Blacken the rest of the fillets, then serve them hot along with whatever go-withs you want.

Be warned that many of the blackening spices are quite hot, especially when used as a thick coating instead of a mere sprinkle. Many people want a glass of ice water at hand as a chaser, but it really won't help much. The heat of chile peppers comes from capsaicin, which isn't diluted by water. It's sort of like pouring water onto a grease fire, making it spread. Dairy products help tame the capsaicin in blackened fish, and I often serve a dollop of sour cream or yogurt on the side.

*Note: Thin fillets from other fish can be used, along with thin slices of beef or venison loin. This is a great recipe for preparing in camp if you mix the spices at home. Most camp cooks are going to burn the fish or meat anyway, so why not do it right?*

# Dutch Oven and Other Cast-Iron Specialties

# CHAPTER

## 12

# Dutch Oven

Ed was one of the great amateur cooks of this world, and with the simplest Florida backwoods ingredients and a Dutch oven, turned out dishes so superlative that when I now prepare one, I grieve that Ed is not here to partake.

—*Marjorie Kinnan Rawlings,* Cross Creek Cookery

There are two kinds of Dutch oven. The one usually found in the modern kitchen has a dome-shaped lid and is flat on the bottom. It is, of course, ideal for cooking on top of a stove, and it is discussed a little later. The other kind, sometimes called a camp oven, is ideal for cooking everything from bread to stew meat over a campfire or at a home fireplace hearth.

The camp Dutch oven became the most important piece of cookware in the westward expansion, simply because it was so versatile. It is still a highly desirable piece of gear for any remote camp, or on camping trips, where an oven and other modern gear is not available. In it, a camper can cook everything he needs—even bread. At home, a camp oven can come in handy, during electric power failures, for cooking on the family hearth or in the yard. Fortunately for the sportsman, the Dutch oven is manufactured today pretty much like it was in the 1800s.

Unlike the stovetop version, the camp oven has legs so that it sits over coals. It also has a flanged lid, which is recessed so that it can hold coals on top. This feature comes in very, very handy for baking bread, for cooking stews for a long time, and for keeping foods warm. The flat lid can also serve as a griddle or a shallow skillet.

The inventor of the original Dutch oven remains in question, and some writers speculate that Paul Revere designed it. In all probability, the more or less final shape of this versatile piece of cookware came about in steps, evolving to suit the needs of the American settler and the westward expansion. Most modern authorities believe the term "Dutch" to have come about because the cookware was sold by Dutch peddlers. But I wonder. The so-called Pennsylvania Dutch settlers also came up with a large oven, made with stone and mortar. These were usually built in connection with a springhouse or a smokehouse, and were not a part of the hearth. A large fire was built inside the oven. When a high temperature was attained, the fire was extinguished and the baking started. The good women of these Pennsylvania settlements gained fame in baking pies, and, who knows, the term "Dutch oven" might have started here. If so, it should be called the "Deutsch oven."

The popular Dutch oven can be used as a stovetop pot or it can be suspended over a campfire. It's great for long, slow cooking.

The real Dutch settlers, who established a trading post on Manhattan Island in 1614, also developed a Dutch oven, which was built into the end of the fireplace. They also used cast-iron pieces for baking. Here's an account from Gertrude I. Thomas's *Foods of Our Forefathers*: "Plenty of baking was carried on in a Dutch oven which was an improvement over the roasting kitchen of Virginia. It was cylindrical and open to the fire on one side, and through it ran a spit for roasting the meat. Bread and cakes were baked in heavy iron kettles with convex, curved lids, into which were piled the live coals."

The old camp Dutch oven was an important piece of gear during frontier days. Hot coals were piled onto the lid in order to brown the biscuits. This original Dutch oven is still being manufactured today for camp or fireplace cookery.

Whatever the truth about the name "Dutch oven," a number of more fanciful explanations have been set forth, sometimes in jest. In a 1971 edition of *Field & Stream*, for example, Ted Trueblood attributed the name to one Dutch O'Leary, a "celebrated frontiersman." And a trapper named Steeljaws Newhouse (Trueblood went on) added the lid with an upturned rim for holding coals on top of the oven. But I suspect that Ted Trueblood had a lot of fun with names, including his own.

In any case, the Dutch oven was an important piece of gear to some of the frontier people. If you do much campfire cooking, or like to cook in your fireplace at home, as I do, I strongly urge you to purchase a Dutch oven of this type. Here are a few recipes.

# EASY CAMP BREAKFAST

The lid to the Dutch oven will do for frying up a little bacon and a chicken egg or two. If you don't have eggs (or have broken them, as often happens in camp), try my recipe for breakfast potatoes and bacon:

bacon, thick-sliced

potatoes, sliced ¼ inch thick, unpeeled

salt

Build a fire and brew some coffee. When you have enough hot coals, rake some aside and form a bed. Place the Dutch oven lid on the coals and put the bacon on it. Stand by while it cooks. If the bacon seems about to burn, pick up the lid with your hook and hold it up while it cools a bit. You may have to repeat this step a few times, but chances are that the heat will be at least in the ballpark. When the bacon is crisp, take it up and put in on a brown paper bag to drain. (If you don't have a brown bag or absorbent paper, put in on a plate or some suitable surface.) Fry the potatoes in the bacon drippings, turning from time to time so they don't burn on the bottom. Take up the sliced potatoes and put them on the brown bag to drain. Salt the potatoes to taste.

I admit that this recipe isn't much for variety, but it's a hearty dish that will stick with you during a hard day afield. And it's easy. Remember also that eggs can be fried to go along with the potatoes and bacon, and toast can also be made in the Dutch oven lid.

*Note: Sliced potatoes fried in bacon grease on a cast-iron griddle or frying pan also make a very tasty addition to a meal cooked at home. If you want to get fancy, separate the potatoes when you put them on paper for draining, then sprinkle the tops lightly with bright red paprika.*

# ALL-DAY POT ROAST

The best way to cook roasts or other large chunks of meat in camp is to dig a hole, put plenty of hot coals in it, put the Dutch oven on top of the coals, and pile more coals on top of the lid. Then cover it all up with the dirt that came out of the hole. Remember, however, that digging a hole in the woods is often something of a problem, especially if roots or rocks, or both, are present. You'll need a scoop. Dig the hole deeper and wider than the Dutch oven, then build a large fire on top of the hole. Then build another fire nearby. (One fire will do, but remember that you will need two batches of coals: one for the bottom of the pit and one to go atop the Dutch oven lid.)

Some people pack along charcoal for cooking purposes, and, of course, it works nicely for pit cooking. But remember that you'll need lots of it, which can make camp cooking a little expensive. On the other hand, I must point out that Dutch oven specialists can define exactly how many briquets are required on top and bottom for cooking a certain recipe in a Dutch oven of a certain size. In any case, here's a good recipe to try:

| | |
|---|---|
| **beef or venison roast, about 6 pounds** | **carrots** |
| **cooking oil** | **onions** |
| **flour** | **salt and pepper** |
| **potatoes** | **water** |

Dig the pit and build the fire early in the morning. When the fire has burned down somewhat, rake out some coals and heat a little oil in the bottom part of the Dutch oven. Sprinkle the roast with flour and brown it on all sides in the hot oil. (In other words, you need to brown the roast in the pot before putting it into the pit.) Salt and pepper the roast. Add 2 cups of water and put the lid on top. Peel the onions and potatoes, then scrape the carrots. Put the potatoes and carrots around the roast, then add the onions on top. Sprinkle on a little salt and pepper. The exact measures of the vegetables aren't too important, so feel free to fill up the pot if you have lots of folks to feed.

From the fire directly over the pit, rake all the coals into the hole. Lower the Dutch oven directly onto the coals. Pile coals from the second fire onto the lid. Then fill up the hole and pile dirt on top. Leave the pot in the hole for 7 to 10 hours, while you are out hunting or fishing or shooting pictures. Before leaving camp, however, make sure that the two fires are out. When you get back, you'll have a complete dinner ready. You'll have gravy, too. Feeds 8 to 12.

*Note: The technique above can be used to cook a number of recipes for large chunks of meat, and it will also work with various recipes calling for stew meat. Remember also that such recipes don't need lots of water or liquid, if the lid fits tightly. (See "Lids," starting on page 210.)*

# CAMP STEW

Although a purely excellent stew can be cooked by the pit method described above, all-day cooking may not always be practical. A good stew can be made in an hour or two on good campfire coals. Having legs, the camp Dutch oven is ideal in that it sits over a bed of coals but not directly on them. (Direct contact with a flat pan will actually extinguish the coals.) Also remember that you can start cooking with a Dutch oven even before the fire has burned down and made coals. The Dutch oven has a bail attached to the pot, which permits it to be hung over the flames. I've always found that a sturdy tripod with a drop chain and an S-hook is by far the best for this purpose, although some people are adept with a dingle stick. If you have a choice, however, wait for the coals. In any case, here's a stew recipe to try in camp:

| | |
|---|---|
| 2 pounds lean stew meat | 2 medium potatoes |
| flour (optional) | 2 carrots |
| cooking oil (optional) | salt and pepper |
| 2 medium onions | water |

I realize that the list of ingredients for this dish is almost the same as for the pot roast. The reason is that onions, potatoes, and carrots are easy to transport and store in camp, as compared with some other vegetables. Also, in the pot roast, these same vegetables were used whole (for very long cooking), whereas in this recipe they are cut up.

If you have oil and are cooking on coals, dust the meat with flour and brown it. Then peel and quarter the potatoes and onions. Scrape and chop the carrots. Add the vegetables to the meat and pour in 2 cups of water. Salt and pepper to taste. Cover and cook for an hour or longer, stirring from time to time to prevent the bottom from burning. Add water if needed. Add more coals around the pot, if needed, and push some underneath. This recipe will feed 4 campers.

*Note: If you have a grill fitted over your campfire, your camp Dutch oven can usually be used on it. The legs will probably fit into the holes or cracks.*

If you plan to start cooking by hanging the Dutch oven over flames, load the pot with carrots, meat, potatoes, and onions, in that order, then add salt, pepper, and water. Cover tightly and suspend the pot over the fire. Omit the cooking oil and the flour. Cook until the meat is done and the potatoes are tender when tested with a fork. It's best to stir the contents from time to time, and add more water if needed. It's also best to swing the pot away from the fire before you remove the lid and stir the dish.

# BIG SCRUB GUINEA HEN

In *Cross Creek Cookery*, Mrs. Rawlings said that it was Ed Hopkins who introduced her to the people in Florida's Big Scrub area, where she set such works as *The Yearling*. Here's a recipe that, I feel, came from Hopkins or from the Scrub people. In any case, I include the recipe in this little book not only because it is good but also because it uses the heated Dutch oven lid to brown the top of a piece of meat while, at the same time, browning the bottom as usual. (I might add that some purely excellent cooks pride themselves in *browning* the bottom of a dish without actually burning it. In Iran, for example, certain rice dishes are browned on the bottom, and the crusty part, considered a delicacy, is saved for the elders.) Heavy cast-iron cookware is ideal for this skill. Don't try it in thin metal cookware coated with Teflon on a campfire, or anywhere else. Here's what you'll need:

### For the Dutch Oven

| | |
|---|---|
| 1 guinea hen | carrots |
| water | medium-size potatoes |

### For Stuffing and Paste

| | |
|---|---|
| bread | ¼ cup butter |
| sage | ½ teaspoon salt |
| chopped onion | salt and pepper |
| ¼ cup flour | |

Mix a stuffing of bread, sage, and chopped onion. Salt and pepper the inside of the guinea hen, then stuff it. (I also like to boil the guinea hen giblets until tender, chop them, and add them to the stuffing.) Make a paste with the butter, flour, and salt. Swab the breast and legs with the paste. Place the bird into the Dutch oven, breast-side up. Add 2 cups of hot water. Put the Dutch oven on hot coals and cover with the lid. Pile hot coals atop the lid. Cook for half an hour. Peel the potatoes and scrape the carrots with your knife, then add both to the pot. (When you remove the lid, check to see whether the guinea hen's breast has browned. If it has, do not replenish coals in the lid. If it hasn't browned, check it again after cooking another 20 minutes or so.) Cover again and cook for an hour. After that time, the potatoes and carrots should be tender. Remove the guinea hen and vegetables.

Ideally, the liquid will have cooked down very low and will have browned on the bottom. If it hasn't, continue cooking over the coals. Do not burn. If you want gravy, stir in 2 tablespoons of flour and ½ teaspoon salt. Stir well. Slowly add 2 cups of water, then continue to cook and stir until you have the gravy as thick as you want it. Serves 2 or 3.

**Note:** *I have been faithful to the list of ingredients used in this dish, but I have elaborated somewhat on the cooking technique. Ed Hopkins might put all this stuff in a Dutch oven and open the lid at the exact time when the pan drippings have browned perfectly on the bottom, but I feel that most of us, without daily practice, will need to take a peek or two.*

*Variations:* If you don't have a guinea hen at your place, or can't catch one, you might try a pullet or a pheasant. I recently used the technique to cook a domestic duck, skinned. It was super-good, and I wished that Mrs. Rawlings and Ed Hopkins were there to partake of it.

# VENISON LIVER AND
# ONIONS ON THE LID

Just because you've got a Dutch oven in camp doesn't mean that you have to use all of it, and build a large fire, in order to cook a good meal. Remember that the lid can be used over coals to pan-fry fish, chops, and so on. One of my favorite camp meals makes use of fresh venison liver, and it can be prepared on a Dutch oven lid. It's easy, and doesn't require a long list of ingredients.

| | |
|---|---|
| venison liver | medium onion |
| bacon | salt and pepper |
| flour | water |

Trim the liver, wash it, and cut it into fingers about ½ inch thick. Salt and pepper the strips and shake them in flour. Leave them in the flour for the time being. Fry the bacon on the lid until browned. Take it up and set it aside to drain, preferably on a brown paper bag. Slice the onion, separate the slices into rings, and sauté them in the bacon drippings for 5 minutes. Take up the onions and put them aside to drain. Brown the strips of liver on both sides for a few minutes. Do not overcook the liver. (If your lid is hot, and produces a good sizzle, cooking the liver for 3 minutes on each side will be about right, if the pieces are ½ inch thick.) When the liver is almost done, crumble the bacon and add it to the lid. Add the onions. Pour on a little water and cook for 5 minutes. Serve from the lid, spooning liver, onions, and pan drippings directly onto plates.

*Variations:* The last time I prepared this dish, I used diced salt pork instead of bacon. I also added a wild turkey liver to the venison liver, along with some fresh mushrooms. It was all very tasty. Rabbit liver is also very good when cooked by this recipe. And fresh chicken liver is almost as good.

# CAMP SNACKS

Your camp Dutch oven is ideal for cooking popcorn, which, of course, is very easy to transport and store. Merely heat the Dutch oven over coals and pour in some popcorn kernels. You might also consider parched corn, which is also easily cooked on a Dutch oven. Here's a quote from an article by Don Holm ("Dutch Oven Cookery") from the October 1972 issue of *Sports Afield*:

"How do you suppose the voyageurs paddled Hudson's Bay Company freight canoes all the way from Montreal to Fort Vancouver, packing most of their rations with them? They practically lived on parched corn.

"Preheat Dutch oven on hot coals. Do not use water or grease. Drop in shelled sweet corn kernels and toast them, turning or stirring frequently to keep from burning. When corn is brown and crunchy it is done.

"Like pemmican, parched corn is an ideal trail food, light and easily stored for long periods. It was a staple of the French-Canadians, the fur traders, and mountain men, as well as Indian tribes like the Arikaras and Mandans."

Parched corn, by the way, can be eaten warm or cold. I prefer mine warm, with a touch of salt and a cold beer.

> In 1813, when mountain man John Colter died of yellow jaundice, his Dutch oven sold for $4, the equivalent of a week's wages then. The iron pots were used not only for cooking but for boiling water to obtain salt at salt licks, melting lead for casting rifle balls, and as ransom to Indians.
>
> —*J. Wayne Fears*, Sports Afield

# CHAPTER 13

## Stovetop Dutch Ovens

**U**nlike the camp Dutch oven, the stovetop model has neither legs nor a flanged lid. It's flat on the bottom and has a domed lid on top. The lid is usually made of cast iron, but glass lids are also available. My personal choice is a heavy cast-iron lid with little equidistant protuberances underneath, so that condensation drips down evenly. Such a lid is called "self-basting."

This kind of Dutch oven was, of course, designed for sitting on top of a kitchen stove. Nevertheless, it can be used in camp and it can also be put into an oven. But it is primarily a stovetop piece, and as such it is hard to beat for cooking pot roasts, stews, fish chowders, and other dishes that gain from slow, even cooking in a tightly covered pot. The Dutch oven can also be used, to great advantage, as a deep fryer. Remember, however, that a large Dutch oven may not work on a small one-burner camp stove simply because it dissipates too much heat.

Thousands of good recipes could be listed below, and any good family cookbook will have directions for various stews and pot roasts. I am, however, adding two of my favorites, both of which happen to be Irish in origin. Personally, I don't make too much of the Irish connection, but I have a friend who says that the Dutch oven was really invented by the Irish—the folks who also, he claims, invented cast iron itself and discovered thyme.

# STRUISIN GAELACH

My friend puffs up and turns red of face when I tell him that Irish potatoes, which is a name often given to ordinary Idaho potatoes, originally came from America. Whatever he says, it follows that Irish stew really ought to be called American stew, since it has a potato base, although, I allow, some people make it with turnip roots instead of potatoes. In any case, my recipe was adapted from *Traditional Irish Recipes* by George L. Thomson.

| | |
|---|---|
| 3 pounds lamb, cubed | ½ tablespoon chopped parsley |
| 2 pounds potatoes | 1 teaspoon thyme |
| 1 pound onions | 1 teaspoon salt |
| 1½ cups meat stock or bouillon | ½ teaspoon pepper |

If feasible, select both large and small potatoes and onions. Preheat the oven to 325 degrees. Slice a large potato and line the bottom of a Dutch oven with the slices. Peel the onions, slice one, and add a layer above the potatoes. Trim the meat and put it on top of the onions. On top of the meat, put the rest of the onions, either whole or quartered. Sprinkle on the parsley, thyme, salt, and pepper. Next, add the rest of the potatoes, either whole or quartered, depending on size; peeled or unpeeled, depending on preference. Add the stock. Cover tightly and put into the preheated oven. Cook for 2 hours without peeking. Serves 6 to 8.

This same recipe also makes a great camp dish, partly because it doesn't require lots of dainty or fragile ingredients, such as chicken eggs. Of course, the recipe can be cooked in a camp Dutch oven.

# ANRAITH BHAINBH

The Irish also have a dish called grunt soup, made with small perch. I tried it with American bluegills and some chopped onions (which were not in the original recipe). It was delicious, and I want to pass it on. Because the name "grunt soup" doesn't sound too good, I'm going back to the Gaelic for the name. If you want to try my version of anraith bhainbh, here's what you'll need:

12 bluegills or other small fish

1 quart water

½ stick margarine

1 medium onion

1 tablespoon flour

½ tablespoon dried chopped parsley

½ tablespoon dried chopped chives

½ teaspoon salt

¼ teaspoon pepper

Scale the fish and clean them. I leave the heads on, but this is optional. Put the fish into a Dutch oven and pour in 1 quart of water. Add the salt. Bring to a boil, then reduce the heat and simmer for a few minutes, or until the fish flake easily from the bone. While the fish are simmering, melt the margarine in a skillet and chop the onion. Sauté the onion for about 3 or 4 minutes, then stir in the flour slowly. Leave the skillet on very low heat. Meanwhile, remove the fish from the Dutch oven and drain in a colander. (Be careful not to leave any fins or parts of the fish in the liquid.) Turn the Dutch oven heat up just a little and gently boil the liquid, uncovered.

Using a fork, carefully pull the meat from the fish bones. And stir the flour from time to time. After about 10 minutes (or quicker if the onions are getting too brown), add the roux to the liquid in the Dutch oven. Also add the chives, parsley, and pepper. Finish pulling the meat from the fish bones. Add the fish to the Dutch oven and simmer for 10 minutes. Serve as an appetizer or as a meal, along with boiled potatoes, bread, green vegetable, and salad.

*Camp Variation:* This recipe can also be cooked with a camp Dutch oven. Merely use the lid of the Dutch oven instead of a skillet to brown the onions and roux. Also, try the recipe with wild onions instead of regular onions, using the fresh green tops instead of the parsley and chives.

*Note: Any good fish of mild flavor can be used in the recipe above. I make it more often with bluegills simply because I, or my children, catch lots of them. I've also made it with crappie heads. Of course, fish heads contain some of the best meat, but most people throw them out. Whether you use heads or whole fish, make sure that you get all the bones out before putting the meat into the soup. Gnawing on fish heads is permitted only in the privacy of the kitchen, not at the dining table.*

# DUTCH OVEN VENISON

The following recipe illustrates how a Dutch oven can be used on top of the stove or in the oven, or both, and how to first brown the meat and then to "braise" it. A meat rack is also used, and, I might add, an 8-inch cast-iron rack (also called a trivet) is manufactured especially for Dutch ovens. The recipe comes from *Alaska Magazine's Cabin Cookbook*, which explains, "Sometimes a deer has lived too long to yield tender steaks and roasts, and that is when we must resort to braising.

"Cut the venison into serving-size pieces and dredge with whole wheat flour. Season with salt, pepper, and any other seasonings you wish. Thyme and marjoram are both good here, as well as dried bell pepper pieces and minced onions. . . .

"Heat about ¼ inch of fat in a Dutch oven and brown the meat slowly in the fat, turning the pieces to ensure even browning. Then put a rack under the meat, add about ¼ cup of water, and cover the pan tightly. Continue cooking over low heat or in a slow oven (300 degrees) until tender (about 1½ to 2 hours). Add a little more water from time to time if necessary to keep the venison from scorching."

The above recipe makes very good gravy, and I am fond of using it to cook lean beef as well as venison.

Cast-iron kettles, once popular for fireplace cooking, make great pots for cooking atop a modern stove.

# VENISON GRILLADES

Here's a breakfast or brunch dish that is customarily made with veal or beef cutlets. My copy of *The Tabasco Cookbook* suggests making the dish with venison—and this is right down my alley. I recommend it to all hunters who want to please the wife and pave the way for future hunts. Take venison loin or tenderloin cutlets, cut about 1 inch thick, and pound down to ¼ inch with a wooden mallet. The measurements below will normally feed four people, but for an anniversary feast, you may want to serve the recipe for two. The dish is usually eaten with cheese grits or spoon bread. I like it with canned whole-kernel hominy, either white or yellow, available in some supermarkets.

Grillades should be refrigerated overnight and reheated in the morning for serving.

5 tablespoons bacon drippings or cooking oil

1½ pounds thin venison cutlets

4 tablespoons flour

1 cup chopped green pepper

1 cup chopped onion

1 cup chopped celery with green tops

2 or 3 toes garlic, minced

1 cup peeled, seeded, and chopped fresh tomatoes

1 cup beef broth

½ cup red wine

2 bay leaves

1 tablespoon Worcestershire sauce

freshly ground sea salt and black pepper to taste

cayenne pepper or Tabasco sauce to taste

¼ cup chopped fresh parsley or cilantro

Heat 3 tablespoons of the bacon drippings or cooking oil in a stovetop Dutch oven. Working in small batches, sear the meat until lightly browned on both sides. Do not overcook. Remove the meat to drain. Add the remaining 2 tablespoons of bacon drippings or oil to the pan drippings, stirring with a wooden spoon to dislodge any little brown grimmilies that may have stuck to the bottom. Add the flour and cook over low heat for 20 or 30 minutes, stirring frequently, to make a roux. Meanwhile, mix the celery, onion, and green pepper—called the holy trinity of Creole cooking.

When the roux is ready, quickly remove the pot from the heat and stir in the holy trinity to arrest the cooking before the bottom of the roux burns. Add the garlic and cook a few minutes longer, stirring as you go with your wooden spoon. Stir

The campfire kettle is ideal for sitting over a bed of hot coals, or for suspending over the fire by the bail.

in the tomatoes, beef broth, wine, bay leaves, Worcestershire, salt, pepper, and cayenne or Tabasco. Return the venison cutlets to the pot, cover, and simmer for an hour or so, stirring from time to time, until the meat is very tender. Throw out the bay leaves. Stir in the parsley or cilantro. Cover and refrigerate overnight. When you are ready to feast in the morning, warm the dish up and serve with cheese grits, spoon bread, or heated whole-kernel hominy.

# MONTANA BISON BOURGUIGNON

Boeuf bourguignon is one of the world's greatest stews, and unlike many French recipes, it doesn't require many sauces and a long list of ingredients. Beef, of course, is used in the classic French boeuf bourguignon, but I think the rich dark meat of bison works even better. Bison meat is available commercially, or you may pay to hunt on dude ranches. For this recipe, use any bison stew meat, but the fatty hump is perfect. Many modern recipes call for tomatoes, carrots, and all manner of stuff. The essence of the classic dish, however, is good red meat, mushrooms, onions, and burgundy wine in some plenty.

| | |
|---|---|
| 1 large onion | 2 cups burgundy wine |
| 1 pound small button mushrooms | 2 cups brown meat stock or canned beef broth |
| ½ cup butter | freshly ground sea salt and peppercorns |
| ¼ pound salt pork, diced | ½ cup cooking oil or lard |
| 4 pounds bison stew meat | 20 to 30 pearl onions |
| 1 teaspoon dried thyme | ½ cup flour |

Mince the large onion and stems from the mushrooms. Heat about half the butter in a stovetop Dutch oven. Sauté the minced onion and mushroom stems to sweeten the pan and get the aroma going. Set the sautéed onions and mushrooms aside to drain.

Sauté the salt pork until you have plenty of cooking grease and some nice cracklings. Drain the cracklings and save them for noshing. Dust the stew meat with flour and brown it in the skillet, working in several small batches. When all the meat is nicely browned, put it into the Dutch oven. Add the thyme, most of the red wine, and all the meat stock. Stir in the sautéed onion and mushroom stems, along with a little salt and pepper. Cover the pot and simmer for an hour and a half, stirring from time to time and adding more salt and pepper if needed.

Meanwhile, reheat the skillet and add some butter to the remaining oil, about half and half. Add a little cooking oil if needed. Sauté the pearl onions and mushroom caps, working in several batches and spooning them into the pot as you go. (If the mushrooms are larger than a golf ball, cut them in half or into quarters.) When all the pearl onions and mushroom caps have been added to the pot, pour most of the oil out of the skillet and deglaze with a swirl of red wine. Pour the fond into the pot, bring to heat, and simmer for a few more minutes, stirring and tasting and adjusting the seasonings if needed. Serve hot with boiled new potatoes, sliced green beans, rice or pasta, and a good bread. Open another bottle of good French burgundy.

**Note:** *This dish is even better the next day, so that it can be made ahead of time. Leftovers are great.*

Some modern cast-iron pots, or saucepans, are convenient for stovetop cooking. The cast-iron handle permits the piece to be put into the oven.

# CHAPTER

## Cooking Cajun

Cajun dishes, for some reason or another, just seem to come out better in cast iron.

—The Frank Davis Seafood Notebook

**C**ajun cooking and Creole cooking, if there is a difference, have gotten into a mess over the years. I'm not going to straighten it out, even if I thought that I could. The Cajuns might blame the rest of the country for corrupting this recipe or that, but the problem is really with the Cajuns themselves. While the general reader wants for definition, so as to know what's what, you can find cookbooks, written by Cajuns or at least by people in lower Louisiana, that contain hundreds of recipes for jambalayas having neither ham nor rice in them, and just as many recipes for gumbos without okra.

For example, I recently counted seven gumbo recipes from *The Justin Wilson Gourmet and Gourmand Cookbook*, and more than half of these don't have okra listed in the ingredients. Without okra, some of these dishes could just have easily been called soup, stew, goulash, or, yes, jambalaya. Wilson no doubt cooks better than he talks, and talks better than he spells and writes, and I suppose he has got license to do pretty much what he wants to do with language or food and call it Cajun.

Moreover, Paul Prudhomme's *Louisiana Kitchen* has lots of gumbo recipes listed and, again, more than half of them contain no okra at all. I confess that I haven't looked deeply or even widely into the matter, and don't intend to do so simply because I've seen all that I want to see. In fact, I hereby wash my hands of the mess, but I must say, before moving on, that I have noticed that Cajun cookbooks have lots of cast-iron cookware pieces in the photographs! The authors may talk about zapping out a roux in a microwave oven, or in a thin Teflon-coated pan, but when it gets down to Cajun on Cajun, they'll reach for cast iron every time.

# JAMBALAYA

A cast-iron frying pan with a large diameter (13 inches or so) and a cover works best for jambalaya, but the dish can also be made in a Dutch oven. Jambalaya should have ham and rice in it, but the other ingredients can, and do, vary from one batch to the next. Here's what I recommend for openers:

| | |
|---|---|
| 1 cup long-grain rice, uncooked | 1 large onion, diced |
| 1 pound smoke-cured ham | 1 green pepper, diced |
| 2 pounds chicken breasts | ½ teaspoon thyme |
| 6 slices bacon | 1 teaspoon salt |
| 1 cup chicken broth, hot | ½ teaspoon black pepper |
| 1 can tomatoes (16-ounce size) | 1 tablespoon Worcestershire sauce |
| 8 ounces fresh mushrooms, whole | Tabasco sauce to taste |
| 1 stalk celery, chopped with leaves | |

Fry the bacon in a large skillet until crisp and set it aside on a brown paper bag to drain. Cut the ham into chunks. Skin and bone the chicken breast; cut the meat into chunks. Brown the meat in the bacon drippings, take it up, and set it aside to drain with the bacon. Add the rice to the bacon drippings in the skillet and cook on low until it starts to brown. Add the onions, celery, mushrooms, and green pepper. Sauté on low heat for 8 minutes. Chop the canned tomatoes and add them to the skillet, along with the juice. Add the chicken broth. Put the chicken, ham, and crumbled bacon into the skillet. Stir in the thyme, salt, black pepper, and Worcestershire sauce. Bring to heat, cover tightly, reduce the heat, and simmer for 30 minutes. About 10 minutes before serving, taste for seasoning. Add Tabasco sauce to taste, along with more salt if needed. Let sit for a few minutes before serving. Feeds 8.

*Variations:* Substitute alligator meat or turtle for the chicken. Add other vegetables, in modest amounts, if you have them at hand and need to clean out the refrigerator. Also, remember that many people like sausage in their jambalaya instead of ham. Try it.

# CREOLE FRIED CHICKEN

Here's an old New Orleans recipe, made without the highly spiced Cajun dust that we see in many modern creations from that important part of the culinary world.

1 fryer (2 to 2½ pounds)

1½ cups fine cracker meal

½ cup flour

2 chicken eggs

milk

salt and white pepper

peanut oil

Cut the chicken into conventional serving pieces. (If you must, substitute breasts, thighs, and so on, prepackaged from the supermarket.) Sprinkle the pieces with salt and white pepper. Whisk the egg, a little milk, and a pinch of salt in a small bowl. Pour the egg wash over the chicken and let it stand for an hour or so, mixing from time to time.

When you are ready to proceed, heat about an inch of peanut oil in a skillet to medium hot. Mix the cracker meal and flour, then roll each piece of chicken in the mixture, shaking off the excess. Fry the chicken a few pieces at a time for about 12 to 15 minutes, or until each piece is done. Serve hot.

Add the water, white wine vinegar, tomato sauce, bell pepper, celery, and onion. Let simmer for 15 minutes. Add the rabbit pieces.

### *Late Additions*

| | |
|---|---|
| 3 cloves garlic, minced | 2 green onions with tops, finely chopped |
| ¼ cup parsley, chopped | rice (cooked separately) |

Sprinkle the dish with minced garlic, parsley, and green onion tops. Stir. Simmer uncovered for 15 minutes. Serve over rice. Feeds 4 to 6.

# CHAPTER

## 15

# Mexican Cooking, Cast-Iron Style

**B**efore the Spanish and the French arrived, native Mexican cooking no doubt developed with the aid of earthenware pots and possibly heated flat rocks. The tortilla, for example, was probably first cooked on a flat rock. And chili was probably stewed in an olla, which would require long, slow cooking. Another speculation: Pinto beans were cooked in an olla for long hours, and leftover beans were mashed up and warmed on a hot flat rock, making the original *frijoles refritos*. In any case, I find that a cast-iron griddle (or skillet) does a great job on tortillas, and cast-iron Dutch ovens or pots work nicely on slow-cooked chili.

## CHILI

The term "chili con carne" means "pepper with meat." Thus, any meat cooked down with chili peppers, or with powder made primarily with dried and ground hot chili peppers, would be the real stuff. Over the years, two other native Mexican ingredients—beans and tomatoes—were naturally added in one way or another. Some modern Americans even assume that chili has beans in it. I suggest that you cook the beans separately, then add them to the chili bowls for those who want them, or serve them as a side dish.

Other grounds for chili arguments arise over the kind of meat. Some want ground meat; others want the meat cut into chunks. Personally, I prefer the chunks, or a mixture. I also like a mixture of meats, as, for example, part venison and part lean pork or javelina. (For convenience, the recipe below calls for pork and beef.)

Chili profits from long, slow cooking, and I think that a cast-iron pot or Dutch oven is ideal.

2 pounds lean beef, trimmed and cubed

1 pound fresh pork, trimmed and cubed

6 slices bacon

1 can tomato sauce (12-ounce size)

1 large onion, chopped

3 cloves garlic, minced

1 large bell pepper, chopped

2 jalapeño peppers, seeded and minced

2 tablespoons prepared chili powder

1 teaspoon salt

½ teaspoon cumin seed, crushed

½ teaspoon dried oregano leaves

2 cups beef broth

In a Dutch oven, fry the bacon until crisp. Put the bacon on a brown paper bag to drain. Crumble when cool. In the bacon drippings, brown the diced beef and pork, stirring in the onion, garlic, and bell pepper. Add the beef broth, chili powder, jalapeño peppers, salt, cumin seeds, and oregano. Stir in the tomato sauce. Bring to a boil. Reduce the heat to very low, cover, and simmer for 4 or 5 hours. Add a little water from time to time, if needed. Note, however, that this particular recipe was designed to be on the thick side. Serve it in a bowl with crackers and pinto beans (cooked separately). Also, try a handful of chopped onion (chilled) on top of each bowl. Or, roll some freshly made, hot tortillas and dunk them into the chili. Feeds 6 to 8.

Some Mexican food experts bake or roast jalapeño peppers until the skin cracks. Then they peel them, cut them in half, seed them, and use them as needed. This might add something to, say, a stuffed pepper snack, but I think it is a waste of time for a dish like chili that is to be cooked for hours.

Remember that chili just doesn't taste right if you don't cook it in an iron pot. I suppose a little of the iron leaches out in the chili and provides that little extra push it needs.

—*Linda West Eckhardt,* The Only Texas Cookbook

# TEXAS CHILI

Be warned that the recipe above has a strong, thick tomato base. You may also want to try another recipe, without any kind of tomato ingredient. I call the recipe below Texas Chili, but, frankly, it's hard to tell where Texas quits and Mexico starts.

| | |
|---|---|
| 3 pounds ground beef (lean) | 6 tablespoons chili powder |
| ½ cup cooking oil | 1 teaspoon cumin seed, crushed |
| 2 large onions, chopped | 6 cups beef stock |
| 3 cloves garlic, minced | salt and pepper to taste |

In a Dutch oven, heat the oil and sauté the onions and garlic for 5 minutes, then take them up with a large spoon. Brown the ground beef, then pour off the oil from the Dutch oven. Return the onions and garlic. Add the beef stock, chili powder, and cumin seeds. Stir and bring to a boil. Reduce the heat, cover, and simmer for at least an hour. Add a little salt to taste. Add pepper if needed. Simmer for a few more minutes and serve. Feeds 6 to 8.

# TORTILLAS

Once I rode across the Rio Grande on a donkey to a small Mexican village. The aroma of good food filled the air, but, to be honest, I didn't see a peasant woman patting out perfectly round tortillas with the palms of her hands. I've tried it myself, and it did not take me long to determine that, in this matter, practice would not make perfect. Fortunately, however, hand patting isn't necessary; anyone can press out a few for home use with the aid of two sheets of waxed paper and a flat-bottomed pie plate, as directed below. If you plan to put up a taco stand in a busy place, however, you would profit by having a mechanical tortilla press.

Some books about Mexican foods specify tamalina or masa harina, which is sometimes available in places that traffic in Mexican ingredients. I use ordinary white stone-ground cornmeal, fine grind, from the grocery store. It should, however, be very fine, like flour. Some of the coarse yellow meals simply won't work, and any meal, white, yellow, or blue, whose label contains the words "self-rising," should be avoided. What you need is ground corn, with nothing put into it—or taken away from it.

**2 cups white cornmeal, fine stone-ground**          **1 cup boiling-hot water**

Mix the cornmeal and the water, making a stiff dough. Shape the dough into balls, using about 1½ tablespoons per ball. (The above measures should make twelve tortillas.) Set the dough balls aside while you heat a cast-iron griddle (or large skillet) on medium heat. Do not grease the griddle or spray it with no-stick stuff.

Tear off some squares of waxed paper. Put one square on a flat, smooth surface. Put a dough ball in the center. Center another piece of waxed paper on top of the dough ball. Position a pie plate over the dough and press straight down. The dough will spread out to a circle of about 6 inches in diameter, and to a thickness of about ⅛ inch. How hard do you press? This is easy, once you get the hang of it. Start with a clear Pyrex pie plate and you can watch the dough spread!

When the griddle is hot, carefully remove the top sheet of waxed paper and flip the uncooked tortilla over onto the surface of the griddle. Carefully remove the waxed paper. Cook for a couple of minutes. Turn and cook the other side for 2 minutes.

For best results, stack the tortillas and keep them hot until you are ready to eat. Mexicans will turn a bowl over them to hold in the heat, and it is also common practice to cover them with a wet, steaming-hot cloth on a warmed plate or platter. If they will be eaten right away, a basket covered with a napkin will do. If the tortillas get cold and somewhat dry, they can be sprinkled lightly with water and reheated before serving.

With the tortillas, you can make tacos or enchiladas or other Mexican specialties. Or you can eat them like bread. First, melt a little butter. Then roll a tortilla, hold it like a bundle between your fingers, dip the end into the melted butter, and take a bite. Repeat the process. When eating tortillas this way, I like a little salt in the butter.

*Corn Chips:* After you cook a batch of tortillas, cut them into strips about ½ inch wide and 2 inches long. Heat 1 inch of peanut oil in a skillet. Carefully put a dozen or so of the strips into the hot oil. Fry until browned, which will take only a minute. Take up and place on a brown paper bag to drain. Salt lightly. Repeat the procedure until all the tortilla strips have been fried. Serve while hot, or warm.

*Tostados:* The corn chips described above are intended to be eaten by themselves. If you have dip or meat sauce, follow the directions for corn chips, but cut the tortillas into triangles before frying.

*Taco Shells:* Heat ½ inch of peanut oil in a skillet. Using tongs, place one tortilla into the hot oil. Carefully hold one edge of the tortilla with the tongs, lift it out of the oil slightly, and fold it over until you form the shape of a taco shell. Hold it in this position until the bottom half cooks and is crisp. Turn the taco over with the tongs and cook the other half until it is crisp.

# FLOUR TORTILLAS

Some folks prefer flour tortillas to those made of cornmeal, and a number of recipes call for them. Here's a good recipe to try on your griddle:

| | |
|---|---|
| **2 cups white flour** | **½ teaspoon salt** |
| **2 tablespoons lard** | **warm water** |

In a bowl, mix the flour and salt. Cut in the lard, then slowly mix in enough warm water to make a soft dough; usually, a tad over ½ cup will be about right. Let the dough sit for 20 minutes, then divide it into eight or nine balls of equal size. Dust a smooth surface with a little flour and roll the balls out. The dough should be at least 8 inches in diameter, and about ⅛ inch thick. (Usually, you can find a bowl top or some dish that will be about the right diameter; this can be used to help cut the dough in a circle.) One at a time, carefully place the flat dough rounds on a heated ungreased griddle. Cook for 1½ to 2 minutes on each side, turning carefully with a pancake spatula. Do not brown either side.

Stack the tortillas on a warm surface and wrap them with a warm, slightly damp cloth until you are ready to serve them, or to use them as an ingredient in other recipes.

# CHAPTER

## 16

# '49er and Sourdough Cooking

Cast-iron skillets were fastened to the backs of covered wagons and carried along when families heeded the advice, "Go West!" The '49ers loaded their black iron and headed out to California to find their fortunes in gold, and many of the miners used small skillets to pan for gold when they got there.

—*Diana Becker Finlay*

**T**he '49ers, and, a little later, the Alaskan camp cooks who became known as "sourdoughs," had to make do in remote areas. Even if their grubstake was large, transportation and replenishment were problems. I'm sure that they made use of native fruits, berries, and greens in season, as well as available fish and game. As I see it, however, these men were too busy looking for gold to waste much time foraging for food. Bread was their sustenance. To make it, they used a sourdough starter, which was kept from one batch to another. I'm sure that they baked loaves of bread and batches of biscuits from time to time, especially when the cabin was snowed under, but I feel that the flapjack was what they cooked more often than not. Just the other night, I was reading a pamphlet called *An Illinois Gold Hunter in the Black Hills*, written in 1876, and the author, Jerry Bryan, made several references to what he called "'49er Slapjacks."

Sourdough breads can still be made in camp, or at home. There must be a thousand sourdough recipes, but all of them have one thing in common: a starter. Most modern people who make sourdough breads save the starter from one batch to the next, partly because sourdough is believed to improve with age. If you lose your starter, you'll have to borrow some from a neighbor in the next wagon, or you'll have to start from scratch. Good starters can be made from potatoes as well as from sour milk, and, of course, many recipes and procedures can be found. Some practitioners make a ritual of sourdough, and insist on making a first batch of starter to sweeten the crock; then they throw it away and make a second batch in the same crock. While one starter may not be quite as good as another, too much depends on other conditions, such as temperature and humidity, for cabin cooks to get the same taste year after year. In short, most modern cooks will come out just as good by using dry yeast to make a starter. Of course, dry yeast is available in small packages at any grocery store. Here's a recipe that's easy to remember.

## SOURDOUGH STARTER

**1 package dry yeast (¼-ounce envelope)**          **2 cups flour**
**2 cups lukewarm water**

Sift your flour if it has got weevils in it. Heat some water until it is warm to the touch, about like milk for babies. In a glass or crockery container, slowly mix all the ingredients and beat well. Cover with a piece of cheesecloth or clean sheeting. Let the starter stand in a warm place for 48 hours. (Do not use aluminum foil or plastic film to cover the starter, and do not keep it in a closed cabinet.) Stir the starter every 8 hours or so. As the starter ferments, bubbles will form, the mixture will rise somewhat, and the characteristic sour smell will develop. After 48 hours, the starter (called a sponge when it is ready to use) can be kept in the refrigerator. A clear liquid may gather on top of the sponge. Stir it back in before using the starter.

After you remove a cup of starter for a recipe, replace it with a fresh batch of flour and water. (No additional yeast is necessary.) Merely mix equal parts of flour and warm water, then stir a cup of the mixture into the remaining starter. Cover the new starter with a cloth and leave it in a warm place for about 10 hours. Then refrigerate it until you are ready to cook more sourdough bread, biscuits, or pancakes. It's best to add new flour and water to the starter once a week. After adding new flour and water, let the starter sit in a warm place for a day or so.

In the method above, several cups of starter are kept at hand, ready to use. Some people, I might add, hold out only a cup of starter, and they mix all of it into a new batch, forming a sponge, the night before cooking with it. Then a cup of the sponge is held back for a starter.

# SOURDOUGH BISCUITS

I haven't seen a lard can lately, but when I was growing up, they were commonly used around the house and farm. If I remember correctly, they held about 5 gallons. Back then, lard was a very popular oil for cooking. But, alas, it is high in cholesterol and has been replaced, on supermarket shelves, almost entirely by vegetable oils.

The old chuck-wagon cooks used lots of lard, as well as oil rendered from salt pork, for baking sourdough breads. But in some remote camps, such as those set up by the mountain men, some of the '49ers, and the "sourdough" cooks of Alaska, lard was sometimes hard to come by. They no doubt substituted other animal fats, and lard made from bear fat was highly regarded. For the record, I'll add that the lightest biscuits I've ever eaten were made with goose grease substituted for the lard in the recipe below. If you don't have hog lard or goose grease, use vegetable shortening or oil, as well as butter, margarine, or bacon drippings.

| | |
|---|---|
| 1 cup sourdough starter (see recipe above) | 1½ teaspoons sugar |
| 1 cup flour | 1 teaspoon baking powder |
| ¼ cup lard | ¼ teaspoon salt |

In a large bowl, mix the flour, sugar, baking powder, and salt. Then cut in the lard or other shortening. This can be accomplished with a pastry blender. If you don't have one of these, try working two knives in a crisscross manner. When you finish, the pastry should resemble bread crumbs. Form a hole in the center of this mixture and pour the cup of sourdough starter into it. Stir the starter with a wooden spoon until all of the flour mixture has been mixed into the starter. Place a handful of flour on a smooth surface and spread it out evenly. Turn the dough out of the bowl onto the flour surface and knead it a few times to make the dough smooth. Do not knead very long, as working it will produce a tough biscuit. Pat the dough gently down to a thickness of about ¾ inch. Grease the bottom and about half the sides of your Dutch oven lightly. Break off pieces of the biscuit dough, about the size of a golf ball, and place them into the Dutch oven. I like for mine to touch, which will produce fluffy pull-apart biscuits. (Your Dutch oven will hold more of these. If you want thinner, crisper biscuits, make the dough ½ inch thick and cut the biscuits out with a biscuit cutter or jar mouth.) Sit the Dutch oven in a warm, draft-free place for 10 minutes so that the dough can rise a little. If you are in camp on a cold night, sit the Dutch oven beside the fire, but not too close, and turn it around after 5 minutes.

While the biscuits are rising, mix 1 cup of flour and 1 cup of warm water. Stir this into your starter so that you will be ready for the next batch of biscuits.

When you are ready to bake, preheat the lid and place it atop the Dutch oven. Rake some coals from the fire and place the Dutch oven on them. Then pile some coals on top of the lid. Check the biscuits after 15 minutes. Add more coals on top, if needed. Check every 5 minutes until the rolls are browned on the top and on the bottom. (Also see Cowboy Biscuits, page 128.)

**Note:** *This recipe will make a dozen large biscuits. If your Dutch oven won't hold this many, cook in two batches.*

# SOURDOUGH FRENCH BREAD

Most sourdough bread that is baked commercially in San Francisco and other places might be made with an age-old, secret recipe and starter (as advertised), but consistent results are obtained only with the aid of sophisticated baking equipment. Such consistency is difficult to obtain in the home kitchen during changeable weather. On the other hand, making bread exactly the same each time makes it a science rather than an art, and takes some of the excitement out of it.

To be honest, sourdough French bread doesn't depend very much on cast iron. True, it can be made in a Dutch oven, but usually it is made in a kitchen oven on tin cookie sheets. On the other hand, the heating properties of cast iron are not without value, and a neat bread pan, shaped like two loaves of bread joined together, is still manufactured of cast iron and is, in fact, called a French bread pan. The recipe below will fit it nicely.

Cast-iron bread pans are available for cooking two perfectly shaped loaves of French bread.

| | |
|---|---|
| 2 cups sourdough starter | 1 tablespoon sugar |
| 4 cups flour | 1 tablespoon cooking oil |
| 1 cup warm water | ¼ teaspoon salt |
| more flour | |

Put 4 cups of flour into a bowl. Mix in 1 tablespoon sugar, ¼ teaspoon salt, and 1 tablespoon cooking oil. Make a hole in the center of the mixture and pour in 2 cups of starter and 1 cup of warm water. With a wooden spoon, stir the starter until all of the flour mixture has been taken in. Add a little more flour if you think the dough will take it.

Turn the dough out onto a smooth, well-floured surface. Knead for 10 minutes or longer, adding a little flour as needed to make a smooth, elastic dough. Let the dough rest for 10 minutes. Divide the dough and shape each half into a long, narrow loaf. Grease the cast-iron French bread pan (or a cookie sheet) and place the loaves in it. With a sharp knife, make 45-degree cuts about 1 inch apart along the length of the loaf. Put the bread in a warm spot and let it rise until it doubles in size, which will usually take about an hour and a half.

Preheat the oven to 450 degrees. Bake the bread on a center rack for 15 minutes. Brush the top of each loaf with cold water. Lower the heat to 350 degrees and bake for 20 to 30 minutes, until the crust begins to brown.

I might point out that this recipe, like many other recipes for breads and meats, starts with a high temperature and ends with a lower temperature—which is exactly what happens in an old Dutch oven.

*Warning:* Sourdough French bread is difficult to make, and you should cook this recipe (or another similar recipe for this bread) several times before inviting guests over to eat it. Be warned, however, that even if you cook it perfectly, some people are not going to appreciate the tough, chewy surface that distinguishes both French and Italian breads. I might add that most French housewives don't normally attempt to bake this bread; instead, they buy it at the bakery. So, be prepared for failure in making this bread, and for hee-haws if you do succeed with it. I like its wonderful flavor, however, and, personally, I've never cooked a loaf that wasn't good at least for dunking in coffee. Except once—and even then my dog Buff liked to chew on it.

# SOURDOUGH FLAPJACKS

My recipe for sourdough flapjacks was influenced heavily by *Alaska Magazine*'s *Cabin Cookbook*, which stated, "Hotcakes are about the most popular of all sourdough recipes, and rightly so. If you have any left over they make good sandwiches to take on the trail, and some birds really go for them in a big way when they are broken into pieces."

This recipe makes a very light flapjack.

| | |
|---|---|
| ½ cup sourdough starter | 1 tablespoon sugar |
| 2 cups flour | 2 teaspoons baking soda |
| 2 cups warm water | 1 teaspoon salt |
| 2 medium chicken eggs | |

The night before you are to have flapjacks for breakfast, mix 2 cups of flour and 2 cups of warm water in a glass or crockery container. With a wooden spoon, stir in ½ cup sourdough starter. Cover the container with cheesecloth and put it into a warm place. Let it work overnight. When you are ready to cook, whisk the eggs lightly and stir them into the sponge, along with the sugar, baking soda, and salt. Heat the cast-iron griddle and cook immediately. Turn once. Serve with wild honey, butter if you have it, and strong black coffee.

*Blueberry Variation:* Alaska is noted for wild berries in season, and blueberries are bountiful in some areas. In any case, they are especially good in sourdough pancakes. I make these by merely adding blueberries to the recipe above. But don't mix the blueberries into the batter. Instead, spoon the batter onto the griddle as usual, then quickly add 8 or 10 blueberries on top of the flapjack. Turn and cook the other side. I prefer to serve blueberry pancakes in stacks of three, with butter between each layer, whipped cream on top, and a thick syrup on the side.

# CHAPTER 17

## Yankee Cooking, Cast-Iron Style

**O**ften we see the terms "cast iron" or "black iron pot" applied to Cajun cooking or Southern cooking or Caribbean cooking. Also, during this country's great westward expansion, the Dutch oven and the cast-iron skillet became associated, in the mind's eye, with the rugged life on the frontier and in the great outdoors. Yet, the real cast-iron cookery in this country just might have been perfected at the domestic hearthside back east, where, I presume, more leisure and less concern for bears and native peoples permitted the creation of good foodstuffs. The popular image is of the good wife in long dress, apron, and bonnet stooping before a hearth while the man of the house sits back puffing on a long-stemmed clay pipe. Maybe, maybe not. The recipes below show that the Yankee men just might have taken an interest in cooking long before the cast-iron patio grill was invented.

# DANIEL WEBSTER'S FISH CHOWDER

Arguments will always crop up about what exactly should go into a fish chowder, and whether or not this recipe or that ought to be called New England chowder, Manhattan chowder, or what. When all the thousands of recipes are counted and the day of reckoning comes, here's one that will surely be high on the list. I found it in the old book *Foods of Our Forefathers*, which in turn quoted it from the 1931 edition of Suzanne Cary Gruver's *The Cape Cod Cook Book*.

The recipe, said to be suitable for a large fishing party, is in Webster's own words:

"Take a cod of ten pounds, well cleaned, leaving on the skin. Cut into pieces one and a half pounds thick, preserving the head whole. Take one and a half pounds of clear, fat, salt pork, cut in thin slices. Do the same with twelve potatoes. Take the largest pot you have. Try out the pork first; then take out the pieces of pork, leaving the drippings. Add to that three parts of water, a layer of fish, so as to cover the bottom of the pot; next, a layer of potatoes, then two tablespoons of salt, 1 teaspoon of pepper, then the pork, another layer of fish, and the remainder of the potatoes.

"Fill the pot with water to cover the ingredients. Put it over a good fire. Let the chowder boil twenty-five minutes. When this is done, have a quart of boiling milk ready, and ten hard crackers split and dipped in cold water. Add milk and crackers. Let the whole boil five minutes. The chowder is then ready and will be first rate if you have followed the directions. An onion may be added if you like the flavor."

By "try," Webster meant to fry or sauté the salt pork until most of the grease cooks out of it, as when making cracklings. Anyway, be sure to try this old recipe in camp or at home. Webster said to use the largest pot that you have. A large cast-iron Dutch oven will be suitable. Cod has always been a popular fish in New England, but any good fish of mild flavor will be fine.

# A YANKEE CORN BREAD

Mark Twain once wrote that Yankees don't know how to make good corn bread. They may think they know, he went on, but they really don't. I agree. Thousands of recipes these days make it hard to tell what's what, but I believe that this recipe, adapted from Sheila Buff's *Corn Cookery*, is the real stuff, for better or worse. The use of chicken eggs, baking powder, milk, wheat flour, and even sugar seems to be typical.

| | |
|---|---|
| 1 cup cornmeal | ¼ cup butter |
| 1 cup flour | 2 chicken eggs |
| 1 cup milk | 1 tablespoon baking powder |
| ¼ cup sugar | ½ teaspoon salt |

Preheat the oven to 400°F. Place the butter in an 8-inch cast-iron skillet and put it into the oven. In a suitable bowl, mix the cornmeal, flour, baking powder, sugar, and salt. In a smaller bowl, whisk together the eggs and milk.

Using your heat-proof glove to hold the hot skillet handle, swirl the melted butter around in the skillet to coat the sides of the skillet, then pour it out of the skillet into the egg mixture. Stir this into the dry mixture and turn the batter out into the hot skillet. Bake in the center of the oven for 20 to 25 minutes, until the top is golden brown and the bread is starting to pull away from the sides of the skillet.

# NANTUCKET FIREMAN'S SUPPER

Here's another recipe that came from *The Cape Cod Cook Book*. It called for a spider, which is nothing more than a cast-iron skillet with a long handle and long legs, designed for sliding in and out of a hot bed of coals at the hearth. As a group, firemen still enjoy the reputation of being good cooks, and this recipe indicates that the tradition is quite old. Try it. If you don't have a spider and a hearth, an ordinary cast-iron skillet and a stove eye will do.

| | |
|---|---|
| pork chops | salt |
| cooking oil | pepper |
| onions, peeled and sliced | water |
| potatoes, peeled and quartered | |

Trim the fat off the pork chops. Heat some cooking oil in a spider, or in a skillet if you are cooking on a stovetop. Slowly brown the chops on both sides. Then cover the top of the chops with sliced onions. Add quartered potatoes. Salt and pepper to taste. Add enough water to barely cover the potatoes, bring to heat, cover tightly, and simmer very slowly until the potatoes are tender, about half an hour.

# NEW ENGLAND BAKED BEANS

Beans were raised by Native Americans and, along with corn, formed a big part of the early American colonial diet. Although there are hundreds of variations on baked bean dishes, often called Boston baked beans, here is one that I highly recommend. Most of the Boston recipes seem to call for molasses, which was shipped up from Jamaica for making rum. This recipe from New Hampshire, however, calls for maple syrup and may be closer to Yankee country cooking. I modified the procedure somewhat to make use of a modern oven with thermostat.

1 quart dry beans (try navy beans)  
½-pound slab salt pork  
½ cup maple syrup  
1 medium onion  

½ tablespoon salt  
½ teaspoon powdered mustard  
water  

Put the beans into a nonmetallic container, cover them with water, and soak them overnight. Drain the beans and put them into a cast-iron pot. Cover with water, bring to a boil, and simmer for an hour. Drain the beans.

Preheat the oven to 250 degrees and put on some water to boil. Chop the onion and put it into the bottom of a cast-iron pot of suitable size. Add the beans to the pot. Mix the maple syrup, mustard, and salt, then spread this mixture over the beans. Put the slab of pork on top of the beans so that the rind is up. Cover the beans and pork with boiling water. Bake at 250 degrees for 8 hours. Add a little water from time to time.

# CHAPTER

## 18

# Large-Batch Cooking

**A** few weeks ago, I went over to my neighbor's place one night to check on a large batch of turtle soup that had begun to fill the neighborhood with its aroma. My cat also wanted to go. When I got there, Dan Webster, David Herndon, and Tommy Murphy were stirring the pot and boning out 50 pounds of turtle meat, all Florida softshell, some of which had a neck as long as your arm. I stirred the pot myself, noting that it had plenty of tomatoes and onions and okra and other good stuff in with the stock and meat. After tasting of it, I said, joking, that a touch of pepper was what it needed. Before Webster could grab his arm, Murphy dumped in another small box of pepper.

From then on, it was stir, taste, and add. We made several trips to a supermarket and to various kitchens and home freezers for more ingredients. It was, I allow, very good. The recipe? Impossible! By midnight, nobody had the slightest idea of what was in that soup. Furthermore, to set forth exact measures here would get Webster, Herndon, or Murphy stirred up at me again, or at one another, with claims that it ought to have more pepper, or less pepper. The truth is that the stir-taste-add method is so much fun that I'm not sure an exact recipe would be advisable. Better, I say, for me to set forth a simple recipe like the Sheep Stew, below, and let the good ol' boys add to it as they go.

Anyhow, the boys entered the turtle soup the next day in a cancer benefit cook-off—and damned if the stuff didn't win first place in the most unusual entry category. A year earlier, the same team won the same trophy in the same annual cook-off with a large batch of fried alligator. The gator meat, as I remember, was marinated overnight in a soak (mostly lemon juice) and then seasoned with salt and pepper, coated in flour, and fried as needed at the cook-off (which lasted all the afternoon). They used two gas burner units, topped with fish fryers. Going full blast, these units can cook lots of alligator, chicken, fish, and so on. One problem the team had, however, was that bits of flour accumulated in the bottom of the fryer and burned. If you plan to use such a deep fryer for an extended period, you might rig some sort of wire basket or scoop to clean the bottom from time to time.

In addition to the commercially available "fish fryers," a number of other cast-iron pots and kettles can be used for large-batch cooking. More than once, I've seen fish fried in vats that were made for scalding hogs. But, thinking back on it, all of these events that I have been to were sponsored by some group of peanut farmers, and I suspect that the peanut oil was provided by a local peanut-processing company. I would hate to have to *buy* enough oil, at today's prices, to cook in one of these vats!

In any case, remember that large cast-iron pieces should be heated slowly and evenly. It's best to add the oil or water cold, then bring it up to heat gradually.

## SHEEP STEW

I found this recipe in *The Progressive Farmer's Southern Cookbook*, first published in 1961, but I suspect that the recipe is much older. It came, the book indicated, from Lunenburg County, Virginia, and was used as a fund-raising event. "Does the school need a piano, library, or new room?" the text asked. "Think nothing of it. Just announce a sheep stew. People come to be served and they bring large containers and buy the surplus. It is amazingly good, we learned at first hand."

50- to 60-pound fat lamb

3 pounds white fat meat (pork)

3 pounds smoked side meat (pork)

50 to 60 pounds onions

3 tablespoons red pepper

7 tablespoons black pepper

10 tablespoons salt

4 to 5 pounds butter or margarine

3½ to 4 loaves of bread

"Dress lamb and place in refrigerator until thoroughly chilled. Saw the sides from the backbone and cut the meat into smaller portions. Place meat in kettle with cold water (a 30- to 35-gallon washpot is good, if you cook it outdoors). Start the fire. Add the finely cubed fat meat and side meat, then add onions. When meat is tender, remove all bones, and add pepper and salt. If more is needed, add it to suit the taste. Then add butter or margarine, and bread that has been broken in small pieces. To stir, use a three- or four-handled fork (a pitchfork with three or four tines). Be sure to stir enough to keep from sticking to pot. In adding water while cooking, use hot water. Cook until thick enough to eat with a fork. This will take 6 hours or longer. Serve hot. Yield: about 75 servings."

# BURGOO

Traditionally made in large batches, this dish can be cooked with an assortment of meats and vegetables, as indicated by the list below. Just for conversation, I always like to throw in something a little out of the ordinary, such as turtle, along with, maybe, a shoulder of venison, a chunk of beef, lean pork, and a hen or two. Sorry cuts of meat, such as shank, can also be used. Of course, I expect everybody who tries this recipe to improve on it as they go along. Start with:

20 pounds turtle, venison shoulder, beef, or hen

3 gallons cold water

10 bay leaves

½ gallon tomatoes, peeled and diced

4 large onions, chopped

3 ribs celery, chopped, tops and all

6 carrots, chopped

1 quart okra, chopped

1 quart whole-kernel corn

2 green peppers, seeded and chopped

1 tablespoon crushed red pepper

3 tablespoons Worcestershire sauce

salt

Tabasco sauce, as needed

Put the cold water and the meats (large chunks) into a small cast-iron washpot or a kettle. (Before adding the chunks of meat, trim off any fat; and skin the hen.) Build the fire under the pot and bring slowly to a boil. (Do not put a cast-iron pot onto a hot wood fire. Fast heating may crack it. It's best to start cold and bring the pot to heat gradually.) Tie the bay leaves in a piece of cloth, or put them into a drawstring tobacco sack, if you've got one empty, and put them into the pot. While the pot is heating, prepare the vegetables. Stir the meat from time to time with a paddle or hickory stick. Cook the meat for an hour or longer. When it is tender, fish out the chunks of meat with a pitchfork. Put the meat aside to drain. Add all the vegetables, pepper, and salt. Bone and chop the meat and add it back to the pot. Discard the bones. Simmer. Stir. Simmer and stir for about 6 hours. Add more water, as needed. Taste the burgoo from time to time and adjust the salt. Add a little Tabasco sauce, as needed for hotness. Half an hour before serving, stir in the Worcestershire sauce. Serve in bowls. Feeds 40 to 60.

# AUNT ANNIE KING'S SOUSE

The best souse, or head cheese, that I've ever eaten was made by my aunt Annie King. She started with a cast-iron washpot, cheesecloth, and the following ingredients.

| | |
|---|---|
| 1 large hog head | ½ teaspoon black pepper |
| 1 tablespoon salt | 1 medium onion |
| ¼ teaspoon powdered sage | 1 cup vinegar |
| ½ teaspoon flaked red pepper | water |

From the hog head, remove the ears, eyes, and brains. Save the brains for scrambling with eggs. Put the rest of the hog head into a cast-iron washpot, under which a good wood fire has been built. If the whole head won't fit into the pot, cut it in half or in quarters. Cover with water and bring to a boil. When the meat is tender and comes from the bones, remove the head from the water and let it cool a bit. (Don't overcook it.) Peel and quarter the onion. Remove the meat from the bones and run it through a food grinder. Run the onion through with the meat. Mix in the vinegar, sage, salt, red pepper, and black pepper.

Shape the mixture into a round ball, which will be about the size of a grapefruit, and wrap it in a square of cheesecloth of suitable dimension. (A piece of old sheet will also work.) Wrap and twist the cloth, putting pressure on the ball of souse. Tie off tightly and hang in a cool place for at least 12 hours. Or longer. (Waiting can be the hard part.) Be sure to put a container under the ball to catch any grease that drips out. Slice the souse and serve it with crackers. It's best at room temperature, but it can be refrigerated and kept for a week or so.

Many cookbook writers tell you to put all manner of stuff into head cheese, such as lemon zest and coriander. Even cinnamon. Suit yourself.

When cleaning the hog head for making souse, some people include the ears. After cooking, the ears can be cut up and used, but the pieces end up being somewhat chewy and, being of a different color than the rest of the mixture, they tend to stand out. I recommend that you omit the ears from your first batch of souse.

But don't omit the trotters. They provide a natural gelatin that helps the souse firm up to cheese consistency. That makes it easier to slice and serve atop good ol' American saltines or other crackers. Toast won't do.

I might add that Swedes often serve head cheese with pickled beets. Indeed, the odd combination is required eating for a Christmas Eve supper. When preparing the pig's head, they singe off any hair or bristle, cut off the ears, and brush the teeth.

# Other Cast-Iron Pieces

**A**lthough the skillet and the Dutch oven are by far the most popular cast-iron pieces found in the modern kitchen, a number of other items are still manufactured and are quite useful. Some of these old pieces are discussed below, along with some newcomers, such as cast-iron woks and ribbed griddles.

## Pie Irons

Pie irons consist of two very small skillet-shaped pieces. Designed for open-fire cooking, the two skillets hinge together and have long handles. You can put pie dough in one unit, add apple pie mix or other suitable filling, top with another piece of dough, close the irons, cook on one side, turn the irons over, cook on the other side, open—and you've got apple turnovers. Although pie irons can still be used successfully for cooking pies, the main use for modern man is in preparing sandwiches and light meals.

I've got two pie irons. One is square, designed to hold two pieces of ordinary loaf bread. The other is round, designed to hold the two halves of a hamburger bun or an English muffin. I sometimes use my pie irons at my kitchen hearth, and they come in handy in a camping situation where you need to cook over an open fire but don't have time to wait for coals to burn down for ideal cooking. By closing the two lids, you can cook directly in the flames.

You can use either half of the pie iron as a miniskillet, just large enough to cook an egg or panfry a small trout that has been cut in half, or maybe for grilling a couple of pieces of fresh venison tenderloin in a deer camp. Frankly, however, long-handled pie irons are a little awkward to take on a camping trip if you are traveling light.

I've cooked a couple of small meat pies on my pie irons, and I've made even more hot sandwiches, such as the Reuben. My favorite, however, is a grilled steak made with a fillet of beef tenderloin. Warm the pie irons. Add butter to one half of the pie iron. Center a few rounds from a slice of onion. Sprinkle a little salt and pepper on the steak and center it over the onion slices. Place a little butter on top, then close the pie irons. Put directly on hot coals and cook for 4 minutes on each side.

Long-handled pie irons, hinged together, are great for cooking small portions over a campfire.

# Cast-Iron Muffin Pans

Cast-iron muffin pans are still being manufactured, along with related pans for cooking popovers and Danish cakes. Any good family-type cookbook has plenty of muffin recipes, but here's an old one that I would like to pass along. Although this recipe calls for huckleberries, you can also use blueberries and other small fruit or chopped fruit.

Also try any good muffin recipe or commercial mix in cast-iron pans. And remember that biscuits and corn breads can be cooked in a muffin pan. And try your favorite recipes for popovers or aebleskievers—unless, of course, you've got a separate aebleskiever pan made of cast iron.

---

| | |
|---|---|
| 2 cups all-purpose flour | 3 tablespoons lard |
| ¾ cup huckleberries | 3 tablespoon sugar |
| 1 chicken egg | 3 teaspoons baking powder |
| 1 cup milk | ½ teaspoon salt |

If the milk, egg, and other ingredients are in the refrigerator, set them out until they reach room temperature. Preheat the oven to 425 degrees. Grease the cast-iron muffin pan. Sift together the flour, sugar, baking powder, and salt. In a bowl, beat the chicken egg and whisk in the milk and lard. Add the flour mixture and huckleberries to the bowl and stir. Fill each cavity in the muffin pan two-thirds full. Bake for 25 to 30 minutes, or until the top of the muffins are lightly browned.

---

Cast-iron muffin pans are available in several sizes and shapes.

Even aebleskiever pans are available in cast iron. These can also be used for ordinary muffins.

Nothing bakes better than cast iron. Try muffins made in our pans and you'll never use a flimsy muffin tin again.

*—Century Cast-Iron Cookware*

# Fluted Cake Pan

The German bundt cake, a sort of pound cake with a topping, is cooked in a circular fluted pan with a solid center. Such a cast-iron pan is also ideal for cooking other cakes, plain and fancy, of the same shape. The pan can also be used for baking breads.

# Bread Sticks and Pans

The familiar bread sticks, some of which are shaped like half an ear of corn, are always popular, and, of course, cast-iron pans to make them are still available. Also, a pan that makes pie-shaped pieces of bread is manufactured in two sizes. All of these pans are used primarily for corn breads.

Pans for baking corn stick pieces of bread have always been popular.

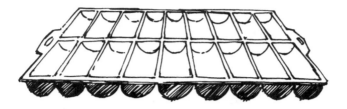

Nothing beats cast iron for cooking corn bread, and a number of special bread pans are available.

My nephew, David Livingston, uses cast-iron "corn stick" pans to mold lead into convenient units. With the lead, he makes fishing lure components, mostly spinnerbaits and buzzbait heads. He buys bulk lead alloy by the ton, and it comes in 65-pound pigs. The 65-pound pigs are melted in a cast-iron pot, then the molten lead is dipped out, with a cast-iron ladle, and poured into cast-iron corn stick pans. Each "stick" weighs a pound, give or take an ounce or two. These sticks of lead are an ideal size and shape to use in 20-pound lead pots made for pouring lead into small molds.

David also makes his own lure molds. First, he melts aluminum in a cast-iron pot, then sand casts the aluminum into roughly shaped molds. Then he has to finish the molds by hand, using dental tools.

Melting lead and other metal in cast iron is an old tradition, and a small melting pot (4½ inches in diameter) is still manufactured. It has a handle and a pouring lip. Comes in handy for keeping barbecue sauce on a grill, too.

## Cast-Iron Woks

Some of the best woks are made in China. Usually, they are fabricated from a flat piece of iron that is hammered down into a mold. It is therefore a more malleable iron than true cast iron. On the other hand, true cast iron probably originated in China some 2,500 years ago, and it was no doubt used for cooking purposes even then. In any case, Lodge Manufacturing has recently introduced a cast-iron wok, and it is truly great. Successful wok cooking depends on having a high heat source in the bottom of the utensil, for which cast iron is just perfect.

There are several good wok books on the market, and I won't offer recipes here. I would, however, like to borrow a text on stir-frying from a brochure from Lodge Manufacturing and House of Tsang:

Cast iron is a good material for wok cooking because it heats evenly and withstands very high temperatures.

"The curved shape of a wok produces graduated temperature zones which allow you to cook many different ingredients without having to remove them from the wok. The bottom of the wok next to the flame is very hot and can be used for searing and sealing. Push food up along the sloping side walls of the wok to keep it warm. This gives you room to stir-fry other ingredients."

Some of the Teflon-coated woks on the market won't hold up to high heat, and are too slick, really, to hold the food up the sides. In this respect, the hammered Chinese wrought-iron version may be better than cast iron. I should hasten to add that the cast-iron wok is "textured," meaning that it is cast in rather rough sand. In any case, the Lodge wok is made with a convenient handle on one side and a lifting grip on the other.

## Deep Fryers

Although I am partial to a good skillet, for the reasons set forth under the section on frying chicken and fish, I allow that some purely excellent cast-iron deep fryers are on the market. These range in size and configuration, depending partly on how they are to be heated. One oblong unit, for example, works best on a grill or grid. Round units work best on stove eyes. The illustrations show some of the more popular models.

Some round deep fryers come with baskets for holding french fries, fish, or chicken.

Large cast-iron deep fryers, oblong-shaped, work nicely over two stove eyes or on a camp stove. Some of these fryers have a lid that can also be used as a griddle.

Frying was covered earlier in this book, but I want to point out here that these cast-iron pieces can be used for other purposes. A 9-by-17-inch "camp fryer," for example, is an excellent piece for baking a large batch of corn bread in the kitchen oven.

## Cast-Iron Kettles

Kettles, with a pouring spout, came in handy for heating and pouring water back when most of the cooking was accomplished at a hearth or on a woodstove. A cast-iron model is still available and is great for making instant coffee or heating water for tea, but, of course, our modern water heaters and indoor plumbing reduce the importance of kettles for cooking and bathing.

Another cast-iron piece, called a country kettle, is used primarily for serving stews and such. It holds only a pint, and has little legs on it. This limits its use as a cooking utensil.

## Fajita Griddles and Sizzleware

I've got what is called a fajita griddle, and I use it for flapjacks, fried eggs, tortillas, pizzas, and other good things. But I'll have to admit that I'm more than a little confused about the term "fajita"—and how to make the real thing. One point is pretty clear: Tortillas are required, often made of flour, and a griddle is ideal for this purpose, as pointed out in the section on Mexican cooking. The rest of the fajita consists of meat, tomatoes, onions, and other fillings, all of which are placed in the center of a warm tortilla and rolled up. Beyond that I hesitate to go, but I will add that some people in Texas refer to the fajita as a Mexican hot dog.

One manufacturer markets what they call sizzleware (Lodge Texas Fajita Sizzleware) and poops it up as a heated serving platter. They also market round and oval "underliners" made of solid wood or rattan, which, of course, prevent the hot cast-iron platter from burning the table or tablecloth. This line of cast iron comes in various

More and more, cast iron is being used for serving as well as for cooking. Some griddles come with wooden or rattan underliners.

sizes and shapes, including a crescent-shaped serving piece. In other words, the main function of sizzleware is in serving the food, not in cooking it. But, of course, some of the pieces can also be used for cooking.

The trick in sizzleware is to preheat the oven to 350 degrees and put the griddle (cast-iron platter) into it for 30 minutes. Then grill the meat or broil it. (If you broil it in the oven, merely switch the heat from bake to broil. Broil the meat on a separate rack, usually very close to the heat source, and leave the griddle on a separate rack down under the meat.) When the meat is done, put it onto the heated griddle and place it on an underliner on the table. Have hot tortillas, chopped tomatoes, and other fajita makings. I tried the method, and find that the cast iron on the table does add a touch of the quaint.

## Double Skillets

A double unit features a griddle that fits perfectly atop a deeper skillet. Either piece may be used separately, or the griddle can be used as a cover. This is, of course, a neat unit for cooking in camp. In addition to being quite versatile, it's great for making smother-fried squirrel and similar dishes that require both frying and steaming.

In this double unit, a shallow skillet fits atop a pot. They can be used together or separately.

## Egg and Bacon Skillet

I'm happy to report that a skillet is made espe-cially for cooking breakfast. It's square—and just the right dimension for bacon. Further, it has a ridge through the middle, separating the bacon side from the egg side. And the egg side is also divided. Thus, it is perfect for cooking four pieces of bacon and two fried eggs.

A convenient cast-iron breakfast skillet will hold two eggs and four slices of bacon.

## The Jumbo Skillet

A 20-inch cast-iron skillet was recently introduced for cooking at family reunions and other such gatherings. It holds over 3 gallons of oil. Unlike other skillets, it doesn't have a one-handed handle and pouring spouts. Rather, it is perfectly round and has short lifting handles on either side. This is a highly specialized piece. It will, to be sure, turn out lots of hamburgers, flapjacks, fried fish, and so on; but it is a difficult skillet to heat on stove eyes. Having no handle, it is difficult to put on and take off a camp fire; most skillets, by comparison, can be lifted off the fire or coals with a handle. On the other hand, this skillet will work nicely on some of the new portable stoves that burn bottled gas.

## Ribbed Griddles and Skillets

In his recipe for pan steak, as discussed earlier in this book, George Herter claimed that many famous restaurants fried steaks for customers, then made grid marks on them with a heated rod in order to keep the custom-ers happy! Now they can use a ribbed skillet or griddle. These are manufactured especially for pan "broiling" and are, I point out, not much good for frying an egg or cooking a flapjack. So don't buy one for its versatility. These units are also said to be good for "grease-free fry-ing." Frankly, I don't know quite what they are

Ribbed cast-iron skillets are used for stovetop broiling.

talking about, and I suspect that some advertising copywriter is either being downright dishonest or is flirting with an oxymoron.

I've got a ribbed griddle, however, and I do like to use it from time to time for cooking strips of bacon and slabs of cured ham.

## Chef's Skillet

This neat piece, about 10 inches in diameter, has more slope to the sides than regular skillets have, and the handle has a more comfortable arch for chefs who like to shake instead of stir. The skillet is ideal for sautéing a few onions, for making sauces, and so on. It can also be used to stir-fry food, and is hereby recommended to those aces who desire to flip a patty of hash browns into the air and catch it, turned and intact, on the way down.

The chef's skillet has sloping sides and a comfortable handle.

## Large Griddles

Several large griddles are manufactured. Some are round, designed for cooking over gas burners, and others are rectangular. Some are made to double as lids for large deep fryers, and these, usually oval in shape, are great for camp use. Some of these units are made especially to fit outdoor cookers.

Some of the larger rectangular griddles work nicely on a two-burner gas stove, and can be used at home on electric ranges. I like to use one for cooking breakfast when no definite serving time has been set. The trick, of course, is to put the large griddle over two stove eyes, one turned up to medium heat and one to warm. Cook on the hotter end and, with a spatula, move the bacon, sausage, eggs, and flapjacks down to the other

# Lids for Cast-Iron Cookware

Cast-iron cookware is usually sold with either cast-iron lids or glass lids. Glass lids usually have a knob on top for handling, whereas cast iron has a suitcase-type handle, arched. Either kind is usually dome-shaped, which is an excellent design for using on a stove, where coals will not be piled on top of the lid. Most of the modern lids are called self-basting, which means that moisture from the food condenses on the dome lid, forms droplets of water, and drips down on the food. The undersides of some of these lids have a number of protuberances from which the droplets fall.

The disadvantage of glass, of course, is that it breaks easily. The disadvantages of cast iron are (1) you can't see through it, (2) it is heavy, (3) it costs almost as much as the pan itself, and (4) it can disflavor dishes during long cooking periods if it is not seasoned properly. Still, I'll take cast iron every time.

More and more, we are seeing plastic lids in cookware retail outlets, no doubt because of the high price of good glass lids or cast-iron lids. While the plastic may be all right for some applications, I much prefer a heavy lid for long, slow cooking, simply because the weight keeps it seated more firmly. In a pinch, metal lids, such as aluminum or tin, can also be used on cast-iron pieces, if they fit.

The better manufacturers of cast-iron products market lids separately for their cookware, and these can be purchased separately in case you lose or break a lid. But these days, many retailers balk at special orders, and some simply will not provide this service. Some independent dealers may order the pieces for you, but, considering their time and high shipping costs for a small order, it is understandable if they utter a strong word or two when you tell them that you bought the original piece from a discount store.

Lids for cookware are available in cast iron as well as glass and plastic.

## Cast-Iron Lids for Camp Dutch Ovens

A camp oven should have a cast-iron lid, not a glass lid. Of course, the handle is in the middle of the lid, and it should be in the form of an arch. Remember that the handle will often be covered up with coals, and that it must be removed with a hook of some sort. Getting the hook in the exact center of the handle, and thereby in the center of the lid, is very important. If the lid tilts when you take it off, ashes may fall into the food. Thus, it should be lifted straight up, and with the hook in the dead center of the lid. To this end, the handle should have a notch centered on the underside. If the lid to your Dutch oven doesn't have a suitable notch, purchase a triangular file and make one.

Also, remember that the lid of a Dutch oven should fit very tightly, especially if the oven is to be left unattended for long periods of time. If the lid doesn't fit tightly, too much moisture gets away and the food could burn. Some lids fit well, and others don't. Your best bet is to follow a tip from an article in the April 1971 issue of *Field & Stream* by Ted Trueblood: "If the lid of a new oven doesn't seat well, smear valve-grinding compound on the rim of the pot and the edge of the lid and rotate it until you have a fit like a bank vault door." Be warned, however, that this is a slow process. But it's well worth the effort, if your lid doesn't seat properly. If you aren't familiar with valve-grinding compound, check with your auto parts retail outlet.

Another trick that will help a loose lid, at least temporarily, is to make a paste of flour and water. After the Dutch oven has been loaded with food, coat the edge of the lid and rim of the Dutch oven with the flour paste. Seat the lid, and leave it be for the duration of the cooking period. If you take a peek, the seal will be broken.

## Camp Oven Lid Hooks

A one-armed man fitted with a good hook can lift a camp Dutch oven lid niftily, but the rest of us need some sort of hook on a handle. Commercial Dutch oven tools, both long and short, are available, or you can make your own by screwing a suitable hook into the end of a wooden handle. The lid hook can also be used to lower a Dutch oven by the bail into a pit of hot coals, or to remove it from the pit. The commercial tools also have a crosspiece that is useful for raking hot coals around.

# Stovetop Dutch Oven Lids

Lids for stovetop Dutch ovens aren't quite as important as for the camp models, simply because they merely cover the pot and never hold coals for heating and cooking purposes. For this reason, they usually have dome-shaped lids. Some of these can be purchased with either glass or cast-iron lids. I prefer self-basting cast iron, but good heatproof glass lids do work very well.

# Skillet Lids

Remember that most cast-iron skillets are manufactured with a pour spout on either side, and a normal lid will not cover this entirely. Special lids are available for cast-iron skillets, but they are expensive and are seldom available in most retail outlets. Usually, lids are not needed for skillet cooking, although there are, of course, exceptions.

Smother-fried meats, for example, work best with a lid, and, under some conditions, a lid is highly desirable for cooking in camp. So, you may want to shop around for a cast-iron skillet with a special lid.

# Other Lids

Lids for such cast-iron pieces as bean pots should fit tightly, especially when food is cooked unattended for long periods of time. Most of the round pots come with lids, or the lids can be purchased separately. Or lids made for other pots may work satisfactorily, either in glass or other material.

Some large cast-iron pieces, such as rectangular fish cookers, often come with lids. Before buying one of these pieces, look around for one that comes with a lid that also serves as a large griddle.

# APPENDIX

## How Cast-Iron Pots Are Made

Lowell Branham, outdoors editor of the *Knoxville News Sentinel*, made a tour of a cast-iron factory in 1988, and here is part of his report:

"The heart of the manufacturing operation is a huge furnace where raw iron is heated to a temperature of 2,800 degrees. At that point, it glows a brilliant yellow orange and flows almost as freely as water.

"The molten iron travels from the furnace to various production points in huge steel pots. To create a cast-iron vessel, the molten metal is poured from the pot into a mold of sand.

"The sand molds are what give cast-iron cookware its characteristic grainy surface. When the metal has solidified and cooled in the mold, the sand is broken away and recycled.

"Pieces coming from the molds are covered with a crust of sand particles that have fused to the metal. To remove the crust, the pieces are sent to a blasting machine and bombarded with fine steel shot.

"A workman then inspects each piece and grinds away any rough edges left from the molding process. From there, the pieces go into a media bath that burnishes away their sandpaper-like roughness and leaves a smooth grain that's pleasing to the touch. As a final step, the pieces are dipped in a wax bath to prevent rusting and then transported to the warehouse area to await shipment."

Some cast-iron pieces are left with a rather rough cooking surface, and others are polished, or machined, to a smoother finish. If I have a choice, I prefer a slick surface for cooking bacon and eggs, but a rough surface works nicely for bread pans and for frying chicken and fish.

## Antique Pieces

Cast iron will last for centuries, and even very old pieces can still be used for cooking. Antiques shops, junk shops, flea markets, and old houses or barns are the most likely places to look for old cast iron. Although antique skillets and Dutch ovens can still be used, the only pieces mentioned below are those that are no longer manufactured. I'm no expert on antiques, and I offer no advice on dating such pieces. But I suspect that the expert can place cast-iron ware pretty closely, and the old stuff is different from the modern. It has a different look about it, a different feel to it. For example, I recently saw some cast-iron pieces hanging on the wall at Choctawhatchee Lodge, and two of the skillets had a ring on the underside. In other words, if they were put on a modern kitchen stove, only the outer ring would touch the stove eye. They were, of course, made for cooking on a wood-burning stove with removable eyes.

In any case, anyone who has an interest in antiques as such will be able to find additional information in any good library. Although my brother, Colonel Ira L. Livingston, is something of an expert on old stuff, I confess that I haven't made even a literary search of such pieces. But I will say that my interest in cast-iron cooking has made my visits to antiques stores and junk shops (usually at the instigation of some woman) more enjoyable. Sometimes, while driving down the highway, I even have an urge to wheel into such a wayside junk shop.

## Waffle Irons

To be sure, waffle irons are still widely used, but most of the ones available today are not cast iron and are made with internal electrical heating elements. The older waffle irons, hinged, were designed for heating over flames or coals. When hot, the irons were removed from the fire and opened. The waffle batter was poured into the proper cavity, and the hinged unit sides were shut. The hot cast iron cooked the waffle, without the unit being over the fire. In fact, the expert could cook two waffles before having to reheat the cast iron.

Typically, antique waffle irons will have very long handles.

## Toasters

Cast-iron pieces of various designs were used for toasting bread at the hearthside. Usually, these were upright pieces that sat on legs and held slices of bread vertically to catch the radiant heat. Most of these had a swivel mechanism, which permitted the browning of first one side and then the other.

## Spiders

Early housewives had spider skillets that were designed especially for cooking on a hearth. They had long legs, for sitting over a bed of coals, and long handles. They were great for hearthside cooking, but would be almost useless on a modern kitchen stove. Nor are they ideal for a campfire, since the legs work best for sliding across a flat surface.

## Trivets

These long-legged pieces were designed for holding a pot or other hot item on the hearth. They were also used to keep pots and pans directly over coals without touching them.

## Andirons

Although modern andirons aren't made with the cook in mind, some of the old ones had built-in hooks for holding spits. If you like to cook in a kitchen fireplace, as I do, keep an eye out for a set. They are sometimes called firedogs.

## Oyster Roasters

Similar in concept to waffle irons, hinged oyster roasters have star-shaped sides for holding six oysters. Anyone who has roasted oysters on a piece of tin or over a grill will appreciate the design. The idea, of course, is to hold the fresh oyster over the heat until the shell opens. Then the oysters are served, hot, on the half shell. Roasting too long will dry out the oysters, taking away their flavor and texture. Only fresh, unshelled oysters should be used for roasting. In any case, this delicacy has almost disappeared from the American scene, and the old cast-iron roasters are things of the past. What a pity.

# METRIC CONVERSION TABLES

## Metric and US Approximate Equivalents

### Liquid Ingredients

| Metric | US Measures | Metric | US Measures |
|---|---|---|---|
| 1.23 ml | ¼ tsp. | 29.57 ml | 2 tbsp. |
| 2.36 ml | ½ tsp. | 44.36 ml | 3 tbsp. |
| 3.70 ml | ¾ tsp. | 59.15 ml | ¼ cup |
| 4.93 ml | 1 tsp. | 118.30 ml | ½ cup |
| 6.16 ml | 1¼ tsp. | 236.59 ml | 1 cup |
| 7.39 ml | 1½ tsp. | 473.18 ml | 2 cups or 1 pt. |
| 8.63 ml | 1¾ tsp. | 709.77 ml | 3 cups |
| 9.86 ml | 2 tsp. | 946.36 ml | 4 cups or 1 qt. |
| 14.79 ml | 1 tbsp. | 3.79 l | 4 qts. or 1 gal. |

### Dry Ingredients

| Metric | US Measures | Metric | US Measures |
|---|---|---|---|
| 2 (1.8) g | ¹⁄₁₆ oz. | 80 g | 2⅘ oz. |
| 3½ (3.5) g | ⅛ oz. | 85 (84.9) g | 3 oz. |
| 7 (7.1) g | ¼ oz. | 100 g | 3½ oz. |
| 15 (14.2) g | ½ oz. | 115 (113.2) g | 4 oz. |
| 21 (21.3) g | ¾ oz. | 125 g | 4½ oz. |
| 25 g | ⅞ oz. | 150 g | 5¼ oz. |
| 30 (28.3) g | 1 oz. | 250 g | 8⅞ oz. |
| 50 g | 1¾ oz. | 454 g | 1 lb.  16 oz. |
| 60 (56.6) g | 2 oz. | 500 g | 1 livre  17⅗ oz. |

# INDEX